# PRAISE FOR
# *A PRACTITIONER'S GUIDE*
# *TO ACCOUNT-BASED MARKETING*

'It is my view that account-based marketing (ABM) is on the threshold of revolutionizing the marketing domain. It shows all the potential of bringing about a much-needed paradigm shift. The undoubted leaders in ABM are ITSMA, led by the authors of this remarkable book. It is an evidence-based book and is replete with practical advice about how to initiate, manage, and profit from ABM. My hope is that everyone who really cares about customers will read it and act on it.' **Professor Malcolm McDonald, Emeritus Professor, Cranfield University School of Management**

'Burgess and Munn do a terrific job of demystifying account-based marketing. They provide practitioners with highly relevant examples, insightful nuggets, and pragmatic suggestions for succeeding in a world where the ability to treat large customers as individual markets really matters.' **Jonathan Copulsky, Global Insights Leader, Deloitte**

'Marketing is only as valuable as its proximity to a customer, and Burgess and Munn have provided the definitive guide to account-based marketing. Very simply, their process works wonders in driving growth. This book should be required reading for all marketing leaders.' **Malcolm Frank, Executive Vice President, Strategy and Marketing, Cognizant, and co-author of *What To Do When Machines Do Everything: How to get ahead in a world of AI, algorithms, bots, and big data***

'The strategies outlined in this book have served as a playbook for our ABM programme, with impressive results. Munn and Burgess are pioneers and thought leaders in the field of account-based marketing and I recommend their approach to any B2B marketing organization that wishes to build a tighter alliance between marketing, sales and their most strategic accounts.' **David Hutchison, SVP and Head of Marketing, SAP North America**

'Finally, a thoughtful map to help all executives create an impactful account-focused approach in the increasingly complex world of marketing. *A Practitioner's Guide to Account-Based Marketing* is grounded in common sense and case-based advice; a must-read.' **Larry Weber, Chairman and CEO, Racepoint Global, and co-author of *The Digital Marketer***

'This is a long overdue, go-to book that marketers can use to implement ABM in their organizations! Whether you practise Strategic, Lite, or Programmatic ABM – or a combination of all three – ITSMA's seven-step process gives you a roadmap for how to understand accounts and use that understanding to execute highly relevant programmes across teams.' **Jon Miller, CEO, Engagio**

'I recommend this book to anyone interested in creating mutual, sustainable value with their strategic accounts.' **John Torrie, CEO UK and Asia, Sopra Steria**

'Bev Burgess with David Munn have written a must-read practical guide for anyone planning for ABM or indeed already on the journey. Read this book to avoid making the mistakes others have made and learn from the pioneers of ABM, with very practical insight from organizations that are really getting value from this approach.' **Peter Lundie, Managing Partner, agent3**

'The proven techniques presented in this book drive innovation and the creation of new value for both companies in a strategic account relationship. As ABM is increasingly adopted in the US and India, I am excited to see what the wider impact will be on the economies of both countries.' **Dr Mukesh Aghi, President, US-India Business Council**

'The competitive landscape for business marketers has become so crowded that account-based marketing is now a must for companies seeking to truly differentiate themselves with their most important customers and prospects. Given their deep knowledge, practical experience, and pioneering role with ABM, Munn and Burgess are the perfect guides for this essential marketing strategy.' **John Hall, Co-Founder, Influence & Co., and author of *Top of Mind***

'As more and more people become interested in what ABM can do for their business, it's refreshing to see such a practical guide to this powerful, insight-led marketing strategy.' **Paul Charmatz, SVP International, Avention OneSource Solutions**

'Having led the two award-winning ABM programmes at BT Global Services and CSC, featured in this book, I know this strategy produces great results. We partnered with Burgess and Munn on both programmes and they have captured all the critical ingredients for success in this comprehensive manifesto on ABM.' **Neil Blakesley, Principal, Consulting CMO and Former CMO, CSC, and Vice President of Marketing, BT Global Services**

'As CEO of the first and only specialist ABM agency I know what good account-based marketing looks like – and Burgess is one of the best in our field. Having witnessed her expertise firsthand, I'm delighted that Burgess has encapsulated this into a must-have read for anyone interested in ABM.' **Alisha Lyndon, CEO, Momentum ABM**

'ABM is a critical marketing strategy for companies serious about putting clients at the heart of their firm to deliver differentiated value over the long term.' **Richard Grove, Global Director of Marketing, Business Development & Communications, Allen & Overy LLP**

'A definitive and groundbreaking book on account-based marketing, written by two of the leading practitioners in the field. This work is highly innovative and practical and provides a roadmap on how to develop lasting client relationships and maximize client lifetime value.' **Professor Adrian Payne, University of New South Wales Business School, Visiting Professor, Cranfield School of Management**

'If there's one person who can take credit for the current upsurge in interest in ABM, it has to be Bev Burgess. Her work to formalize, evangelize and galvanize the disparate people talking about and working in ABM has been inspirational and transformational – without her ABM wouldn't be the hot topic that it is today.' **Joel Harrison, Editor-in-chief, B2B Marketing**

'Successful account-based marketing involves so much more than just repurposing existing marketing materials for your top accounts. Anyone can do that. If you truly want to differentiate your marketing from others', embrace the ABM tidal wave and learn how to do it the right way. This book is a great primer on how to create an effective and sustainable ABM programme, based on years of ITSMA research, experience, and practitioner input.' **John Lenzen, CMO, CareerBuilder**

# A Practitioner's Guide to Account-Based Marketing

Accelerating growth in strategic accounts

Bev Burgess
Dave Munn

KoganPage

First published in Great Britain and the United States in 2017 by Kogan Page Limited

| | | |
|---|---|---|
| 2nd Floor, 45 Gee Street | c/o Martin P Hill Consulting | 4737/23 Ansari Road |
| London | 122 W 27th St, 10th Floor | Daryaganj |
| EC1V 3RS | New York, NY 10001 | New Delhi 110002 |
| United Kingdom | USA | India |

www.koganpage.com

© Bev Burgess and Dave Munn, 2017

The right of Bev Burgess and Dave Munn to be identified as the authors of this work has been asserted by them in accordance with the Copyright, Designs and Patents Act 1988.

ISBN    978 0 7494 7989 3
E-ISBN  978 0 7494 7990 9

**British Library Cataloguing-in-Publication Data**

A CIP record for this book is available from the British Library.

**Library of Congress Cataloging-in-Publication Data**

Names: Burgess, Bev, author. | Munn, Dave, author.
Title: A practitioner's guide to account-based marketing : accelerating
    growth in strategic accounts / Bev Burgess, Dave Munn.
Description: New York : Kogan Page Limited, [2017] | Includes bibliographical
    references and index.
Identifiers: LCCN 2016050881 (print) | LCCN 2017002847 (ebook) |
    ISBN 9780749479893 (alk. paper) | ISBN 9780749479909 (ebook)
Subjects: LCSH: Marketing--Key accounts. | Selling--Key accounts. |
    Relationship marketing. | Industrial marketing--Management.
Classification: LCC HF5415.122 .B867 2017 (print) | LCC HF5415.122 (ebook) |
    DDC 658.8/04--dc23

Typeset by Integra Software Services, Pondicherry
Print production managed by Jellyfish
Printed and bound by CPI Group (UK) Ltd, Croydon, CR0 4YY

# CONTENTS

# ABOUT THE AUTHORS

 **Bev Burgess** is an accomplished marketer and business-woman. She is passionate about the critical role of marketing in business growth. Her specialism is the marketing and selling of business services, built through a combination of postgraduate study and 25 years' experience of both running and marketing service companies.

Bev's background includes senior roles at British Gas, Epson and Fujitsu. She has also run her own strategic marketing consultancy. Today Bev leads ITSMA's European business and its Global ABM Practice, delivering consulting and training to companies around the world that are designing, developing and implementing ABM programmes. Bev first developed this more focused marketing approach while managing director of ITSMA Europe in 2003.

Bev holds an MBA in strategic marketing and a BSc Honours degree in business and ergonomics. She is a Fellow of the Chartered Institute of Marketing and has served as an international trustee.

Her first book, *Marketing Technology as a Service*, was published by Wiley in 2010, exploring proven techniques to create value through services based on an infrastructure of technology.

 **Dave Munn** is President and CEO of ITSMA (www.itsma.com), a research-based community for B2B marketing leaders that pioneered the ABM approach in the early 2000s. A tireless advocate and networker, Dave has spent the last 20 years bringing together marketers from top technology, communications and professional services firms to advance the theory and practice of B2B services and solutions marketing.

Since taking over leadership of ITSMA in 2001, Dave has broadened and deepened the company's research, consulting, training and community programmes in such essential and innovative aspects of marketing as ABM, thought leadership, solutions marketing, brand differentiation, buyer personas, and customer success.

Prior to joining ITSMA in 1995, Dave held senior-level field positions with Oracle and Apple, and was a senior analyst at the Ledgeway Group, an innovative research firm that laid the foundation for the growth of technology services business research in the 1990s.

Dave holds a BA degree in Economics from Denison University and an MBA from Kellogg School of Management at Northwestern University.

# FOREWORD

Clients are now so complex, and so large in scale, that they are effectively markets in their own right. Being markets, they have all the characteristics of markets: multiple segments, different buyers and cultures – and multiple opportunities. Individual client companies and organizations require the same marketing analysis and management as would normally be applied to traditional market segments. Account-based marketing (ABM) is a way of addressing this opportunity and also of bridging the gap between traditional sales management and marketing.

ABM, at its core, is essentially treating individual accounts as markets in their own right, and then acting with all the tools of marketing to position the company and its services with the aim of ultimately acquiring a greater share of clients' business and earning their continuing loyalty.

I have seen ABM take shape as a distinct marketing discipline over many years. Having worked for six major companies in six different industries across three continents in 30 years, I have had many opportunities to observe and engage with local, national and international companies within different industries, and to get to understand both their consistent similarities as well as their unique differences.

During my time at one of these companies – Accenture – I realized that the business-to-business approach to traditional industry marketing was limited. It was always going to be difficult to be seen as an 'industry expert' if the supplier company was not actually part of the same industry as the buyer company. Also, it was clear that, even within an industry sector, despite similar competitive dynamics, every industry player is different, with unique cultures and challenges. Therefore, a much deeper understanding of the client, a far more sophisticated segmentation, right down to the individual level, was needed rather than a simple analysis of 'industry trends' in order to uncover more opportunity.

My international work experience had given me an understanding and appreciation of the role that individual and national characteristics had played in major business events. Therefore, it seemed natural to me to apply this analysis of differences within a larger industry sector. It was going to be necessary to re-orientate traditional 'industry research' towards understanding individual buyer clients within single companies and segmenting them accordingly.

Understanding the interconnections between individuals within the power structure of the buyer company and how they related to their target markets – and how all of this impacted the supplier company – is fascinating. After all, at the core of what at Accenture we called client-centric marketing, or what we now call account-based marketing, is deep research into how individuals react within institutions, and how both are affected by market dynamics and competition – and what opportunities this presents.

ABM also represents a new way of changing perceptions of the supplier company with the buyer company. As such it represents a new frontier in brand development beyond the traditional brand-building tools. Getting a fuller and deeper understanding of how a brand is perceived in the core client group is a rich learning experience and fundamental to all good brand strategies.

I have learned about ABM and the benefits it can bring in my day-to-day working life – and continue to apply this learning today in my current global CMO role. Globalization has increased and there are few clients who are unaffected by forces larger than their domestic territory. As we were pioneering in the field, we had no general theory to draw upon, so I applaud the authors of this work for bringing a general framework and methodology for ABM to a new generation of marketing professionals.

It is a good time to begin to master this fascinating ABM discipline within professional marketing. It is no longer a discipline that can be left to the tactical salesperson with their short-term targets. Marketing professionals can use the techniques of ABM, both to bridge the great divide between marketing and sales, and also to maximize their career potential – and bring a longer-term strategic approach to client development.

The exploratory and pioneering work on ABM has now been done. So I would advise that all marketers take advantage and occupy the high ground of client development and relationship building. It represents more than just a toolkit for short-term sales targets. It is more than just winning a greater percentage of clients' spend relative to competitors. It is about arranging your products and services into something valuable that is of long-term relevance and which is measurable in terms that the client understands. It is your world organized according to your clients' perspective rather than your own. This is what builds trust and long-term relationships.

*Dr Charles Doyle, Group Chief Marketing and*
*Communications Officer, JLL, and author,*
Oxford Dictionary of Marketing

# ABOUT THIS BOOK

A few years ago, one of the marketers attending an ITSMA event on a relatively new marketing strategy – account-based marketing, or ABM – came up at the end of the session and asked us a simple question. 'Can you recommend a good book I can buy to learn more about how to do ABM in practice?' The answer was no, we couldn't, because no one had yet written a book on ABM – not even us!

In truth, ABM as a discipline was still new. Today there is more written online about ABM every day than there was in a year back then. It is billed as the new big thing, the answer to every B2B marketer's dream, every company's must-have marketing strategy. The reason for all this ABM enthusiasm is simple. It works.

So now that everyone is getting interested in what ABM can do for them, it's time to bring all our experience, research, and case study examples together and write that book. This book. A practitioner's guide to ABM.

This book is for you if you have just heard the term ABM and want to find out more about it. It's for you if your company has asked you to look into ABM and set up a pilot programme. And it's for you if you've been working in ABM for a while, but want to keep yourself fresh and extend your programme.

In Part One we discuss the basics of ABM – what is driving its adoption and how it has evolved to the point where today there are three different types of ABM in use around the world. We look at the fundamentals to get in place as you get started with an ABM programme – objectives, positioning, governance, funding, metrics – and the all-important decision of which accounts to prioritize for ABM support. We take you through the technologies you can use to support your programme as it gets started and as it scales. And we explore how most companies move from their first pilot accounts through to a standardized and scaled approach across their business.

In Part Two we look at how to do ABM on an individual strategic account. Working through ITSMA's seven-step process, we explain how to start by building an in-depth understanding of the account and the key stakeholders within it. The insights from your analysis are used to decide where your best opportunities are for growth in the account and to map your own offers and solutions against your client's issues.

Then, after identifying and profiling the decision-makers and influencers for your solutions, we take you through the process of creating targeted and compelling value propositions for these key stakeholders. Next, we demonstrate how to build an integrated sales and marketing campaign for your account and to execute your campaign shoulder-to-shoulder with your sales colleagues. Finally, we offer some ideas for the metrics you can use to evaluate your ABM results and report your success.

Part Three of this book is focused on the skills and attributes you need to be a good account-based marketer. We introduce ITSMA's ABM competency model, and discuss the profile of the typical ABM-er, highlighting both their strengths and their areas for development. We also look at how to manage the agency resources that you can use to access the specialist skills you may need for your ABM plan or to help you deliver ABM at scale. Our final chapter presents some ideas for managing your own ABM career, based on the collected wisdom of seven marketers working at the forefront of ABM today. A profile of each of our 'Magnificent Seven' is included to round off the book. Each one of them has a key piece of advice for you so that you can benefit from their experience and deliver results faster.

At the end of every chapter we provide you with a handy list of the key points for you to remember: your ABM checklist.

We recognize that ABM won't stand still once this book is written. So we encourage you to continue the conversation and your exploration of ABM with us at our events, or online at www.itsma.com, on LinkedIn (ABM for B2B Marketing Professionals) or on Twitter @ITSMA_B2B #ABMpower. It is so great to be part of something this exciting, so please share your journey with us and help us to continue to shape the development of account-based marketing as a professional discipline.

# ACKNOWLEDGEMENTS

We have many people to thank for their help in writing this book.

First, thanks so much to Charles Doyle for working with us in the early days on the ABM concept and for coming with us on the journey right up to the present day. His Foreword sets the perfect tone for this book, and his invaluable advice continues as one of our 'Magnificent Seven' interviews with leading ABM practitioners in Chapter 14.

In a similar way, we also want to thank all those who have participated in our membership activities with ABM, and have shared their perspectives and stories with us over the years to ensure that ABM continues to evolve successfully as a discipline. Some of your stories appear in this book as case studies. As a membership community, ITSMA is built on this collaborative development of new ideas and best practices.

In particular, we'd like to thank the members of our Global ABM Council for their ongoing contribution. Interviews with several of the members are featured in Chapter 14: Raianne Reiss at Juniper, Dorothea Gosling at CSC, Andy Pedack at Microsoft, Eric Martin at SAP, and Julie Johnson at KPMG. They join Charles Doyle in this impressive line-up. Our final member of the 'Magnificent Seven' and all-round ABM star is Andrea Clatworthy at Fujitsu. Thanks to you all!

Our colleagues at ITSMA have played a key role in the development of this book. Julie Schwartz, our SVP Research and Thought Leadership, has run all of our ABM research studies and written many of our resulting publications on ABM. Jeff Sands, VP and ABM Practice Co-Lead, for many years has been involved in developing many of the models you see in this book. SVP Rob Leavitt has helped to shape both the thinking and the articles that ITSMA has published on the topic. Ashley Turcotte provided invaluable proof reading support.

Our associates who work with us on ABM projects also deserve a mention, since they too have debated and developed ABM thinking with us over the years. From Kathy Macchi in the USA (the go-to person for ABM campaigns and technology advice) and Lisa Dennis, through to Louise Jefferson, Lynda Chambers and Gerry Davies in Europe (all of whom have done ABM in their day jobs as well as helped others to do the same over the years). A special mention goes to Sara Sheppard, who worked on the initial ABM discovery project with Bev back in 2003 and has been a sounding board for ideas ever since.

Finally, there are five people without whom this book simply would not have been published and to whom we are especially grateful. Laura Mazur at Writers 4 Management, whose help with drafting and editing was invaluable as the book took shape, and Kathy Hunter at ITSMA, who created all of the tables and figures you see in the book while delivering witty one-liners through the day to keep us going. Our final and warm thanks go to the publishers, Kogan Page: Charlotte Owen, whose advice throughout the writing of the book has been so helpful, Philippa Fiszzon, who managed the production process so professionally despite some last minute adjustments to the text, and Jenny Volich, for commissioning the book and recognizing the need for a book on ABM now.

*For Andy, Katherine and Lauren, with thanks
for your love and support.
Bev*

*For Dick Munn, with thanks for your wisdom, inspiration,
and passion for marketing.
Dave*

# PART ONE
# Setting up an account-based marketing programme

## Introduction to Part One

This first part of this book describes what account-based marketing (ABM) is, how and why it evolved and how companies are using it to accelerate growth in their strategic accounts today. It then leverages ITSMA's research and experience with account-based marketers around the world to bring you the guidance you need to set up and scale an ABM programme for your own company.

In Chapter 1 we dig into the driving forces behind ABM and look at the benefits it has delivered for those adopting it into their marketing strategy. We look at how ABM as a practice has evolved since it was first codified by the Information Technology Services Marketing Association (ITSMA) in 2003, and how three types of ABM have recently emerged in response to demand for more from the business, enabled by technologies that can help you adopt ABM principles at greater scale. This chapter helps you to think about whether ABM is right for your business, and if so, which type or types will work best for you.

Chapter 2 moves on to explore the foundations you will need to put in place if you're planning an ABM programme. We cover the fundamentals, from being clear on what you want to achieve, through positioning ABM as a business initiative (not just a marketing initiative), building your governance framework, identifying your sources of funding to defining what success will look like.

The technologies that could support your programme are the subject of Chapter 3. We look at technologies supporting communications between marketing and sales, those that help uncover insights about the accounts in your programme, those that help in the planning and execution of campaigns and the systems that allow you to track and report on your ABM results.

Deciding which accounts to include in your programme can appear simple but actually can be problematic, sometimes making the difference between your programme's success and failure. Chapter 4 introduces an objective process for prioritizing accounts with your business and sales colleagues. We demonstrate how you can use a multifactor matrix to help you decide the appropriate levels of investment and attention for each account in a collaborative way.

Thinking ahead to the success of your programme, Chapter 5 sets out ITSMA's ABM adoption model, built with our Global ABM Council to show the phases companies go through as they launch and scale ABM. We share the characteristics and tasks in each phase, together with the drivers for moving from one phase to the next, so that you can be prepared as you start on your ABM journey.

# The essentials    01
# of account-based
# marketing

## Why account-based marketing matters

In 2015, Wal-Mart's revenues stood at $486 billion, Toyota's at $247 billion and Apple's at $183 billion. The global revenues of just four of the leading information technology service companies[1] – IBM, Fujitsu, Accenture and NEC – were almost $196 billion, which is just over 11 per cent of the gross domestic product of the United States. To put this into perspective, the combined GDP of the bottom 50 of the world's 214 countries as defined by the World Bank equalled just $158 million in 2015.[2]

Common sense alone should tell anyone determined to establish new business relationships or cement existing ones with organizations of this breadth and depth in the highly complex and competitive business-to-business (B2B) arena that traditional marketing approaches will have limited returns. Glossy corporate campaigns are proving to be increasingly less effective for winning business, driving growth and keeping performance on track. This is exacerbated by an environment characterized by volatility, uncertainty, discontinuity and the changing demands of customers (see box 'Driving forces').

The realization of this has led a growing number of forward-looking companies to embrace the principles of account-based marketing, or ABM, for their biggest accounts. First defined by ITSMA as 'treating individual accounts as markets in their own right', it is now well established in some of the world's largest technology companies, such as Cisco, Fujitsu, Microsoft and SAP, while its reach extends beyond the technology sector into professional services (eg KPMG) and other business sectors (eg engineering consultancy Black & Veatch).

And it is proving its worth. An ITSMA 2016 ABM benchmarking survey[3] found that 84 per cent of marketers who measure return on investment (ROI) described ABM as delivering higher returns than any other marketing approach. Almost 80 per cent of those marketers surveyed said that ABM is important or very important to their overall marketing strategy, while 86 per cent said it had increased in importance in the past two years. The majority (69 per cent) expected investment in ABM to increase in 2016 (Figures 1.1 and 1.2).

**Figure 1.1**   ABM and ROI

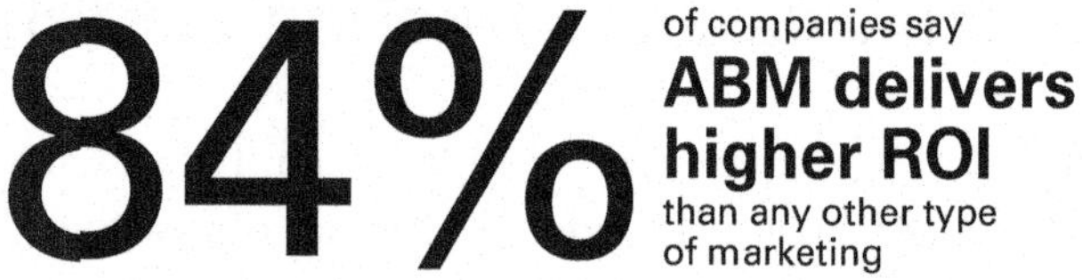

**84%** of companies say
**ABM delivers higher ROI**
than any other type of marketing

SOURCE  ITSMA, Account-Based Marketing Benchmarking Survey, March 2016 (N=51)

**Figure 1.2**   ABM is on fire

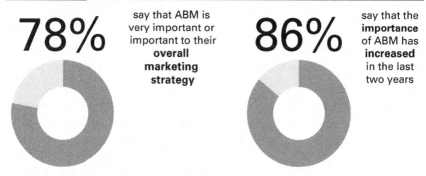

**78%** say that ABM is very important or important to their **overall marketing strategy**

**86%** say that the **importance** of ABM has **increased** in the last two years

SOURCE  ITSMA, Account-Based Marketing Benchmarking Survey, March 2016 (N=112)

ABM makes such a measurable difference because it is designed with specific objectives aimed at a tightly targeted audience. Externally, it is an integrated, coordinated programme of activities that brings valuable propositions and relevant ideas to clients. Internally, it encourages closer cooperation between marketing, account management, sales and delivery teams because it is only truly effective when everyone involved with a client works collaboratively.

## Driving forces

There are some powerful economic, technological and social trends that are driving the need to incorporate ABM into your marketing strategy. These include:

- **Commoditization**. Combatting the commoditization of products and services demands differentiation through more personalized service and building close relationships.

- **Competitive disruption** is becoming a fact of business life as fast-moving technology gives new entrants the ability to enter previously closed markets.

- **Globalization and complexity**. Big B2B contracts can stretch over many years and cover a number of geographies. These long-term relationships demand careful nurturing.

- **Buyer expectations**. Customers are not only more knowledgeable and demanding but they can be more fickle as well, benchmarking service and quality across sectors and expecting similar levels from existing suppliers. Potential suppliers have to do enough homework on the business to be able to craft a bespoke value proposition that stands out as relevant and which will deliver the right business outcomes.

- **Widening decision-making units**. As corporate governance tightens up and procurement practices become more sophisticated, more people are involved in B2B buying decisions. In technology, this is best represented by business buyers becoming more influential compared with their IT peers.

- **Customization and personalization.** The concept of one-to-one marketing came to prominence through the work of Don Peppers and Martha Rogers,[4] who argued that as technology increasingly enabled a one-to-one relationship, business-to-business organizations have to do a lot more than just sell. They have to get more deeply involved at all levels of the individual customer organization and the customer's business, helping each client to manage its own business ever more efficiently and effectively.

# Defining account-based marketing

Reflecting the ITSMA definition of 'treating individual accounts as markets in their own right', ABM is a structured process for developing and implementing highly-customized marketing programmes to strategic accounts, partners or prospects. It is by its very nature a long-term programme that demands a commitment of resources since it can take more than a year to deliver substantial returns. It is underpinned by a close analysis of the key business issues facing the client.

ABM should be built on an ethos that encourages people to work together to the common goal. Building cross-functional teams that collaborate effectively is increasingly recognized as a source of innovation and agility in successful businesses, and ABM engages all relevant functions to determine how best to meet client's particular business needs and goals. Marketing acts as a core member of the account team, adding value in a number of ways:

- examining the key business issues facing the account;
- mapping them to the individuals responsible;
- developing customized, integrated sales and marketing campaigns to take relevant propositions into the account.

This can have important outcomes for the client, and for sales and marketing. Figure 1.3 shows some of these benefits.

Sales teams seem to welcome it. Figure 1.4 shows the result of an ITSMA survey of members asked for the main benefits for sales teams of ABM.

It is important to stress that ABM is not just about doing marketing differently. It is a business change initiative to drive growth. As Table 1.1 (see p 10) illustrates, this is more fundamental than a redrawing of marketing plans. It shifts the focus of attention from inside-out to outside-in, starting with the account and its problems, then working back into the supplier company and how it can help to solve those problems.

ABM should be closely aligned with key/strategic account management. A key account plan, at its best, operates like a business plan, including objectives, sales targets, positioning, delivery and dependencies. But what it often lacks is a specific marketing element. Adding marketing expertise into account teams can help them move beyond a narrow operational focus and be in a better position to spot potentially lucrative opportunities.

**Figure 1.3** Benefits of an ABM programme

## Client

- Client feels better understood as a result of the in-depth analysis you have undertaken
- Conversations with the client focus more on them than on you
- Client has broader awareness and understanding of your offerings, strategy, and solutions
- Increase in customer satisfaction and experience because of tailored approach
- Client tends to position and sell you across the organization as a partner in concert with their needs

## Sales

- Transitions perception of company from vendor to a trusted partner and advisor (status is earned, not simply claimed)
- Richer conversations aligned around account needs
- Uncovers new opportunities
- Accelerates customer buying cycles (longer-term)
- Expands reach into the account
- Increases revenue, margin, and wallet share
- More sole-sourced opportunities
- One message to the customer: all account team members in agreement on priorities and message

## Marketing

- Aligns marketing and sales in a unified account strategy
- Helps orchestrate all relevant lines of business appropriate to the account into a coherent message and position
- Increased marketing ROI
- Consistent tailored campaigns and messages into individual accounts and targets
- Client more inclined to provide references

**Figure 1.4** Key benefits of ABM for sales

What are the key benefits of your ABM programme for sales?
% of respondents (N = 62)

| Benefit | % |
|---|---|
| Sales uncovers more new opportunities within accounts | 57 |
| Increased account penetration: wallet share, revenue, and margin | 57 |
| Sales is able to have richer conversations with customers | 48 |
| More consistent and aligned BU/brand/offer messaging into accounts | 45 |
| Improved marketing and sales alignment | 42 |
| Sales is viewed as a trusted advisor | 11 |
| More sole-sourced opportunities | 8 |
| More referenceable accounts | 7 |
| Shorter sales cycles | 3 |

**NOTE** Multiple responses allowed
**SOURCE** ITSMA, Account-Based Marketing Benchmarking Survey, October 2013

**Figure 1.5** Common ABM misconceptions

| Misconception | Reality |
|---|---|
| Account-based marketing is a standalone marketing programme: mutually exclusive from other marketing programmes | Account-based marketing is a customer-driven marketing methodology that uses any and all marketing and sales tactics to give clients what they want and need |
| Account-based marketing is just another form of account planning and thus is a duplication of effort by the sales teams | Account-based marketing does not replace but rather builds on good account planning to create actionable marketing and sales strategies |
| Account-based marketing can be done successfully without customer intelligence | Customer intelligence is what makes it 'account-based'; otherwise, it's still 'spray and pray' marketing |
| Account-based marketing is appropriate for every large account | Account-based marketing is an INVESTMENT and thus best for those accounts that can provide a suitable ROI |
| Account-based marketing is just a 'marketing thing' | Account-based marketing must be executed hand-in-hand with sales – and be thought of as a key sales enabler |
| Account-based marketing replaces your current selling model or methodology and replaces your account planning process | Account-based marketing complements your selling model, makes account planning real, and creates a shared living document |

**Table 1.1**   Product marketing versus ABM

|  | **Product marketing** | **ABM** |
| --- | --- | --- |
| Focus | Features<br>Benefits | Problems<br>Solutions |
| Information | Price<br>Promotion | Awareness<br>Education |
| Timing | One-off | Ongoing |
| Objective | Reduce inventory | Increase share of mind and wallet |

**SOURCE** ITSMA, 2016

Gaining insights from thorough research ensures that plans are timely and relevant and encourages value co-creation, with the biggest accounts treated individually based on their potential lifetime value. Figure 1.5 illustrates the gap between common perceptions of ABM and the reality.

Admittedly, this more collaborative marketing approach sometimes encounters strong resistance among organizational silos. This can be even more of a challenge when teams are virtual, brought together through the seamlessness of modern technology rather than face-to-face meetings alone. Dealing with what can be difficult 'people' issues will be discussed further on in the book.

# The evolution of ABM to the next generation

The global professional services firm Accenture was one of the first to grasp the power of ABM back in 2003. It was championed by Dr Charles Doyle, who was in charge of marketing for its global high-tech practice. He believed that the firm's most important accounts should have special attention, including a specific marketing plan, to build a more multifaceted relationship. He developed his 'client-centric' marketing programme based on ITSMA's Marketing Framework (see box 'Dr Charles Doyle: pioneering a new approach').

## Dr Charles Doyle: pioneering a new approach

In an interview in 2005,[5] Dr Charles Doyle discussed the ABM programme he introduced into Accenture to build business and strengthen relationships individually with major accounts. The key points summarized here are still as relevant today.

### Q: How would you define client-centric marketing?

Client-centric marketing, simply put, is about the management and development of perceptions – perceptions that we manage just like market share, just like revenue. [It] is a programme to enhance clients' perceptions of your company's abilities and delivered value. It includes a full range of marketing techniques applied to each client or prospect.

### Q: What are the main objectives of client-centric marketing?

I would say there are three main objectives behind client-centric marketing. First, the management of long-term perceptions – helping build perception over the long haul, over a three-year period. This also involves creating awareness.

Second, client-centric marketing aims to create differentiated positioning. Some of the clients that we deal with have the GNP equivalent of Third World countries and are much more complex than some Third World countries, and we tend to call them accounts and customers. They're actually vast, complex worlds in their own right. So we have to think of that client as a market in its own right. That is the common denominator through which we marketers will build demand in the future.

A final objective of client-centric marketing is to create demand. The client knows you do this, they know roughly what you've done in the past, but what can you specifically do for them? What can you specifically do for their division, their business line, the group of people that they work with? What credentials have you got and have you done it before; and who says you've done it before, and can I go and see it?

### Q: How did you design the Accenture model based on the ITSMA Marketing Framework?

To do good client-centric marketing, you need to do good research. You're effectively applying the techniques to a client that you would apply to the market. So good research, analysis, segmentation, work out your gap, reposition. The second thing is the alignment of what you have, more customized, to cover those gaps and to close the perception gaps.

The third thing is the execution, where we use traditional marketing techniques at the level of the client, all the usual things you see, but with the accent on customization. No more going to big industry shows and trying to get clients to come along. This time, you customize the show, the roundtable and the thought leadership for the group of clients that you have worked out. You still have to do the shows to create the awareness, but it's no longer the basis of the professional services marketing.

Then you start to monitor. Your perception research that you did at the start gets refined during the year. Did this client's perception of what we do in outsourcing go up 10 per cent over the last year from what it was? And isn't that much more powerful than monitoring a share of voice with analysts or media or other kinds of traditional things that we use? Again, same sort of technique, working out the gap, trying to close the gap, applying programmes – only the context changes.

Then you have to have an infrastructure that supports it – databases, tools, techniques. You have to have all the things that can support sales campaigns and your alliance partners working closing with you.

**Q: How do you get started on client-centric marketing for a major client?**

You need a good understanding of the following:

- the current state of the relationship;
- the client's perception of your company;
- the client's business needs;
- the client's views on your work;
- the client's culture;
- the client's buyer values.

You also need to follow an action plan. Immediate items on that action plan should include conducting primary perception research, determining perceptual gaps and setting the metrics that will be captured. Short-term items include building the client-centric marketing plan around the assessment results and creating programmes by client segmentation and targeted individuals within each business unit.

More long-term items on the action plan should be refreshing the marketing plan, building campaigns and tools to enable enhanced engagements with clients, and measuring and publicizing successes and results.

Over the next few years ABM began to be taken up by big companies in the wider technology sector as companies such as BT, Fujitsu, HP and IBM embraced the idea. Those determined to exploit the full potential of ABM began to look at developing value propositions based on sales and marketing plans aimed at individual clients. Because ABM is undeniably resource-intensive, companies trying to scale up their programmes were quick to analyse the usefulness of the growing number of marketing technologies and tools to scale efficiently without damaging the one-to-one nature of ABM. Figure 1.6, overleaf, illustrates the ABM timeline.

As these tools have become more sophisticated, they offer more scope, although on a relatively limited basis, in areas such as IP-based personalization or account intelligence and stakeholder profiling. However, as Chapter 3 will show, we are now moving into what could be called 'next generation' ABM. Technology platforms are appearing specifically geared to support ABM and help scale it up more cost-efficiently, exploiting transformational advances such as big data, digital engagement with customers and cloud computing.

## ABM history top ten

1993: Peppers and Rogers publish *The One to One Future*.

1997: CSC lands mega-deals with ABM-like pursuit marketing.

2003: ITSMA introduces and names account-based marketing concept and approach.

2006: ITSMA launches ABM Council; Xerox and Northrup Grumman win first ABM Marketing Excellence Awards.

2007: ITSMA introduces three-phase model for ABM programme development.

2009: ITSMA introduces Collaborative Account Planning model.

2011: BT is first to automate account insight for ABM.

2012: ITSMA introduces first marketing certification programme for ABM.

2015: ABM catches fire with VC funding for technology-enabled ABM.

2016: ITSMA study documents rise of three types of ABM.

**Figure 1.6** The ABM timeline

**1993**

Don Peppers and Martha Rogers publish their seminal book, *The One to One Future*

**1997**

CSC launches full-court press pursuit marketing, lands two highly visible 10-year outsourcing contracts worth approximately $170 million

CSC

**2002**

Accenture and Unisys pioneer Client Centric Marketing: Account manager demand outpaces supply

accenture
UNISYS

ITSMA conducts first-ever survey on Account Management and the Role of Marketing

**2003**

ITSMA introduces the concept of Account-Based Marketing (ABM) igniting a groundswell in B2B marketing

**2004**

ITSMA publishes ground-breaking paper, *Account-Based Marketing: The New Frontier*

ITSMA
Account Based Marketing

Charles Doyle of Accenture presents the three objectives of Client-Centric Marketing at ITSMA's Annual Conference: manage perception, create a differentiated position, generate demand

**2006**

Xerox Global Services and Northup Grumman win the first ITSMA Marketing Excellence Awards for ABM

MARKETING EXCELLENCE

ITSMA ABM Council launched with founding members Avaya, BearingPoint, EDS, First Data, Hewlett-Packard, IBM, Lucent, Unisys, and Xerox

**2007**

ITSMA introduces Three-Phase Model for ABM development

**2008**

BEA, Capgemini, Cisco, Deloitte, and Oracle join the ITSMA ABM Council

ITSMA conducts the first-ever ABM Benchmarking Study, highlights success with scaling ABM

Continued»

## 2009

ITSMA introduces the Collaborative Account Planning Model, to help marketers and salespeople accelerate opportunities with existing customers and high priority prospects

BT Global Services and AT&T win the ITSMA Marketing Excellence Award for ABM

CA and CSC join the ITSMA ABM Council

## 2010

BT and Microsoft join the ITSMA ABM Council

## 2011

BT is first to automate gathering account insight for ABM; KAM Live, based on Agent 3, enhances the conversation among marketing, sales, and the client

Cognizant and KPMG join the ITSMA ABM Council

## 2012

ITSMA identifies the four steps for successful ABM adoption: ITSMA Account-Based Marketing^SM Adoption Model

ITSMA introduces the first Certification Program for Account Based Marketers in North America (and has now certified hundreds of ABMers)

## 2013

ITSMA introduces the first Certification Program for Account-Based Marketers in Europe

ITSMA conducts a second ABM Benchmarking Study. Key finding: Companies positioning ABM as strategic business initiative rather than tactical marketing program show best results

## 2014

Juniper and Cognizant win the ITSMA Marketing Excellence Award for Accelerating Growth with Account-Based Marketing

## 2015

ITSMA inaugurates ABM Skills Competency Model and Assessment

ABM catches fire! Venture capitalists uncover the potential for technology enabled ABM, investing in Engagio, Demandbase, and more

SAP America, Cisco, and KPMG win the ITSMA Marketing Excellence Award for Accelerating Growth with ABM

Avanade, Dell, Juniper, and SAP join the ITSMA ABM Council

## 2016

ITSMA documents the rise of three distinct types of ABM: Strategic ABM, ABM Lite, and Programmatic ABM

New study confirms that 84% of marketers find ABM delivers higher ROI than other marketing initiatives

**SOURCE** © 2017 ITSMA. For source material and more information, see www.itsma.com/abm/

**Figure 1.7**   Three types of ABM

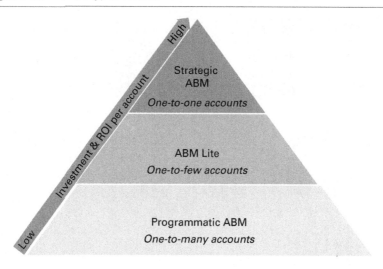

The result is that today three types of ABM have emerged, supported by these technologies, as shown in Figure 1.7. The first, which we've focused on so far, is usually reserved for strategic accounts and executed on a one-to-one basis. This is Strategic ABM.

Here's where you find one marketer responsible for one to five accounts and becoming an integral part of the account team.

The second type is ABM Lite. This is a one-to-few model, often focused on a wider group of strategic accounts or the next tier down of accounts. Technology becomes more important here, helping to automate the account insight process, campaign execution and measurement. The advantage of ABM Lite is that it is less resource-intensive – both in people and budgets – than strategic ABM. But inevitably, a 'Liter' approach leads to 'Liter' returns.

The third type of ABM, regarded as the 'new kid on the block', is Programmatic ABM. Enabled by technologies that automate ABM-inspired tactics at scale across hundreds or even thousands of identified accounts, this is where most of today's hype about ABM is coming from.

Some companies just do one type of ABM. Some do a combination. Increasingly, companies are exploring all three, as some elements of the programmatic approach can be used in the other two types of ABM as tactical activity support.

# Is ABM right for my organization?

Embarking on ABM should be an important strategic consideration for any organization. It is closely tied with the objectives of the business and its sales team, and usually used to support:

- Cross-selling/upselling for account penetration. This uses a more structured, planned approach geared to increasing share of wallet and share of mind through better and deeper relationships.

- Changing perception or positioning. Enhancing positioning and/or changing perceptions, often important when a company goes through a rebranding or is recovering from a service issue.

- Developing new accounts. Creating an integrated approach with sales to penetrate new accounts.

- Pursuing identified major opportunities. Supporting accounts based on requests for proposals (RFPs) or identified major sales opportunities. Marketing's link with sales is more tactical and short term for the duration of the bid process. Often called 'opportunity-centric marketing', any of the other reasons for doing ABM should eventually lead to this one.

If your ABM programme is to be successful beyond a concept and small pilot, it has to be positioned as a coordinated, appropriately-funded business change programme to deliver these objectives. It will have an impact on people, processes and systems, as further chapters will show. The quickest way to go wrong is to position ABM as a tactical marketing programme without the support and collaboration of the business.

Research conducted by ITSMA in 2014[6] found that:

- Positioning ABM as a company-wide business initiative correlates with higher ROI.

- Positioning ABM as a marketing initiative, rather than as a company-wide business initiative, may lead to under-investment and unrealistic expectations of quick returns.

- ABM is not a funnel-filling tactic. It is a strategic, mid- to long-term relationship-building programme that requires investment.

The long-term, resource-intensive nature of ABM means that it is so important to have the sponsorship of business and sales leaders for your ABM programme. In addition, if there is a culture of 'inside-out' thinking in your company, or marketing is seen as a tactical, sales support activity that remains distinctly separate from sales, then ABM may not be right for you.

Ultimately, your decision about the best marketing or ABM approaches to take should be made in the same way that your decisions on the best sales and account management model are made, based on the potential of the accounts in the market with which you could do business. Figure 1.8 helps to illustrate the most effective marketing strategy to deploy for each level of accounts within a market and industry sector.

## Strategic ABM

Strategic ABM sits at the top of your ABM pyramid as the most appropriate strategy for those accounts grouped by their revenue potential, or whose proportion of your future revenues is so important that it will make or break your future business. Another way to look at this is customer lifetime value. The objective is either to grow your small share of a large wallet or to defend your already large share of that wallet.

Seventy per cent of people use strategic ABM to increase business with existing clients, with only 30 per cent using it to break into new accounts.[7] Strategic ABM only makes sense in accounts with large budgets because it is so resource-intensive, with marketers looking after between three and five

**Figure 1.8**   Choosing the right marketing strategy for your accounts

Mass-customized marketing
(All audiences)

Segment marketing
(eg, All retailers)

Programmatic ABM
(Named retailers)

ABM Lite
(Cluster of key retail
accounts with similar
issues)

Strategic ABM
(Top retail
accounts)

accounts, or sometimes a single, large account. Creating jointly-developed, integrated sales and marketing plans which are both relevant and personalized for clients demands in-depth knowledge, such as what is going on in their industry, the key issues in the company itself, the initiatives they are working on, and what individuals are responsible for what activities.

In strategic ABM, the marketing plan becomes a core part of the account plan and is reviewed alongside the other elements of the plan within account governance processes. While technology is often used to help gather insights, target communications or track progress on both the sales and marketing fronts, there is a significant amount of creativity used in strategic ABM, from innovative value propositions to new thought leadership and content developed for each account. Almost all (92 per cent) of marketers say that strategic ABM delivers a higher return on investment than any other form of marketing.

In strategic ABM, an account-based marketer is an integral part of the account team.

## ABM Lite

ABM 'Lite' will be made up of accounts which are either still strategic, but unable to be addressed with full ABM due to resource constraints, or are a second tier of accounts that, while still significant, do not warrant the investment of the top tier. They will have common issues and/or other similar characteristics that enable a form of 'cluster' marketing, such as a group of grocery retailers who are all developing click-and-collect capabilities to become multichannel retailers.

According to research,[8] ABM Lite is not just used for existing accounts (56 per cent compared with 70 per cent for strategic ABM), but is often a way to break into new accounts.

It uses the same ABM process, but one marketer will run the process for a small group of companies that have similar business issues and initiatives. Each marketer will handle up to around 25 accounts, grouping them into smaller 'clusters' and working with sales at key decision points such as agreeing which accounts to target, agreeing the most relevant propositions to promote and tailoring existing content for the marketing and sales campaigns. Just over two-thirds (68 per cent) of marketers who measure return on investment and use ABM Lite say that it delivers higher ROI than any other marketing approach.[9] The ABM marketer works the sales teams on a limited number of accounts (usually three to five in a cluster across maybe 25 accounts in total).

## *Programmatic ABM*

In companies with high-value, complex sales, programmatic ABM is reserved for accounts that do not yet warrant the individual investment of the other two types. In companies with lower value sales that still want to adopt ABM principles to improve their campaign effectiveness, it is usually the only form of ABM done. There is a 50:50 split of the use of programmatic ABM for existing clients and new accounts.[10]

In this type of ABM marketers can automate some of the more strategic ABM steps, such as the collection of insight through social listening technologies, or the delivery of targeted advertising through reverse-IP recognition. With just one marketer working across tens, or perhaps hundreds, of accounts to support whole sales teams, programmatic ABM is much less resource-intensive, and more applicable for businesses that don't have the same complex, large, multi-year deals of those which have been using strategic ABM.

Today, programmatic ABM is described by just over two-thirds (67 per cent) of marketers who measure return on investment as delivering higher ROI than any other marketing approach.[11] This is the lowest proportion among the three types of ABM, and close to ABM Lite, perhaps because both are moving away from the focus of strategic ABM towards the 'one-to-many' span of more traditional mass-marketing campaigns. But programmatic ABM is still evolving to help align sales and marketing more closely into the demand generation process.

Note that in companies with large deal sizes, programmatic ABM is often used to improve the way that segment marketing is done – such as into industries like the retail or healthcare sectors – or alternatively used to mass-customize more horizontal marketing campaigns, such as brand or offering campaigns. It can also be used as tactical support within strategic and ABM Lite campaign execution.

An ABM marketer, sector marketer or campaign manager should align with sales teams to focus on tens to hundreds of named accounts to generate better quality leads.

**CASE STUDY**   Making the difference at SAP North America

SAP North America, a subsidiary of SAP, is a market leader in enterprise software, helping companies of all sizes and industries to operate more effectively and efficiently from their back offices to boardrooms, warehouses to store fronts and desktop to mobile devices.

In 2014 SAP North America developed an account-based marketing (ABM) programme to focus and customize marketing efforts for large, strategic customers. Like many mature B2B companies, SAP receives a very high percentage of revenue from a small number of strategic accounts. With the top 10 per cent of accounts delivering up to 80 per cent of revenue in North America, it became clear that field marketers needed to become true 'business partners' to sales and customers in order to drive sustainable account growth, accelerate opportunities and cultivate customer relationships.

SAP's challenge was to consolidate and modify previously unfocused marketing efforts, create a common methodology to its approach across regions and maintain consistency by sharing best practices.

### Programme objectives

SAP's main objective was to add strategic value to its relationships with top accounts and to become true business partners to sales and to its customers. The team also focused on building a future pipeline through marketing practices rather than focusing on near-term needs. The programme was designed to deliver value to sales in two primary ways: by enabling customers to accelerate decision-making processes; and expanding the SAP presence within these large accounts.

Another ABM driver was the need to extend support to more of a sustainable, year-long programme of activities which demonstrated to customers and sales teams alike how marketing can support a partnership with SAP – not just be viewed simply as a vendor. By utilizing the ABM marketing strategy, SAP could achieve its objective of increasing the level and quality of customer engagement as well as ensuring a long-term value recognition and growth from customers.

### Programme execution

SAP NA addressed this need through establishing a centralized ABM programme office and creation of a comprehensive ABM programme in 2014. ABM marketing efforts utilized a strategic approach in which highly targeted awareness and demand generation programmes were executed for a specific customer. The SAP team delivered formalized training programmes for a core group of marketing professionals, studied external best practices around ABM, worked closely with sales colleagues on account selection and establishing rules of engagement and created a marketing bill of materials as well as an execution engine to deliver against those tactics.

Implementation of account planning sessions helped to identify new opportunities, as well as to ensure sales and marketing alignment. New tactics were implemented into the ABM programme, such as employing a dedicated marketer, developing an 18-month plan and securing a budget for customized activities. Other tactics included customized newsletters and webcasts, dedicated enterprise social networking sites, account-specific digital marketing and onsite one-to-one events.

One of the most effective tactics, known as customer co-Innovation days, brought a customized, onsite event directly to the customer. The overall focus of these events was to inform customers about how they can co-innovate with SAP.

## Business results

The ABM marketing strategy exceeded its goals across all key objectives. The indicators used to measure what has been accomplished include pipeline touched, new pipeline created (value and number of opportunities) as well as quality contacts created in new buying centres.

2014 results demonstrated significant, incremental impact:

- marketing pipeline touched (MPT): $209 million touched, $27.6 million closed;
- marketing progressed pipeline (MPP): $57 million progressed, $30.3 million closed;
- new opportunities created: 49 for $27 million in new pipeline;
- 1,200 new line-of-business (LOB) contacts.

As a result of ABM success, the programme expanded to include 55 accounts in 2015, with additional budget and headcount allocated to the effort. SAP also established a Global ABM Programme Office to leverage the success of the North American region and syndicate it throughout other regional marketing teams.

In addition, the 2015 ABM programme evolved from one dedicated person to four, as well as an extended team of 15, and ABM funding increased by 50 per cent over 2014. The results derived from the impressive effects of ABM marketing demonstrated to customers and sales how marketing can support account growth, accelerate opportunities and deliver customer value.

# Your ABM checklist

**1** ABM is a structured process for developing and implementing highly-customized marketing programmes to strategic accounts, partners or prospects.

**2** ABM makes such a measurable difference because it is designed with specific objectives aimed at a tightly targeted audience. Marketers describe ABM as delivering higher returns than any other marketing approach.

**3** ABM has to be seen as a business change initiative to drive growth and be closely aligned with key/strategic account management.

**4** Three types of ABM have emerged thanks to technological advances: strategic ABM, ABM Lite and programmatic ABM.

**5** ABM is used to support cross-selling/upselling for account penetration, changing perception/positioning, developing new accounts or pursuing identified major opportunities.

# Notes

**1** http://fortune.com/global500/

**2** http://data.worldbank.org/data-catalog/GNI-Atlas-method-table

**3** ITSMA (2016) *Account-Based Marketing Benchmarking Survey*

**4** Peppers, D and Rogers, M (2001) *The One to One B2B: Customer Relationship Management Strategies for the Real Economy*, Crown Business

**5** *ITSMA Viewpoint* (2005) An in-depth look at Accenture's client-centric marketing

**6** *ITSMA Online Survey ABM and ROI: Building the Case for Investment Benchmarking*, January 2014

**7, 8, 9, 10, 11** ITSMA (2016) *Account-Based Marketing Benchmarking Survey*

# Building the right foundations for account-based marketing

## Taking the first steps

As Chapter 1 showed, three main categories of ABM are emerging as technological advances enable a wider degree of personalization more cost effectively.

At the top level, strategic ABM is aimed at those big, complex, critical accounts which could contribute a disproportionately large amount of your revenue. Strategic ABM is far more than an automated personalized marketing initiative or account-based advertising, although both of these can play a role in the campaign execution phase and underpin today's Programmatic ABM. To offer the payback that such an investment warrants, ABM has to be tightly interlinked with the broader overall goals of the business.

It has to be based on collaboration, engaging sales, marketing and delivery teams, along with key executives in the client account, to determine how best to meet the client's particular needs and goals. It should be viewed from the start as a change management programme and allocated sufficient resources to work effectively.

There are six elements to consider when building the foundations for your ABM programme:

- deciding what you want to achieve with ABM;
- positioning ABM as a strategic business initiative;

- creating the right framework for effective governance;
- making the metrics count;
- devoting sufficient funding and allocating the budget intelligently;
- selecting the appropriate tools and technologies.

These first six elements were integral to Fujitsu's ability to set up and scale its ABM programme (see case study 'Scaling ABM – a new approach at Fujitsu'). The final element is dealt with in the next chapter.

## CASE STUDY  Scaling ABM – a new approach at Fujitsu

Fujitsu is the leading Japanese information and communication technology (ICT) company, offering a full range of technology products, solutions and services. When Fujitsu UK & Ireland decided to put a higher priority on gaining more business with existing customers as a key part of its business strategy, the challenge for the marketing team was to devise the most effective framework to achieve this.

For Andrea Clatworthy, head of client marketing at Fujitsu, there was an easy answer. Having piloted account-based marketing with three accounts with great results in parts of the business already, the best answer was to rapidly increase the scale of this customer-focused marketing strategy. 'We welcomed the request to do something different with open arms, as we knew we'd wasted significant amounts of money in previous years generating "sales-accepted leads" that went nowhere,' according to Clatworthy.

But Clatworthy knew that there would also be significant challenges in scaling up the ABM programme from a pilot to the centrepiece of the team's marketing plan. Finding the staff, identifying the accounts, developing templates and providing adequate support for a widely expanded programme all figured prominently in Clatworthy's list of issues to address. And while the business was setting the direction, she still needed to convince them that ABM was the vehicle to achieve the company's goals.

To get the business to buy into a wider ABM programme, Clatworthy evangelized the approach, shared the results achieved by other companies, provided benchmarking data from ITSMA, and created a new marketing strategy that illustrated how the money they'd been wasting on lead generation could be invested more wisely in ABM. This new approach was communicated during the company's three-year planning process and positioned as the natural bridge between the business strategy and the marketing strategy.

### Designing the programme

#### 1. Identifying ABM accounts

The team worked with the business to identify customers and targets for ABM where there was real potential or they could see potential over the next 18 months to two years. They started with two lists – the list from the business and the list from marketing – which highlighted some commonalities. That was followed by a discussion to develop the accounts for the ABM list: first at the line-of-business level and then with agreement at the business-unit director level. The criteria used included:

- size of wallet;
- share of wallet;
- the amount of change going on in the account;
- whether Fujitsu could add some value;
- whether marketing could work with the account team.

This analysis generated a final list of 58 accounts in the UK and Ireland for the financial year starting April 2014, including a select few target customers.

#### 2. Building the right ABM framework

Clatworthy consulted with ITSMA to refine the ABM process used in pilots and build a strategy for scaling the process. 'We sat down and we designed an ABM training programme for our marketers. Through that process we designed the account-based marketing plan template. That drove the type of thinking that I wanted the ABM-ers to go through.'

Clatworthy was clear that she didn't want to get to a point where Fujitsu just had a whole load of people doing tailored communications, because as she put it:

> …that's not ABM. I wanted marketing to be the driving force behind understanding the customer so that we could take the right message to the right people at the right time. At no point were we going to include people in a generic campaign because that didn't make sense. We wanted to develop ideas and create campaigns for an account that recognize their needs and demonstrate we were responding to those needs.

The team did, however, make prodigious use of existing corporate programmes within their ABM plans. The emphasis was on specifically tailored sets of engagements and communications that leveraged pre-existing corporate activities, whether publications, like *iCIO* magazine, or events.

One important example was Fujitsu's Executive Discussion Evening (EDE) series, which encompassed a number of events throughout the year on varying topics with high-profile speakers. The events offered an opportunity for key stake-holders in customer accounts to participate in substantive discussions with outside experts, Fujitsu executives and each other.

For the ABM team, the 'ABM skill,' as Clatworthy called it, was in identifying the specific events and topics that would be of most interest to their accounts and intelligently incorporating those into the broader ABM plan. They focused on positioning individual events with their accounts so that customers were primed and motivated to attend.

The result was not only more effective engagement with ABM accounts but also improved performance of the corporate programmes. Where the EDE programme, for example, previously had targets for number of attendees from various industry sectors, there were now targets for number of attendees from ABM accounts. All of those targets, for EDEs and other corporate programmes, were achieved.

### 3. Programme governance

Critical parts of Clatworthy's approach to scaling the ABM programme were a clear set of required templates and milestones for each account. The first step was to go deeply into each account, led by the ABM-ers with the account team. Armed with a template and some training on how to conduct these sessions, ABM-ers used the necessary background and account information to start building their plans.

Plans were due at the end of the first quarter. They were reviewed first by the appropriate buddy (industry marketers with relevant sector and ABM experience) and then by Clatworthy before going to the account manager for sign-off. Once the account manager was happy, Clatworthy had ultimate sign-off on the plan. This allowed both marketing and sales to contribute to the plan and accept it.

Plans were reviewed quarterly thereafter. The fourth quarter review looked at the experience and results of the previous 12 months, lessons learned, and initial thoughts for the year to come. All of these reviews were publicly available to sales and marketing on a SharePoint site for review, ensuring transparency on all sides.

**A new innovation: the transfer window**    Halfway through the year, the newly expanded ABM strategy was getting good traction with account teams and business units. Clatworthy's next challenge was that some business units were asking for more ABM and others wanted to swap accounts. To respond to these demands, Clatworthy borrowed from professional sports: she instituted a transfer window.

The rules were extremely strict, and with good reason. For one, said Clatworthy, 'I was really clear that ABM is not about swapping accounts all the time. That's

called deal-based marketing, for a particular opportunity.' This is especially important because it takes time for ABM-ers to get up to speed on new accounts, said
Clatworthy. 'If you think about it, for the first two to three months as an ABM-er
you're learning about your customer and you're doing your planning.'

Nevertheless, she wanted to be able to address the rare instances where there
had been a genuine mistake or a major change in the account since selection,
which meant that ABM resources were being squandered on an account that
wasn't going anywhere. Likewise, if the business unit decided that a much bigger
prize emerged that wasn't part of the ABM programme, it should be allowed to
drop another account in favour of that one.

With all of that in mind, she put these rules in place:

- There is only one transfer window per year for the whole programme.
- You can't swap all of your accounts.
- Any swap must be based on discussion and agreement between the business
  unit manager and Clatworthy.

The transfer window concept proved a workable idea. It helped to keep the account
teams and business units on board and, in the end, only two accounts out of 58
were swapped the first year, resulting in only a small impact on the ABM team.

**Funding**    The expanded ABM programme benefitted from a pragmatic approach
to funding ABM activities. For healthy customer accounts that the business had
already deemed strategic prior to the programme, the business unit paid for any
incremental costs incurred by the ABM programme. For accounts that were not
funded by the business unit, Clatworthy had a dedicated amount of marketing
budget. To access this budget, ABM-ers had to go through an application process
that involved confirming that the activity was in the ABM plan and completing a
light business case based on a template.

To Clatworthy's surprise, this budget was not exhausted before the end of the
year. As it turned out, 'A lot of the activity we executed was around making better
use of corporate programmes, tailoring the messaging and adding wraparound
activities.' The things that made this ABM programme so effective – understanding the needs and priorities of individual accounts and addressing them
accordingly – didn't necessarily require any significant additional investment to
make them work.

**Continuous improvement and engagement**    An issue that was particularly important to Clatworthy was keeping all the marketing community engaged. Two
tools helped her do this. One was an ABM-er-of-the-month programme, which

recognized the great work of individuals and highlighted their achievements. The other was actively soliciting feedback from the ABM team. To do this, Clatworthy employed a stop/start/continue construct that she first took the team through at the end of the third quarter. This approach not only reinforced the fact that the ABM team was shaping the direction of the programme but also provided crucial input to continuously improve the programme itself.

**Leveraging core marketing skills**    In addition to working closely with the corporate marketing programmes and events, ABM pulled heavily on many of the central marketing functions at Fujitsu. For example, the ABM-ers worked closely with the market intelligence team to produce annual reports for each ABM customer. With input from market intelligence on key industry and technology trends, and insights from the ABM-er on specific customer engagements and customer priorities, the resulting output provided a summary (indeed, almost a case study) of what Fujitsu had done for the customer in the last year and some forward thinking about future issues and opportunities.

In collaboration with the digital team, these annual reports were published in a sleek e-book template that looked impressive and was easy to deliver. The digital team also adapted some of its social listening activity to track important activity at an account level and share it with the appropriate ABM-er.

### Results

The ABM programme's performance was tracked broadly under three areas – reputation, relationships and revenue – though marketing didn't have a hard target in the third:

- **Revenues** – the revenue results were strong enough that the business units clamoured for even more ABM.
- **Relationships** – while the company's regular 'voice of the customer' programme would over time offer a hard measure, in the interim Clatworthy tracked many proxy data points. For example, one characteristic of a good customer relationship was that individuals reply quickly to an invitation, even if they couldn't attend. If they didn't respond at all, then there was no relationship with them.
- **Reputation** – this was very difficult to measure, especially the customer advocacy journey that she defined at the start of the programme. So she put in some hard measures on making sure the team had what was called a 'reference summary' updated for every ABM customer, where they were an existing customer within the year. Although the ABM team didn't manage to hit the

target completely in the first year, it did succeed in creating updated reference summaries for 86 per cent of their ABM accounts, with the target of 100 per cent for the following year.

**Lessons learned**

There were a number of lessons learned along the way. These were what Clatworthy considered the most important:

- Get buy-in early on from the business, sales and account management and delivery communities – and engage with them at the right level. Although Clatworthy had done a thorough job of gaining the support of the senior executives, she didn't initially plan anything to help educate the sales and business development teams. As a result, she and her team ended up putting a great deal of effort into educating these groups along the way. Her advice? Run sales education programmes from the start.
- Select accounts carefully. Evaluate potential opportunity over 18 to 24 months, not just three to six, and make sure there is good potential to work well with the account team. The business opportunity has to be there, but so does the compatibility between the marketing and sales teams.
- Integrate with the account planning process and work closely with the account team. Where no account plan existed, the ABM plan became the document everyone worked to. The biggest challenge in most accounts was creating a plan that would support opportunities but not put marketing on the line for actually closing them, since that job belonged to sales.
- Get every marketer properly trained in ABM. Even if individuals decided not to go ahead, they at least understood what the ABM team was trying to do.
- Provide ABM refresher training throughout the year. Clatworthy wished she had planned a one-day ABM refresher for the marketing team in the third quarter. 'Some of the stuff you teach people at the start of the process they're not actually starting to use until three to six months in, so you need to remind them,' she noted.
- Be clear on what makes a really good ABM-er. Attitude, enthusiasm and a willingness to interact directly with customers are all essential. Having the appropriate mix of marketing skills is table stakes, but great ABM-ers understand that customers are people, not a theoretical concept.
- Do fewer accounts, better. Clatworthy was adamant that quality trumps quantity in ABM, so she dramatically scaled back the number of ABM accounts in the region from 58 to 36 in the 2015/16 financial year.

- Innovation workshops are a powerful way of driving opportunities. For new accounts in particular, ABM is a powerful way to get prospects to the point of engaging in one of these workshops.
- Be clear about the difference between deal-based marketing and ABM. Some accounts initially selected for ABM had major bids running, so the effort was focused on supporting those opportunities rather than the full ABM process. Once these deals were concluded, Clatworthy and her team were looking forward to expanding the scope of marketing efforts to build on the successful bid marketing done to date.

# Deciding what you want to achieve with ABM

The first step is to determine the specific objectives for your ABM programme. This is critical to prevent a wasteful diffusion of resources and lacklustre outcomes. As suggested in the previous chapter, there are four main contexts in which ABM can be used and your programme may address one or more of these:

- Cross-selling/upselling for account penetration. This uses a more structured, planned approach geared to increasing share of wallet and share of mind through better and deeper relationships and potentially can be done with partners. In companies that sell services to clients based on the premise of continuing cost improvement, there is often a need to cross-sell and upsell further solutions to strategic accounts to augment falling revenues from the core outsourcing contract.

- Changing perception or positioning. Enhancing positioning and/or changing perceptions, often important when a company goes through a rebranding, a merger or acquisition, or is shifting from a transactional product focus to a solutions-based company.

- Developing new accounts. A key characteristic of ABM is about creating an integrated approach with sales to penetrate new accounts. For companies looking to grow market share rapidly, ABM can be used to target attractive new blue-chip clients.

- Pursuing identified major opportunities. ABM can support accounts based on requests for proposals (RFPs) or identified major sales opportunities. Marketing's link with sales is more tactical and short-term here and can be the result of an established central 'tiger team'.

While the following chapters will take a more detailed look at implementing the ABM philosophy and methodology, it's worth taking some time to ensure you are clear about your strategic goals for the programme before you start down the ABM path.

# Positioning ABM as a strategic business initiative

The quickest way to go wrong with ABM is to position it as a marketing-led initiative without the support and collaboration of the business at the highest level. ITSMA benchmark studies[1] have found that many companies still struggle to get this right:

- Almost three-quarters saw ABM as predominantly marketing-led, rather than a business-led initiative.

- Two-thirds of respondents had multiple, uncoordinated ABM initiatives in different geographies, business units or both.

- Most ABM practitioners were doing it without a governing council or programme management office.

- ABM initiatives were funded primarily by field marketing, which meant ABM remained a localized, tactical activity.

While the latter three points will be addressed further on in this chapter, it is worth emphasizing the point about ABM's positioning. It can be far too common for organizations, particularly in the B2B arena, to position marketing as a support for sales. But companies where marketers are viewed solely as, say, event planners and brochure writers will struggle to find success with ABM because marketing and sales have to be equal partners to engage effectively.

ABM is most successful when positioned as a strategic growth programme in the same way as new key account management or sales approaches are positioned. This has become even more important in the face of the powerful driving forces first outlined in the previous chapter, such as commoditization, hyper-competition, technology, globalization and changing buyer behaviour. It demands that companies work in a joined-up way from the market *in* rather than from the company *out* (see box 'Marketing's changing role').

## Marketing's changing role

Research carried out for ITSMA's *State of the Marketing Profession 2016* report[2] found that marketing appears to be evolving from its original brand and reputation focus to more of an emphasis on revenue growth through a range of lead-generation/lead-nurturing activities. This, in turn, is leading to a greater focus on deepening engagement and relationships with customers at all stages of the buying cycle.

The survey showed that marketing is adding value to organizations in a number of ways:

- Marketing precision is improving with new marketing tools, new approaches and more ways of reaching and engaging with clients and prospects, with the resulting shift from mass marketing to segment/targeted marketing and through to account-based marketing.

- The scope of marketing is expanding as marketing leaders and marketing teams are adding new responsibilities, from customer engagement programmes to alliance management to business development and account planning, having revenue contribution goals and owning marketing technology.

- Marketers are becoming more involved in predicting outcomes and not just tracking activity. They are harnessing data from internal systems to spot trends, determine who's more likely to buy, or who's less likely to renew, and what prospects are ready to buy using new tools to build models to predict behaviour.

- Marketing is nurturing relationships well beyond just lead creation or lead nurturing. Nurturing leads is tactical. It can be done automatically using a piece of software on a schedule. Nurturing relationships is more strategic and requires human contact. Buyers increasingly want their suppliers/partners to know them and based on that knowledge provide relevant content and proactively bring them ideas that will solve their business problems or open opportunities. Above all, they demand open and honest two-way conversations about where the business is going.

- Marketing is emerging as a driver of growth as more and more marketers are able to show the link between marketing activities and business outcomes and business impact.

- Marketing at its best can act as the central hub for customer information, much like the central nervous system in the body, by building the right information systems, implementing agile processes and leveraging sophisticated analytics tools, supported with the best talent.

- Marketing can be the catalyst for culture change in other parts of the organization by influencing sales processes, account prioritization, customer engagement and through gathering insights from data analysis to spot problems and opportunities.

# Creating the right framework for effective governance

Once the strategic momentum is there, building the foundation for ABM success is about creating the right framework for ABM, including governance, funding and employing the most appropriate tools and technologies.

The starting point is to find the appropriate business sponsor. As has been repeatedly emphasized, the quickest way to go wrong is to position ABM as the latest marketing-led 'fad' without strong support and active collaboration from the business as a whole. Centralizing and formalizing ABM governance is essential for a number of reasons:

- An ABM programme will be a core part of the company's strategic plan. Over time it needs to become part of the corporate culture.

- Tough decisions need to be made between dedicated or shared resources.

- Marketing and sales should be working toward a common set of management objectives based on team performance.

- Growth and expansion need to be closely monitored and controlled.

One approach used successfully by a number of companies is to create a senior-level ABM leadership governing council or steering group representing marketing, sales, business units and delivery teams (Figure 2.1). This leadership council will oversee the adoption, execution and alignment of the ABM programme by:

- defining the rules of engagement;
- serving as the hub for strategic decision making for all ABM activities;

**Figure 2.1**    ABM programme governance bodies

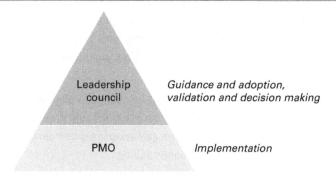

- allocating required resources;
- resolving conflicts;
- identifying systems needed to manage and track progress.

Take time to decide who will be on the steering committee, since that will send strong signals about top-level commitment.

Implementation can then be put in the hands of a programme management office (PMO) which will be charged with:

- supporting the alignment, integration and prioritization of all ABM activities across practices;
- managing and driving the implementation of client-focused ABM campaigns locally;
- managing the application of resources.

## Making the metrics count

With research by ITSMA over the last decade consistently showing that ABM generates the highest return on investment (ROI) of any B2B marketing programme, why isn't every company doing it – or, at the very least, more of it?

The answer is probably a failure to lay the appropriate groundwork by developing a strong set of metrics for measuring and communicating the performance of ABM from the start. Once the steering group is in place, the members need to agree on the objectives and metrics which will frame the ABM programme.

There are three fundamental challenges that all organizations face in delivering and demonstrating the powerful returns ABM can generate:

- First, marketing must accurately measure and evaluate the ROI of ABM programmes, which is not always as straightforward a task as it might seem.

- Second, marketing leaders must establish a point of comparison to other marketing programmes.

- Finally, and most importantly, stakeholders need to agree a realistic time-line for ABM to deliver results. ABM programmes usually, although not always, take longer to achieve ROI than other marketing approaches, such as segment-based campaigns that have concrete objectives, wider target audiences, and quarterly time horizons (Figure 2.2).

You need to establish a standardized, account-level metrics dashboard to track success, measuring both qualitative and quantitative results that can be aggregated up to a programme level. ABM metrics should cover three main categories:

- Relationships: which indicate broader and deeper penetration within accounts.

- Reputation: which may include changing or improving perception and/or educating accounts about your full portfolio of offerings or capabilities.

- Revenues: including growth in total pipeline as well as specific, identified sales opportunities.

**Figure 2.2**    Marketing ROI over time

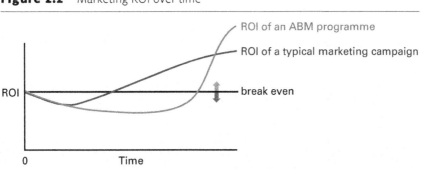

Any ABM programme should regularly track performance both for individual accounts and at the programme level. Although the metrics used for account-level and programme-level evaluation may be the same, they tend to vary in importance. Hard metrics, like pipeline growth, total revenue tied to ABM initiatives, and revenue growth, are among the most important programme metrics. Most of the programme metrics tend to be lagging indicators: in other words, measurement of results achieved.

In addition, specific metrics can often differ from account to account, just as the specific objectives for the ABM plan in the account will differ. In ITSMA's 2016 benchmarking study,[3] the most popular account metrics used in strategic, Lite and programmatic ABM varied, with a broader set of metrics common at the strategic level (see Chapter 12 for more detail on this).

Account metrics usually include a number of soft metrics as well, which can encompass leading indicators of ABM performance. These can include the number of new executive relationships within the account, number of executive meetings, number of new relationships in new lines of business, and quality of relationships. These metrics are predictors of future success, particularly where ABM has not been in place long enough to deliver concrete financial results.

**Table 2.1**   Top metrics used to evaluate ABM

|  | **Strategic ABM (N = 47)** | **ABM Lite (N = 45)** | **Programmatic ABM (N = 29)** |
|---|---|---|---|
| 1 | Pipeline growth (68%) | Pipeline growth (67%) | Revenue growth (55%) |
| 2 | Revenue growth (57%) | Revenue growth (58%) | Pipeline growth (52%) |
| 3 | Sales rep feedback (34%) | Win rate (33%) | Client engagement (41%) |
| 4 | Client engagement (34%) | Sales rep feedback (31%) | Total revenue tied to ABM initiatives (41%) |
| 5 | Customer satisfaction (32%) | Total revenue tied to ABM initiatives (31%) | |

**NOTE** Up to five responses allowed
**SOURCE** ITSMA, Account-Based Marketing Benchmarking Survey, March 2016

Note the top metrics used to evaluate the three types of ABM by around a third or more of companies (Table 2.1).

# Devoting sufficient funding and allocating the budget intelligently

An ABM programme demands resources. It can take, on average, up to a fifth of the marketing budget. Nevertheless, almost 70 per cent of marketers were expecting to increase investment in 2016[4] (Figures 2.3 and 2.4).

**Figure 2.3**   Size of the 2015 ABM budget (as % of total marketing budget)

In FY2015, approximately what percentage of your marketing budget was spent on ABM?
% of respondents (N = 44)

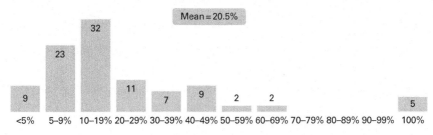

SOURCE ITSMA, Account-Based Marketing Benchmarking Survey, March 2016

**Figure 2.4**   Change in the ABM budget for 2016

What are your spending plans in FY2016 for account-based marketing?
% of respondents (N = 94)

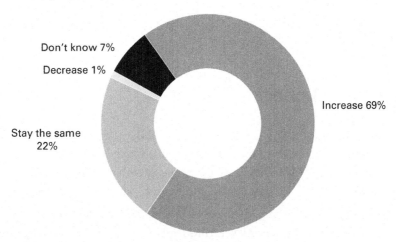

Don't know 7%
Decrease 1%
Increase 69%
Stay the same 22%

SOURCE ITSMA, Account-Based Marketing Benchmarking Survey, March 2016

**Figure 2.5**   Biggest ABM challenges

What is your biggest ABM challenge? % of respondents (N=61)

| | |
|---|---|
| Getting adequate budget to support programmes and resources | 38 |
| Justifying the programme costs/ proving ROI | 21 |
| Hiring marketers with the right experience and talent | 18 |
| Collaborating with sales | 15 |

**NOTE** Differences are significantly different
**SOURCE** ITSMA, Account-Based Marketing Benchmarking Survey, March 2016

Deciding on the initial funding and how the budget will be allocated can make or break an ABM programme. Ideally, both marketing and sales will be committed enough to the initiative to contribute the necessary resources to ensure cooperation.

Decisions have to be taken about a number of issues. For example:

- Who pays for the initial research needed to collect in-depth client insights?
- How many marketers can we afford to allocate to the programme? Do we need to hire more?
- Which department will fund the marketing communications activities?
- Who will fund the central tools and templates that help make each individual ABM plan more effective to deliver?

ITSMA research has found that securing adequate budget and resources is the main challenge for marketers in strategic ABM, the second biggest challenge in ABM Lite, and the third biggest challenge in programmatic ABM. Earlier benchmarking studies[5] showed that a lack of budget and resources can prevent ABM programmes from building, standardizing, achieving scale and ultimately realizing sufficient ROI (Figure 2.5). This has been a consistent finding.

# Your ABM checklist

1 Determine specific objectives for your ABM programme to prevent a wasteful diffusion of resources and lacklustre outcomes.
2 Position your ABM initiative as a strategic growth programme in the same way that new key account management or sales approaches are positioned.
3 Create the appropriate governance framework including the right business sponsor and a senior-level ABM leadership council or steering group representing marketing, sales, business units and delivery teams.

4 Develop a strong set of metrics for measuring and communicating ABM performance from the start.

5 Remember: deciding on the initial funding and how the budget will be allocated can make or break an ABM programme.

## Notes

1 ITSMA (2014) *Account-Based Marketing Benchmarking Study*

2 ITSMA (2016) *State of the Marketing Profession*

**3, 4** ITSMA (2016) *Account-Based Marketing Benchmarking Survey*

5 ITSMA (2013) *Account-Based Marketing Benchmarking Survey*

# Investing in the right tools and technologies

## 03

## Challenges and opportunities of modern technology

Modern developments in marketing technology offer organizations keen to implement an ABM programme the tantalizing promise of lightening the load and, more significantly, the cost, particularly as their programmes scale up. More companies can now consider implementing elements of ABM in a programmatic approach, thanks to the advances in areas such as IP-based personalization or account intelligence and stakeholder profiling.

The two main questions those overseeing a strategic ABM initiative should ask as marketing technologies become mainstream and ABM programmes face pressure to expand are:

- How can we put existing marketing technology to use in an ABM programme?
- What else is out there to support ABM?

Any technology tool that can help improve the efficiency of what can be a resource-intensive investment, extend programme reach and can potentially generate significant returns should be welcome. But there is a danger it can do more harm than good, such as automated horizontal marketing campaigns, which, although well intentioned, are poorly thought through in terms of the impact on carefully-selected ABM accounts. Sending generic e-mails to contacts who have been carefully cultivated through a coordinated ABM programme can quickly undo months of effort.

Part of the challenge is that many marketing automation systems, a cornerstone of marketing technology infrastructure, have been designed to do anything but ABM. While these are without doubt critical tools, making them work effectively in an ABM context requires both considerable creativity and patience. For example, there is no way to create an overall account view in these systems. However, a growing number of new tools are now being developed to support ABM specifically. More importantly, there are many ways in which existing technology can make operating ABM programmes more efficient and effective.

There are two main areas in which technology tools are important: 1) supporting ABM initiatives in individual accounts; 2) managing ABM initiatives at a programme level across multiple accounts.

# Supporting ABM in individual accounts

The many and varied activities that go into planning and executing ABM can be grouped at a high level into five main categories:

**1** Communicating between marketing and sales.

**2** Gathering market, account and stakeholder intelligence.

**3** Creating plays and value propositions.

**4** Defining and executing tailored campaigns.

**5** Measuring and tracking progress.

Figure 3.1 shows where the various technology tools available today could be used to support these ABM activities.

**Figure 3.1**  Mapping marketing technology to ABM activities

| Gather market, account, and stakeholder intelligence | Create plays and value propositions | Define and execute campaigns | Measure and track progress |
| --- | --- | --- | --- |
| Digital advertising & retargeting | | | |
| Personalization (website, content) | | | Business intelligence |
| Social listening/social media | | | |
| Insight platforms | | | |
| CRM and marketing automation | | | |
| Communicate between marketing and sales | | | |

**SOURCE** ITSMA and Inverta, 2015

**Figure 3.2** Technology platforms supporting ABM programmes

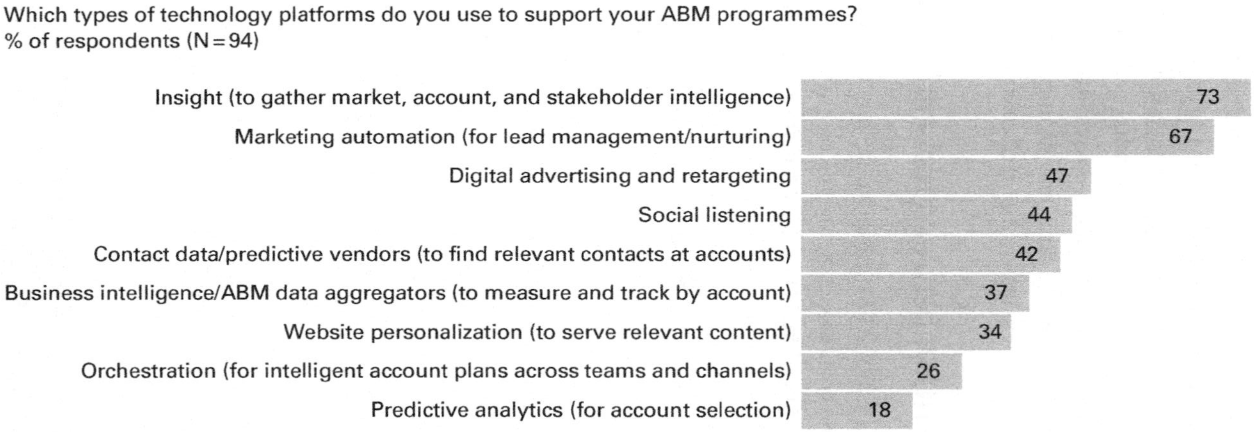

Which types of technology platforms do you use to support your ABM programmes?
% of respondents (N = 94)

| Platform | % |
|---|---|
| Insight (to gather market, account, and stakeholder intelligence) | 73 |
| Marketing automation (for lead management/nurturing) | 67 |
| Digital advertising and retargeting | 47 |
| Social listening | 44 |
| Contact data/predictive vendors (to find relevant contacts at accounts) | 42 |
| Business intelligence/ABM data aggregators (to measure and track by account) | 37 |
| Website personalization (to serve relevant content) | 34 |
| Orchestration (for intelligent account plans across teams and channels) | 26 |
| Predictive analytics (for account selection) | 18 |

NOTE Multiple responses allowed
SOURCE ITSMA, Account-Based Marketing Benchmarking Survey, March 2016

However, the latest ITSMA research into this area[1] shows that technology platforms are not used in each of these areas to support ABM programmes yet. Instead, they are most commonly used to gather market, account and stakeholder insight. Almost three-quarters of ABM-ers use technology in this way. The next most popular are marketing automation tools for lead management and nurturing, used by two-thirds of marketers. Around half use digital advertising and retargeting technology platforms. Figure 3.2 provides a more comprehensive view of what is being used today.

As marketing as a whole becomes increasingly enabled by technology, ABM will no doubt follow the same adoption curve, until each of the main areas are more comprehensively supported with digital tools.

## 1. Communication between marketing and sales

The foundation of any ABM initiative is the collaborative effort between marketing and sales. This depends on clear, consistent communication. Essential information, like account and market intelligence, value propositions, account plans, updates on campaign execution and information on what content individuals have consumed online should be readily available and easy to access. It is even better if it is in one place.

In reality, of course, these different bits of information are coming from many different sources. Some are generated by systems such as marketing automation and content management while others are project outputs, which may be manually refreshed periodically, like the account plan. The goal is to make sure everyone who needs access to the information can find it whenever and wherever they need it.

The other challenge is ensuring they have access to the right level of information. It is certainly possible to integrate data from marketing automation systems into customer relationship management (CRM) systems so that the sales team has a view of the marketing activity targeted to individuals in their accounts. The problem is often choosing between providing too much detailed information like opens, click-throughs, bounce-backs and unsubscribes, or too little, where there is a very high level view of responses to marketing contact that misses critical insights.

## 2. Gathering and managing marketing, account and stakeholder intelligence

Once the account has been selected and the marketing and sales team assembled, the next step in any ABM initiative, whether existing client or new account, is to gather information to create an up-to-date under-standing of the account and to profile stakeholders. The problem isn't so much tapping into the huge wealth of information available as determin-ing which elements are useful or important and placing them into the right context.

- Insight platforms. Specialist research companies like Avention, Lead-Bridge, CRISIL and M-Brain have long been useful sources of account intelligence. In the last few years a new category of research compa-nies has emerged, such as agent3, which uses traditional market research methods and web tools to help build account profiles and has developed technology platforms to help ABM teams to maintain, communicate, and build on initial insights.

- Social listening tools. Although many research and marketing intelligence providers will include social listening in their project work, this is some-thing ABM teams can do for themselves on an ongoing basis. It is a great source of insight on companies and key individuals, particularly if they are active on social media sites such as Twitter and LinkedIn. A wide variety of social listening tools is available. Many marketing organiza-tions will already have one or two in operation to monitor mentions and trends. For ABM, it is just a question of adding a new set of parameters specific to the accounts and stakeholders that matter.

- Content personalization systems. A growing number of technologies on the market are designed to serve personalized content to individuals based on their demonstrated preferences. These systems not only can improve engagement because they offer better-targeted content but also provide more detailed feedback on what kinds of materials and subjects indi-vidual stakeholders find most engaging and respond to more frequently.

- Digital advertising and retargeting. Although we usually think of digi-tal advertising as a tool in campaign execution – and it is – it is also an increasingly valuable source of information on individuals and accounts. Using reverse-IP look-up and cookies, different tools can tell you who is looking at what on your website as well as what else they are looking at online. This offers a view of, for example, which offer-ings may be most compelling and what competitors they may also be evaluating. While the main goal for digital advertising and retargeting is awareness, these tools can also offer a means of gathering intent data. You can acquire useful intelligence by reviewing the number and type of search terms made by a given company as a by-product of digital ads and retargeting.

## 3. Creating plays and value propositions

Perhaps the most fundamental elements of ABM – developing the plays that sales and marketing will execute into the account and creating targeted value propositions – are the ones that are least addressed by existing technology. With the exception of agent3's insight platform, which maps account issues against your offering portfolio, there are very few, if any, specialized technology tools to help.

Creating plays and targeted value propositions represents the 'heavy lifting' of ABM. This is where the bulk of the analysis and creative thinking come into play. And, for the foreseeable future, there are no technology tools that will significantly change that.

## 4. Planning and executing ABM campaigns

Most marketing technologies today are designed for campaign execution, whether that's in the context of ABM or not. And while they can certainly be put to good use in ABM, there is a big gap that nothing out there really addresses at this point: campaign planning. While we do expect this gap to be filled at some point, no tool will ever be able to substitute the intuition and creative thinking that ABM teams contribute to designing campaigns.

Executing ABM campaigns, however, is the central area in which marketing technology can help. The recurring theme is that these tools are not designed to meet the particular needs of ABM, but they can be configured and applied in such a way to support your ABM initiatives.

Listed below are the key areas in terms of ABM campaigns. Some of these tools are foundations of marketing technology infrastructure while others are quickly becoming so. If these seem very similar to the technologies that are most helpful in gathering account intelligence, that's because they are. The advantage of these technologies is that they create what is effectively a feedback loop, if used correctly. The key technologies are:

- Marketing automation and CRM. Marketing automation is the cornerstone of marketing technology infrastructure, but its benefit is severely limited unless it is well integrated with CRM systems. This is particularly evident in ABM.

- Website and content personalization. If you have invested the time and effort to develop account-specific plays, value propositions, and even supporting content, it makes sense to invest in marketing technology tools that will help to promote those personalized messages to the account and individuals they are intended for. There are two primary types of customization tools that can help. One type of tool is website customization. Through IP address look-up, these tools allow you, in real time, to shape the content that particular visitors see on your website. Content personalization, the other type of tool, helps to promote content in two ways: determining which content pieces should be sent in a push mode (eg e-mail) and suggesting related content to individuals in a pull mode (eg browsing or reading on your website or microsite).

- Digital advertising and retargeting. Digital advertising and retargeting offer the ability to place highly targeted ads and to gain insight, through retargeting, into where stakeholders in an account are spending their time online and what they're interested in. Taken together, they are a powerful source of intelligence and an excellent means of promoting brand awareness.

- Social media. These media offer different channels for direct communication with individuals in key accounts. They are also a means for communicating personalized messages frequently, directly, and cost effectively.

## 5. Measuring and tracking results

A critical element of applying marketing technology to ABM is ensuring that your tools are integrated in such a way that you can review and track what is happening on an ongoing basis. As with all marketing and sales programmes, a plethora of information comes from numerous systems, posing significant challenges to measuring and tracking results, particularly for ABM.

At the account level, CRM systems are the most obvious place to review and track ABM progress. They provide a view of activities, interactions, and opportunities or deals – the last of which are, ultimately, the most important metrics for measuring ABM impact.

The drawback of using CRM systems to track ABM results is that they are only part of the picture. You'll need to pull information from other systems as well, particularly marketing automation and personalization systems. Since there really isn't an easy way to integrate this into a CRM dashboard, that means reviewing multiple dashboards to get the full perspective.

While there are a variety of flexible and often inexpensive dashboard tools available on the market – many of which are cloud-based – the better answer may well be to evaluate tools that operate at the ABM programme level and can provide dashboards and analysis at the account level as well, such as Engagio. Regardless of the tool you use, the biggest hurdle is getting data clean enough to provide useful analysis (see case study 'CSC – Linking marketing activity to business results').

# Managing ABM programmes across accounts

The challenge of measuring and monitoring ABM results becomes even more critical when looking across multiple accounts at the ABM programme overall. At the programme level, you need to be able to do several things well, preferably with up-to-date information:

- monitor individual ABM accounts;
- track overall programme performance;
- compare performance of ABM accounts versus non-ABM accounts;
- prioritize current and potential ABM accounts.

To perform this kind of analysis requires a wide range of information that comes from multiple systems, not just the CRM and marketing tools, but corporate information systems as well. In particular, financial systems are likely to be a key source of information. Your finance and corporate functions are probably already using an enterprise-class business intelligence (BI) tool to conduct other kinds of reporting and analysis. The best option for most marketing organizations is to extend these corporate BI tools to cover the specific requirements of ABM reporting and analysis. This makes reporting to the executive team that much easier, while offering another means of reinforcing the point that ABM is really a business strategy like any other.

**CASE STUDY**  CSC – Linking marketing activity to business results

CSC had succeeded over the years selling complex, technology-based services to a handful of clients. The company had been flying under the radar, with 80 per cent of revenue from fewer than 1,000 long-standing clients. Advertising was an anathema to the company founders and marketing a relatively new addition to the corporate bailiwick.

When Nick Panayi, CSC's Head of digital marketing and global brand, joined the company in June 2011, he hoped for a sizeable advertising budget to accomplish his mission of shoring up CSC's brand awareness. The budget never materialized. Instead, Panayi got a senior management mandate to leapfrog the competition by building a best-practice model for demand generation and lead management.

CSC recognized that buyer behaviour was changing and the buying process was going digital. Even within CSC's small group of large clients, the company was missing opportunities. The first thing marketing had to do was to build the infrastructure to track the digital footsteps and body language of every prospect and client.

'I set out to prove the model of how sales and marketing could work together, doubling down in some areas and making decisions to divest in others. If I showed the value of marketing, then the money would come,' said Panayi. The marketing dashboard was born.

### A robust digital ecosystem

The power behind the CSC dashboard was the integrated digital ecosystem that enabled tiered data. Everything rolled up into one number: total contract value (TCV). From that number the dashboard user could click to drill into detail: the name and contact of every lead, where he or she was in the buying process, assets viewed on the website, events attended and responses to campaign calls-to-action. Or the user could dissect individual campaigns or the sales pipeline, analyse content quality based on usage or determine the contribution of social media over live events.

'The most difficult part was not the dashboard itself. It was collecting all the underlying elements,' according to Panayi. 'If you looked at CSC two years before, you would see a company caught in a 1990s time warp. No digital marketing or sales infrastructure to speak of. Pockets of digital brilliance, but a decentralized marketing organization that gave rise to siloed systems.'

That all changed. A new chief marketing officer (CMO), Neil Blakesley, spear-headed a marketing centralization initiative soon after he arrived in June 2013 to improve support to the business units. The company developed a new website, a marketing automation platform, and content management platforms, as well as numerous analytics tools. Based on over 50 different digital systems, which, remarkably, were all integrated, the company built a true digital infrastructure in about a year. Without this integrated digital infrastructure there would be no dashboard. As Chris Marin, director of the digital marketing platform, said, 'There's a lot more behind the dashboard than most people realize'.

### A best-of-breed solution

Fifty different digital systems might seem excessive. Wouldn't it be better to purchase a more comprehensive solution that did not have to be stitched together? But, as Panayi pointed out, the marketing technology landscape was in constant flux, with new players appearing daily. Consolidation was happening, but waiting was not an option.

Besides, Panayi was a firm believer in best-of-breed solutions. Every new player might have a feature or benefit that would give CSC a new advantage. He didn't want to miss these opportunities. Rather, his approach was to build a flexible, integrated digital ecosystem in which CSC could plug and unplug different elements.

### Sales and marketing under one roof

'Marketing needed to show the sales team how marketing could be a powerful tool to help sales,' said Dorothea Gosling, Account-Based Marketing (ABM) and Pursuit Marketing Centre of Excellence leader. In fact, CSC put sales and marketing on the same  team, reporting to the same senior vice president and establishing marketing as a player.

Marketing at CSC was responsible for generating quality leads and working hand-in-hand with sales to move them through the pipeline. Marketing automation had to connect with sales automation. Building the lead-generation and management model was a collaborative process, from the establishment of the initial definitions through to the implementation and rollout. Consequently, the marketing dashboard showed a seamless linkage between sales and marketing.

The most important stitch in the digital ecosystem was the bond between sales and marketing. Many marketing organizations talk about marketing handing off leads to sales. At CSC, marketing didn't hand off leads. It stayed involved to nurture the lead to revenue and beyond. Sales and marketing developed formal service-level agreements (SLAs) based on well-documented definitions and processes: What is a lead? What is a qualified lead? Who gets credit for generating the lead? What are the reasons a lead can be rejected? What happens to a lead once it is rejected? All of this and more were codified in the system.

## Getting the analytics in shape

CSC found that the ability to analyse and interpret data didn't go far enough. 'The ability to use data to build models to predict the future will be the next proving ground for marketing science,' believed Panayi. Without predictive analytics, dashboards were nothing more than rear-view mirrors. Predictive models would separate good marketing from great. CSC started with a few simple models to be added to over time:

- Lead score. Assigned a number based on a prospect's digital behaviour, level of engagement, demographics, and firmographics. The lead score allowed CSC to identify potential leads before they 'raised their hand'.
- Multichannel attribution. Determined which marketing channels (eg social media, SEO, e-mail, live event) were working by assigning points every time a lead was advanced. All the touches were aggregated to determine which channel carried the most weight.
- Content score. Assigned a content score based on visits, downloads, page views, average time onsite, and cross-visits. CSC calculated a score for 30,000 pieces of content on its website and ranked them. The scores were recalculated daily.
- Valued visits. Predicted future lead activity by modelling website visits. Value visits were based on the aggregated behaviours that correlated with a prospect becoming a marketing lead. The model excluded visits from students, partners, job seekers, and others unlikely to buy.
- Personalization. Presented or suggested appropriate website content after identifying the company based on IP address, determining the industry and interpreting the visitor's behaviours.

## Building the dashboard

The main objective was to build a dashboard that was consumable and digestible by busy people with limited time because no one wanted to deal with the thousands of reports produced by the digital ecosystem. So Panayi and his team set out to build a global marketing dashboard that would bring together all the key business metrics the executive team wanted to see as well as high-level summary charts of marketing metrics they might also be interested in. They wanted a dashboard that could be updated daily, dynamically and automatically.

To ensure that the dashboard was used every day, it needed to be intuitive and visually pleasing. Here's where the art of marketing was just as important as the science. Marketers put their design skills to work creating a dashboard that not only had important, useful information but also looked good and reflected the CSC brand.

CSC started with a plan, and the plan started by defining key performance indicators (KPIs). Having to define which metrics to use on the dashboard forced everybody to get on the same page and articulate why they mattered and how they tied into the bigger picture.

It took five months to choose and define KPIs. Only after the plan was fully fleshed out did the search for specialized software begin. The final choice was a dashboard product from GoodData, which recommended a consultant to guide them through the process. The decision to buy a product rather than build a proprietary system enabled CSC to get the dashboard up and running in three months.

### The KPIs senior leadership cares about

The CSC executive mandate to marketing was clear: generate leads that resulted in closed business both with new accounts and the existing client base. The KPIs CSC's senior leadership cared about most were:

- total contract value (TCV);
- marketing-qualified leads (MQLs);
- marketing-sourced pipeline (MSP);
- marketing-assisted pipeline (MAP).

The top level of the dashboard – the marketing overview tab – showed these four measures, with MQLs and their derivation displayed prominently. These were the metrics that business executives most wanted to see.

If the executive wanted more detail, the dashboard also provided drill-down capability, thanks to the integrated CSC digital ecosystem. Everything rolled up into total contract value. From there, the executive could click through to find the detail: the name and contact of every lead, where they were in the buying process, assets viewed on the website, events attended, responses to campaign calls-to-action, and so on. Additional tabs summarized KPIs for global marketing: web, brand, content, social media, leads and attribution.

### Metrics that matter

CSC didn't report solely on what was easy to measure and didn't throw in metrics simply because it could. Instead, CSC measured only what affected total contract value. For instance, some web traffic was tied to TCV and some was not. Visitors who looked for case studies and descriptions of offerings were more likely to be buyers than those who looked at management team bios and press releases. So the definition of valued visits, which in turn tied into marketing-influenced leads, excluded visitors who failed to engage with critical web content.

The dashboard had a mirror set of metrics just for key customers and targets that were part of the CSC ABM programme. As Marin explained, 'It is the 80:20 rule. We care about these visits more than our average visitors.' They were also looking at funnel advancement, whether it was forward or backward, to pinpoint which assets worked the best, where there were gaps and where prospects were getting stuck and why.

### Lessons learned

CSC attributed the success of the dashboards to four factors. None were primarily about technology, and all had more to do with people, and, in particular, with collaboration, communication, and process:

- Establish a common vocabulary. Marketing worked collaboratively with the sales team to identify and define the metrics, pipeline stages, and processes. That way, sales, sales operations, corporate marketing, field marketing, marketing operations, and IT were all speaking the same language.
- Over-communicate. When everything is new, there needs to be plenty of communication. CSC marketing used to be decentralized, with each business unit or team doing its own thing. Now everyone used a common set of processes and tools. Senior leadership never had much need to follow marketing metrics; now marketing metrics functioned as leading indicators for the business. All of these changes required education – lots of it.
- Recognize that developing dashboards is an iterative process. Although the marketing team planned the dashboard and defined all KPIs prior to implementation, the plan had to accommodate critiques from sales, marketing leaders, and senior executives. CSC started with a soft launch among the digital brand and marketing teams to evaluate the information collected and the look and feel. Following the soft launch, the dashboard was rolled out to the entire organization.
- Hire the smartest people you can find. Creating a robust digital infrastructure, integrating marketing automation and salesforce management systems, and building predictive analytical models may not be rocket science, but it's close. You need people who can integrate the technology and algorithms into a business context. Add the need to collaborate and communicate, and the applicant pool narrows even further. But the people are out there. You just have to find them.

# Your ABM checklist

**1** There are a growing number of new tools being developed to support ABM specifically. But make sure that using marketing automation tools doesn't detract from the purpose of ABM.

**2** Choose the right tool for the right job in terms of planning and executing ABM for individual accounts:

- communicating between marketing and sales;
- gathering market, account and stakeholder intelligence;
- creating plays and value propositions;
- defining and executing tailored campaigns;
- measuring and tracking progress.

**3** The challenge of monitoring and measuring ABM results becomes even more critical when looking across multiple accounts and requires not just employing CRM and marketing tools but corporate information systems as well.

# Note

**1** ITSMA (2016) *Account-Based Marketing Benchmarking Survey*

# Deciding which accounts to focus on

04

## Not all accounts are equal

Account selection has a major impact on your potential success with ABM, regardless of whether you are just getting started, increasing your programme's size and scope or managing a mature programme. You can give yourself the greatest chance of meeting your objectives for ABM by selecting those accounts which have the best potential to achieve your ABM goals.

If your main priority is account growth, for example, it is essential to select accounts that have an appropriate level of spending (sometimes referred to as 'size of wallet') to support your growth ambitions. Also, you're unlikely to get significant growth in an account where your customer is already spending 90 per cent of their available budget with you. If your main priority is to win some flagship companies, or anchor accounts in a market or sector, you need to select those that have influence over their peers and the confidence of analysts for their foreseeable future.

Regardless of your near-term objective for ABM, the long-term goal ultimately boils down to supporting the growth strategy of your business in every case.

While the size of the account's available budget is an important criterion, it is only one of several that should be taken into account. Determining which criteria to evaluate and what weight to give each of them is a key part of the selection process and will vary from organization to organization.

In many cases, your company will already have been through an account prioritization process, to enable decisions as to where to invest sales and account management resources, or even commercial, finance, HR and other functional support.

Where this tiering of accounts exists is your starting point for selecting ABM accounts. Typically, there will be a list of strategic accounts receiving account management attention (either one or more people dedicated to a major account or a one-to-few model where an account manager is responsible for a handful of accounts).

Beneath this top tier comes a list of key accounts which have the potential to become strategic to the business in the medium term, or are buying all they can from you today so are worth defending. These are usually managed in a one-to-few model, or given to salespeople or service delivery managers to look after.

After this second tier comes a list of 'named' accounts that the company is interested in doing business with. These accounts often form a salesperson's patch to pursue or prospect in.

Underneath these three tiers comes the rest of the universe of accounts that exist in the market. These accounts are not usually managed in any way, but always offer the possibility of an incoming lead or 'bluebird' opportunity to be considered and responded to by the sales team.

The three-tier model for accounts corresponds nicely to the three types of ABM, and allows marketers to align corresponding investment and attention to pre-screened accounts as part of an integrated business development value chain.

One health warning to bear in mind though is that often these tiers have been created based on an account's current value to your company rather than with a view to its potential lifetime value or long-term strategic fit. So, even if a tiering of accounts already exists in your company, it's worth spending some time prioritizing them for ABM investment within their tiers, or indeed offering to facilitate a more robust prioritization of accounts for the business as a whole.

## Defining the account selection process

There is a proven and rigorous process to evaluate and select accounts to be included in your ABM programme, based on the directional policy matrix developed by McKinsey for GE (see Figure 4.1 on page 61):

**Step 1**: Screen your long list of accounts at a high level to develop a shortlist that will be evaluated in detail.

**Step 2**: Assess your shortlist according to two factors: 1) the account's attractiveness; and 2) your organization's relative business strength as a potential supplier in that account.

**Step 3**: Select the accounts to be included according to their combined scores in Step 2.

**Step 4**: Use the results of your prioritization process to plan your go-to-market strategy and ABM approach for accounts depending on their final scores.

If you are rolling out an ABM programme across multiple divisions or industry sectors, you may decide to evaluate the attractiveness of individual market segments or industries first in order to focus your efforts. To do this, follow the same process as for account evaluation in Steps 2–4, but evaluate market segments instead of individual companies. Then complete the account prioritization process for accounts that fall into the markets or industries you have prioritized, as detailed in the process below.

## Step 1: Create your shortlist of accounts

The first step in selecting accounts for ABM is to define a manageable list. Since you'll be investing significant time in evaluating individual accounts in some detail, it's wise to limit that initial list to accounts that have good potential for ABM.

Start with an easily evaluated metric that acts as a good proxy for the type of account that you want to do business with. The one we see most frequently is company size: it's easy and quick to measure and is a good indication of budget. But you may decide to choose something that is better aligned with your organization's goals. For example, if you're using ABM to grow business with accounts that are leading-edge adopters, you might determine your shortlist by looking at accounts that are the most innovative or highest-growth in their sectors.

There is no hard-and-fast rule for how many accounts you should be evaluating. That number depends on several sets of circumstances:

- The stage of your ABM programme: whether you are selecting a small number of pilot accounts, expanding the scope of your programme to cover a larger number of accounts or evaluating an existing ABM portfolio to exclude accounts or include new ones.

- The resources available to assess individual accounts.

- The timeline for completing the evaluation.

Clearly the greater the number of resources and the longer the timeline, the more accounts you can evaluate in detail. At ITSMA, we usually recommend limiting the number of accounts to 50 per industry sector or division for a programme that is being rolled out company-wide. If you are evaluating only a small number of accounts for an ABM pilot, starting with 25–50 in total will still give you plenty of room for generating a shortlist to run through more comprehensive assessment.

## Step 2: Assess your shortlist

There are two main factors to determine the priority of potential ABM accounts: 1) how attractive the account is to you; and 2) your relative business strengths as a potential supplier in that account.

Much of the decision making, outside of the analysis or number crunching, is best done in a workshop environment with your key stakeholders, to ensure their buy-in to both the process and the results.

### 1. Agree assessment criteria

First, agree a set of criteria by which to define and measure both factors. The group agreeing on these criteria may be your ABM steering committee or project management office (PMO), ideally incorporating representatives from both sales and the business unit leadership team, in a workshop.

To help you facilitate the workshop and determine the right criteria, here are some questions to prompt the group's thinking:

- Where have we sold most effectively in the past?
- Which kinds of accounts have proven most profitable over time?
- Which sub-industries do we work with today?
- What characteristics are most predictive of sales success?
- What attributes make for the best fit with our offerings?
- What traits should rule out an account?
- What kind of accounts play best to our unique strengths?
- Which accounts do we already have an advantage in?
- What accounts deliver the most value?

To define account attractiveness, brainstorm and agree the criteria you will use. Examples of criteria used by others include:

- business size (employees/revenues);
- size of spend (or wallet);

- predicted business growth/analyst rating;
- number of contract renewals in the next two to three years;
- compelling event (such as a merger or acquisition, change of leadership) in the foreseeable future;
- local or global decision making;
- procurement approach (eg use of framework agreements).

Then do the same for your relative strength in an account. Examples of criteria used to determine this include:

- relevant intellectual property assets;
- overlap of geographic footprint;
- lack of competitor advocacy and/or advocacy for our company;
- existing senior relationships;
- track record in similar accounts;
- cultural fit.

Each account will be scored against the agreed criteria and evaluated using a version of the GE/McKinsey directional policy matrix (Figure 4.1). The resulting prioritization will guide your decision-making process.

**Figure 4.1**   Illustrative directional matrix supporting ABM/marketing investment decisions

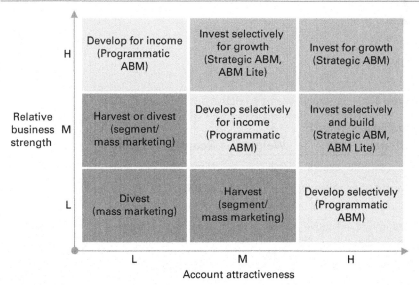

**SOURCE** ITSMA, 2017

## 2. Define your metrics and measures

Next, define the importance weighting and the scoring model you will use for each criterion, against which you will score each account (Tables 4.1 and 4.2).

Each criterion should be weighted in terms of its relative importance compared to the others in the attractiveness or business strength category in which it sits. The key is to ensure that the individual weightings in each category add up to 1.0 (or 100 per cent). So, for example, you may decide that in defining how attractive an account is to you, the size of its IT spend is the most important, so is weighted 0.4 (or 40 per cent). Its medium-term growth over the next three years and the number of relevant contracts renewing are equally important, and so are weighted 0.3 (30 per cent) each.

**Table 4.1**  Illustrative example account attractiveness criteria

| Segment attractiveness criteria | Weight | Score 1 | Score 3 | Score 5 |
|---|---|---|---|---|
| Size of IT spend | 0.4 | <$1B | $1–2B | >$2B |
| Medium-term growth in spend (over the next 3 years) | 0.3 | Below average | Average | Above average |
| Number of relevant contracts renewing within 3 years | 0.3 | 1–3 | 4–6 | >6 |

**SOURCE** ITSMA, 2017

**Table 4.2**  Illustrative example relative business strength criteria

| Business strength criteria | Weight | Score 1 | Score 3 | Score 5 |
|---|---|---|---|---|
| Relevant IP or assets | 0.2 | None | Some | Many |
| Overlap of geographic footprint | 0.4 | <25% | 25–50% | >50% |
| Strength of executive relationships compared to competitors | 0.4 | Weaker | Same | Stronger |

**SOURCE** ITSMA, 2017

Once the criteria are weighted, it's time to develop a scoring system for each criterion. In some cases the criteria will have a specific, quantitative measure, such as the number of relevant contracts coming up for renewal in an account within the next three years. In these cases, if an account had one to three contracts coming up, it would score 1. If it had four to six, it would score 3, and if it had more than six, it would score 5.

In other cases, you will assign a qualitative assessment. For example, strength of existing executive relationships may be weaker, the same, or stronger than competitors.

With your criteria weighted and a scoring system developed for each, it's time to run your shortlist of accounts through the analysis. For each account, multiply the score it achieves on each criterion by the weighting assigned to that criterion, then sum up the total scores the account achieves within the attractiveness category, and then within the business strength category. The easiest way to do this is through a simple spreadsheet model.

## Step 3: Select your ABM accounts

Now that you have evaluated each of your accounts, and each one has a total score for attractiveness and a total score for your relative business strength, you can plot them on the matrix along the x and y axes to determine which have the highest potential and therefore are highest priority for strategic ABM, versus ABM Lite, programmatic ABM or more broadly-based marketing approaches (Figure 4.2).

When plotting the accounts on the matrix, it's useful to use a 'bubble chart' approach, so that the size of the bubbles represents either the size of the account's revenues or its spend. (It is also possible to show the bubble as a pie chart, with a slice/wedge showing the share of spend that your company already has in the account.)

Accounts that are in the upper-right quadrants of the matrix are the most attractive and should therefore be the highest priority for strategic ABM. Any decision to include any accounts in your strategic ABM approach that are outside of the three most attractive boxes should be treated with caution. This is where a blend of the three types of ABM may be useful in your programme, as you tier your levels of marketing investment across the prioritization matrix according to the resources you have available.

Reviewing the results of your analysis is again best done with a wider group in a workshop. Business unit and sales leaders may disagree with where an account falls on the matrix, and therefore the recommended marketing

**Figure 4.2**   Plotting accounts for ABM investment

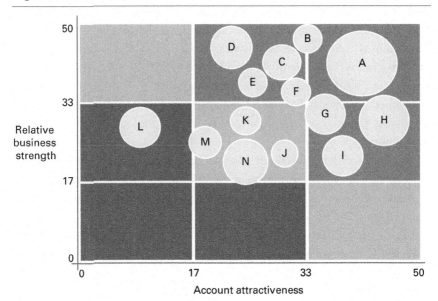

**SOURCE** ITSMA, 2017

approach and investment it receives. This often happens when individuals are particularly close to an account. The advantage of this process means that you show logically why an account has fallen where it has, so, in order to move the account to a different position on the matrix, the team would need to agree a change to the criteria, weightings, scoring approach or way that the account has been scored. You can't simply move the account's bubble!

Now that you have determined the most attractive accounts to include in your ABM programme based on the accounts' characteristics and your organization's relative strengths, there is one more assessment you may want to consider before deciding on your final list. How receptive is the account manager or sales team to ABM, and how well are they likely to work with marketing?

Though certainly not a requirement, we have evidence from the field that suggests the account team's receptiveness can be a significant determinant of how effective your ABM efforts will be. You can waste a lot of time chasing the account manager and salespeople for an account, and get nowhere, when those at another account are more willing to engage and could deliver better business results.

## Step 4: Build your go-to-market plan

With the prioritization exercise complete, it should be clear which accounts qualify for an ABM approach. You will also have an indication of the relative importance of the remaining accounts and can use it to decide your go-to-market plan for these, be it segment or mass-customized marketing.

Accounts falling in the top-left to bottom-right diagonal boxes are probably most suited to an ABM or segment marketing programmatic approach. And those that fall into the bottom-left corner boxes are best suited to segment or mass-customized marketing. It all depends on the resources you have or are willing to invest across all types of marketing in your go-to-market strategy.

The analysis you have done will be a valuable asset to feed into the process of determining your individual account plans. The information contained in your assessment provides a good starting point for the more detailed account insight and stakeholder intelligence you'll need. The Fujitsu case study is a great example of how it can work.

**CASE STUDY**   Fujitsu – Using segmentation to prioritize sales opportunities

In 2007, leading information and communications technology company Fujitsu realized that it was spreading its attention too thinly across the UK market. It knew that there were existing and potential customers that were worth a more focused selling effort, but it wasn't sure where to apply the resources to get the most payback. 'We had everyone spread across too many opportunities,' according to Peter Barrett, then head of marketing for financial services at Fujitsu.

'And the danger was that we had a lack of focus. People were making decisions at the sales level or the contractual level as to what they would do with sales opportunities. The challenge was to focus on a smaller number of opportunities where we could get more business and where it would be mutually beneficial to both parties.'

So Fujitsu's marketing leaders set out to segment its private-sector customers and prospects (mainly large corporations) within the various industries it serves – what Fujitsu called sector mapping. The goal of the effort was simple: win bigger deals more often by focusing on the most important opportunities and by building longer-term relationships with a target group of 30–40 companies. 'We had to figure out how we proactively tell people which prospects to focus on to build relationships and which existing customers are most worth trying to expand business in,' said Barrett.

Of course, carrying out the goal was anything but simple. Mapping your customers by segment requires careful planning and a near-mystical ability to develop parameters for segmentation that will result in real insight. It also requires permission and cooperation from sales. 'We needed to make sure we got buy-in from the sales and account management people who control the accounts within the particular sectors we were focusing on,' said Barrett.

Fujitsu developed a sector-mapping process and designed parameters that revealed the most attractive opportunities across multiple industries. As is the case in many services companies, Fujitsu is organized to go to market by industry. Therefore, it made sense to focus the effort on revealing the best opportunities for Fujitsu within the various industries it serves.

### Identify the right targets

The first task was to identify companies within each industry that were attractive to Fujitsu and that at least had the potential to view Fujitsu in the same way. There were five steps in this process:

1 Developing a list of potential companies from *Forbes* magazine's Global 2000 list and the FTSE (*Financial Times* London Stock Exchange list of largest UK companies) with capitalization greater than £1 billion.
2 Filtering that list by excluding companies that did not have an estimated IT spend of at least £100 million.
3 Vetting the list with the various business unit directors and managers and allowing them to add back in accounts that did not meet the initial criteria but that they viewed as important (eg based on personal knowledge of the account).
4 Creating criteria for client attractiveness and Fujitsu business position in collaboration with sales, account managers, and business unit directors.
5 Collecting data against each of these criteria through research, sales, account managers, and business unit managers.

### Rate the industries

With limited resources to put towards selling big deals, Fujitsu needed to determine which industries had the highest concentration of attractive deals, compared with Fujitsu's reputation and penetration within each industry. Fujitsu developed a scoring system for each of the criteria and a weighting system to rank the relative importance of the various criteria (the specific scores and weights Fujitsu used for the different criteria are proprietary and not revealed here).

To find the most attractive industries, the company used the following criteria:

- average operating profit of companies in the industry;
- regulation/legislation driving significant need for IT investment;
- size of industry IT spend;
- growth rate of industry (annual);
- number of firms accounting for 80 per cent of industry revenues.

## Create criteria to test your industry reputation

Selling strategies can't be based only on picking targets with the biggest revenue potential. It's also important to gauge the likelihood that those targets will consider you a viable alternative. Here are the criteria that Fujitsu used to determine which industries would be most receptive:

- number of reference clients in the industry;
- current market share;
- existing intellectual property assets;
- degree to which the industry is globalized.

Using these criteria, Fujitsu was able to plot the industries it served on a graph by industry attractiveness, competitive position, and opportunity size within each industry (Figure 4.3).

## Finding the key clients to pursue

It's not enough to uncover the best industries to target. You must take the analysis deeper and find the best target clients within each industry. Using the same framework as the industry sector analysis, Fujitsu created the following criteria to determine client attractiveness:

**Figure 4.3**   Industry sector mapping at Fujitsu

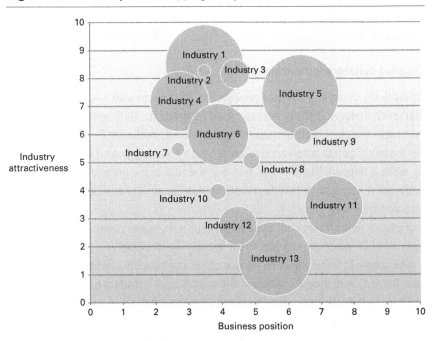

- predicted compelling event leading to £25 million+ buying decision;
- trend in sales, general and administrative expenses (overheads) relative to revenue over past 18 months;
- scope of geographical decision making and deployment;
- typically buys proven, cost-effective IT and/or business process outsourcing solutions;
- has a good cultural fit: long-term view, straightforward, realistic.

## Do they like us?

Good segmentation requires a good look in the mirror. Providers need to be brutally honest in assessing their specific delivery strengths and weaknesses and their past track records with clients. Fujitsu developed these characteristics to rate its chances with clients:

- a £25 million opportunity over the next three years in Fujitsu's three core delivery areas;
- a proven track record of delivering good-quality service to this client;
- privileged access to key decision makers;
- current share of external IT spend.

Using the combination of internal criteria and external reputation criteria, Fujitsu was able to map its most attractive opportunities within the major industries it serves. As a result, marketing was able to offer valuable guidance, based on data developed jointly with sales, on the accounts that could benefit from more attention.

### Ensuring collaboration and buy-in

By involving salespeople in the development of the framework and in the research, marketing ensured that the results would be credible. 'Getting buy-in from sales was really the most important aspect of this for me,' reckoned Barrett. 'In the past we tended to go into a darkened room, produce a strategy, come out, and say, let's go make it happen. But then you find that the rest of the organization says, well, that's great, you spent a few days working this out on your own, but we've had no involvement in that.'

Fujitsu's new strategy did not come out of a darkened room, however. It was easy to trace its origin and test the thinking. 'The process was transparent and it was simple to understand, so people could see how the results were derived,' said Barrett. 'And they were part of the process, so it made it easier for them to engage. That made a massive difference psychologically.'

The clarity of the process and salespeople's buy-in had the effect that Fujitsu wanted: it changed people's behaviour. Salespeople focused more of their energies on a smaller number of accounts that scored highly in the segmenting process. 'The resources we have are more limited, but we can put more impact into specific bid opportunities than we did in the past,' Barrett declared. 'So it's a bit more effective in terms of results. Because we understand our sales priorities better, we can allocate resources much more effectively.'

# Your ABM checklist

**1** Give yourself the greatest chance of meeting your objectives for ABM by selecting those accounts which have the best potential to achieve your ABM goals.

**2** While the size of the account's available budget is an important criterion, it is only one of several. Determine what weight in terms of organizational priority to give each factor as a key part of the selection process.

**3** Use the proven and rigorous four-step process detailed in this chapter to evaluate and select accounts collaboratively with the business.

**4** Use the information from your assessment as a starting point for the more detailed account insight and stakeholder intelligence you will need to build successful ABM plans.

# The ABM adoption model

## A recognized approach

The last four chapters have discussed the compelling reasons for making ABM a key part of your strategic armoury in dealing with your most important clients and how to select the accounts that will form part of your programme. In this chapter we explain the key stages involved in starting and growing your ABM programme to allow you to reach a scale that delivers a significant return on your investment.

Since ITSMA first developed ABM as a formalized framework in 2003, consistent patterns have emerged in the ways that companies think about and adopt ABM. Perhaps the most important is that ABM has gone from being an experimental new marketing approach to a proven way for companies to build long-term influence and trusted advisor status in their most important accounts. In other words, ABM has become a key part of the company's *strategic growth initiatives.*

The best evidence of its impact is that companies have continued to boost their ABM budgets. For example, the ITSMA Benchmarking Survey[1] found that respondents allocated an average of 20 per cent of their marketing budget to ABM in 2015, and 69 per cent of them planned increases to that budget for 2016 (see Figure 5.1).

The main driver behind the increased investment in ABM is the fact that the business has recognized the results it delivers and wants more (see Figure 5.2).

Over time, a big shift has come from the perception of ABM as an expensive investment suitable only for the biggest accounts with endless potential for increased wallet share. ITSMA research has shown that ABM is scalable by adopting a 'one-to-few' approach as well (ABM Lite). And technology-enabled programmatic ABM is taking the principles of the approach even wider through targeted marketing at an account level. Through careful

**Figure 5.1** A virtuous circle of ABM

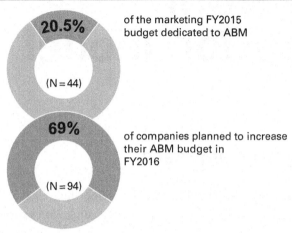

20.5%

(N = 44)

of the marketing FY2015
budget dedicated to ABM

69%

(N = 94)

of companies planned to increase
their ABM budget in
FY2016

**SOURCE** ITSMA, Account-Based Marketing Benchmarking Survey, March 2016

governance, many companies are able to reuse (with tailoring) existing programmes and content for their ABM accounts. Some of the costs for ABM can thus be already covered by existing programmes.

There are several challenges involved in scaling your programme (see Figure 5.3). The most widely felt is the lack of available people/headcount within marketing to continue to scale ABM with the same ratio of people to accounts that was initially used in the pilot or proof of concept. More than one-third of ABM-ers cite this as their primary limiting factor when looking to scale. Just over a quarter of marketers cite the limited investment or budget available as their top challenge, while one-fifth quote the lack of ABM skills in the marketing function. Sales buy-in and engagement is another factor mentioned.

If you know what challenges to expect at the start of your ABM journey and take the right steps going in, you have more chance of success with your programme. Clearly, agreeing investment and training or hiring the right skills are two things to build into your business case early on.

This chapter identifies the four steps for ABM adoption, developed with the ITSMA Global ABM Council and based on research, experience, and best practice. We highlight the things to think about to maximize your chances of success at each step, as well as the drivers that will lead you to move on to the next step.

**Figure 5.2** Businesses are demanding more ABM

What is the one primary
driver behind scaling your
ABM programmes?
% of respondents (N=66)

Results have been so good that the business
and/or sales is demanding more — 41

We need to expand beyond the initial geography
to have a truly global programme — 17

We need to address additional vertical markets — 15

We need to be more targeted in our overall
marketing approach — 12

We have the technology to scale — 9

**SOURCE** ITSMA, Account-Based Marketing Benchmarking Survey, March 2016

**Figure 5.3**  Challenges in scaling ABM

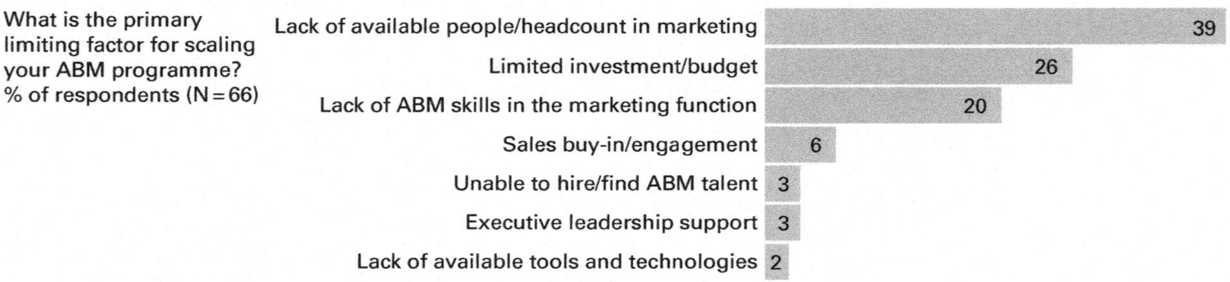

What is the primary
limiting factor for scaling
your ABM programme?
% of respondents (N = 66)

| | |
|---|---|
| Lack of available people/headcount in marketing | 39 |
| Limited investment/budget | 26 |
| Lack of ABM skills in the marketing function | 20 |
| Sales buy-in/engagement | 6 |
| Unable to hire/find ABM talent | 3 |
| Executive leadership support | 3 |
| Lack of available tools and technologies | 2 |

**SOURCE** ITSMA, Account-Based Marketing Benchmarking Survey, March 2016

# The prerequisites for ABM

Because ABM is a strategy rather than a marketing tactic, the company as a whole must be ready for it. Companies fail at ABM when they don't have the right prerequisites in place before launching their programme, some of which, by now, should be familiar to you from previous chapters:

- **A flexible approach to selling.** Successful ABM companies have sellers who are able to do more than fulfil transactions. They are able to take a consultative approach with customers as well.

- **Cultural acceptance of a customer-led selling strategy.** ABM success requires that companies understand that they must sell by understanding and solving customers' problems rather than pushing offerings – and have the patience for this more time-consuming approach. Meanwhile, customers inside these accounts must be willing to invest their time in relationships with providers who can provide help with larger business problems.

- **Marketing is seen as strategic.** Companies where marketers are viewed solely as event planners and brochure writers won't be implementing ABM any time soon. For ABM to be truly effective, marketing has to be perceived by sales as an equal partner. That's because ABM relies on both sales and marketing to be part of the ABM process and to take on complementary roles while being part of a team of equals.

- **A sufficient number of large, high-potential customers.** ABM investments do not pay off with small customers.

- **Tiered accounts.** Most companies that embark on an ABM programme have already created tiers of accounts that separate more important accounts from the rest. Some have a formal process for creating tiers, while others take an informal approach based on revenue potential and feedback from account managers.

- **Sellers assigned to one or a few accounts.** ABM works best when the company has a history of assigning sellers and/or account managers exclusively to a single account or handful of accounts. Otherwise, there are unlikely to be relationships with accounts that are broad and deep enough to warrant investment.

- **Hunger to expand share of wallet.** Sellers and their management are hungry for ways to go wider and deeper in top accounts and the business growth strategy is built around this approach.

- **Well-rounded marketers.** The marketing organization must have 'end-to-end' marketers with business knowledge and consultative abilities along with tactical knowledge.

- **Shared responsibility between sales and marketing.** Sellers support the involvement of marketing at the account level to do things that sellers are unable to do themselves (eg thought leadership, events, etc).

- **Focus on lifetime customer relationships.** Companies with a strong commitment to focusing on lifetime customer value are best suited for ABM. If quarterly sales numbers are the only major driver, ABM will not succeed.

## The ABM programme roadmap

With the right conditions in place, companies are ready to start the ABM journey. Trying to get ahead of yourself by skipping steps or moving too fast could jeopardize your programme. Go too slow and you risk losing momentum and support in the company. Like most change programmes, it's a balancing act to get the pace right.

There are four distinct stages to ABM adoption (Figure 5.4):

**1** Pilot:

- determine pilot accounts;
- develop metrics;
- research and analyse pilot accounts;
- build and execute integrated account plans;
- publicize the results.

**2** Build:

- gather learnings from pilots;
- refine account selection criteria;
- begin defining common metrics and success criteria;
- identify funding sources and resources;
- create growth criteria;
- deepen executive sponsorship.

**Figure 5.4** ITSMA's ABM adoption model

| Pilot | Build | Standardize | Scale |
|---|---|---|---|
| • Determine pilot accounts<br>• Develop metrics<br>• Research and analyse pilot accounts<br>• Build integrated account plan and execute<br>• Measure and review<br>• Publicize results | • Gather learnings from pilots<br>• Refine account selection criteria<br>• Begin defining common metrics and success criteria<br>• Identify funding sources and resources<br>• Create growth criteria<br>• Deepen executive sponsorship | • Create PMO and governance model<br>• Determine standard metrics and success criteria across all accounts<br>• Develop staffing process<br>• Integrate ABM into the overall reward/recognition system | • Achieve economies of scale through standard processes, shared services, and automation<br>• Create ABM knowledge management system<br>• Leverage ABM practices in other areas of marketing |
| **Drivers to pilot** | **Drivers to build** | **Drivers to standardize** | **Drivers to scale** |
| • *Opportunity to increase wallet share and mindshare*<br>• *Increased competition in accounts*<br>• *Account relationships at risk*<br>• *Lack of cohesive strategy for deepening account relationships* | • *Positive results from pilots*<br>• *Encouraging feedback from sales*<br>• *Account planning process improves*<br>• *Increased executive support for ABM strategy* | • *Account managers demand ABM*<br>• *ABM sparks career interest*<br>• *Account relationships improve*<br>• *ABM accounts outperform others* | • *ABM results lift the overall business*<br>• *Recognition of need to expand globally from original geography/sector* |

**SOURCE** © 2017 ITSMA

**3** Standardize:

- create a programme management office (PMO) and governance model;
- determine standard metrics and success criteria across all accounts;
- develop a staffing process;
- integrate ABM into the overall reward/recognition system.

**4** Scale:

- achieve economies of scale through standard processes, shared services and automation;
- create an ABM knowledge management system;
- leverage ABM practices in other areas of marketing.

The rest of this chapter looks at each of these stages in more detail.

# Stage One: Pilot

## Key drivers to pilot ABM

Companies that move forward with ABM programmes see a number of common issues inside their top accounts that drive them to experiment with an ABM pilot, including:

- **Opportunity to increase wallet share and mindshare.** Frustration is the signal here. Look for it on the faces of the account team as they struggle to break into new divisions of the account using selling efforts alone.

- **Account relationships at risk.** Sales account managers report that they are getting fewer meetings with key people inside key accounts. Just as importantly, they notice that accounts are asking for help and advice less often than in the past. These companies aren't having fewer problems but are going to other sources due to a perception that you can't help them.

- **Turnover brings little change.** As relationships with accounts stagnate, companies bring in new account managers, hoping that the problems lie with the people. But because marketing and sales are not collaborating on a more targeted approach that puts customer needs first, the new people are unable to reverse the trend.

- Lack of cohesive strategy for deepening account relationships. Some account relationships, even successful ones, may be more a result of ad hoc opportunities than a cohesive strategy to build upon past successes. When growth slows, this lack of long-term planning may become painfully apparent.

## Piloting ABM in select accounts

Few companies are willing or able to make a full commitment to ABM without testing the concept first. They typically begin by carefully choosing a select number of the company's most important accounts. For Strategic ABM, three is the magic number in most cases, while a cluster of five accounts works for ABM Lite and a sample group of named accounts for Programmatic ABM. It's important that these accounts be

---

### Key members of the strategic ABM team

There can be many members of an account team, but generally only one is responsible for managing the ABM plan: the account marketer. The account team marketer, in concert with the sales account leader, coordinates the activities of the team.

The core team typically includes:

- account executive and sales team members;
- solutions and services consultants/delivery personnel;
- marketing representatives from solutions, industry, communications and the field;
- other potential support/participants such as technical or management colleagues from the professional service and support organizations.

Based on the account and your team composition you may also need to bring other skills onto the team:

- product management;
- consulting representative;
- industry representative;
- solution engineer;
- sales enablement;
- partners.

a representative sampling so that the outcomes of the pilots will be credible evidence for deciding whether to build a fully-fledged programme using one or more of the ABM types.

ABM is a team sport, and so it's worth thinking about the people you will involve in the pilots up front. Their engagement and support will make or break the pilot, so be sure to invest enough time to brief them and get their buy-in to the pilot before you start.

Here are some other important aspects of the pilot phase:

- **Develop metrics.** Before piloting ABM, companies need to come up with a definition of success. They must create a 'before and after' picture of an account that achieves the goals of the pilot. After defining success, it's time to create metrics that reflect this definition. In ITSMA research, we have seen qualitative metrics, quantitative metrics, and a mixture of both.

- **Select pilot accounts.** Selection criteria for ABM pilots will vary from company to company. There are, however, a few universal selection criteria for pilot accounts which shortcut the more extensive process detailed in Chapter 4:

  - **Pick accounts where you have strong relationships or that have high revenue potential.** It's much harder to break into accounts where you don't have at least one contact that might advocate on your behalf. Prospect accounts where you don't do business currently are tough for that reason, but an investment in in-depth research could make the difference.

  - **Pick marketing-savvy account managers.** It's tough to work with a sales team that doesn't know – or doesn't believe in – the value that marketing can bring.

  - **Avoid problem accounts.** If an account relationship is badly strained, ABM shouldn't be the way to salvage it. Without a fully-developed programme and experience behind the pilot effort, it's likely that the relationship will not improve.

  - **Pick accounts where the customer sees the potential to do more.** A good candidate for an ABM pilot is a customer who sees the potential to do more with you but has not been given the opportunity to explore more ways to work together or has simply not invested the time before.

- **Research and analyse pilot accounts.** In preparation for working with the pilot accounts, companies need to conduct secondary research about the company and its markets and about the key stakeholders in the company. The purpose of the research is to be able to come into the pilot accounts ready to have a more relevant, credible conversation about their problems and issues.

- **Build integrated account plans.** Each strategic ABM pilot account must have a joint account planning process that includes an ABM-er, the sales account manager, and the sales representative(s). ABM Lite and Programmatic ABM need integration at a multi-account level.

- **Measure and review.** While anecdotal reports of success in ABM pilot accounts are important to build support within the company, it's essential to conduct a formal review of the accounts to compare successes across accounts. The consolidated findings are necessary to make a persuasive case for expanding the programme beyond the pilot stage.

- **Publicize results.** It's important that the rest of the organization hears about the successes of the pilot programme. First, publicize across sales by word-of-mouth. Salespeople are competitive and communicative. If a tactic or strategy is working for a colleague, word gets around through the salesforce. If that success is more than a fluke or a matter of individual talent – ie ABM is proven to work across a number of different pilot accounts – salespeople will begin demanding access to the same advantages that their colleagues have. Second, publicize ABM success outside of sales and marketing. Creating internal case studies about ABM success helps convince sceptical executives that it's worth investing in the programme.

# Stage Two: Build

## *Key drivers to building the ABM programme*

In our experience, there are few instances where devoting more attention to accounts with relevant, targeted research and advice does not bring positive results. But companies must make sure that they capitalize on the goodwill and momentum of success in ABM pilot accounts before it fades. ABM leaders use the experiences and results from the pilots to start lobbying for a larger programme right away.

Here are the key drivers to look for:

- **Positive results from pilots.** Nothing builds momentum for expansion of the programme better than clear, demonstrable proof that the pilots have led to success in the goals and metrics selected for the accounts.

- **Encouraging feedback from sales.** Salespeople in the pilot accounts generally report that after beginning ABM, they no longer feel like Sisyphus pushing the rock up the hill. They are seeing improvements in the key relationships within the account and are getting meetings with executives in areas of the account that they had not been able to penetrate before.

- **Account planning process improves.** Strategic ABM has a formal process for collaborative account planning with sales and marketing. Having an aligned process rather than approaching accounts in an ad hoc or opportunistic way improves performance.

- **Increased executive support for ABM strategy.** Success within the pilot accounts leads executives in marketing and sales to pay attention and consider expanding the programme.

## Building the foundation

As you move from a few successful pilots to building a formal programme, don't let enthusiasm and passion get ahead of planning. What worked in the pilots might not necessarily work when building a programme that is meant to scale. The overall objectives shift from an emphasis on specific account success to include an emphasis on practices and metrics that will bring success to multiple, diverse accounts at the same time. If the programme can't scale economically, it won't make it past the pilot stage.

It's also important to ensure that ABM does not descend into becoming a tactical, short-term funnel-filling exercise. This is a strategic programme that should be linked to the broader overall goals of the business. So there shouldn't be five different flavours of ABM programmes with different goals within a particular business unit, for example.

Other important steps in building the programme foundation include the following:

- **Gather research from pilots.** Programmes that require organizational change as ABM does must have a narrative. ABM advocates package up the successes and best practices into stories and presentations for those who want a detailed defence of the strategy and brief elevator pitches for spreading the word among salespeople and other employees.

- **Refine account selection criteria.** During the pilot phase, account selection is dictated as much by the need to prove the concept as by the true goal of ABM: accelerating growth. As companies move beyond the pilot phase, they will want to adjust their account selection criteria accordingly.

- **Begin defining common metrics and success criteria.** Pilot accounts provide a rough blueprint of overall success criteria and goals for ABM, but again, the blueprint is blurred by the need to prove the case for ABM. You will need goals and metrics that will remain relevant as the programme grows. Also, during the pilot phase, it's fine to focus on measuring at the individual account level. But as you build the foundation for scaling the programme, measure both at the individual account level, by ABM type, and at the overall programme level.

- **Identify funding sources and resources.** One of the advantages of ABM is that it does not always require the creation of new marketing campaigns. The relationship programmes, the loyalty programmes and the thought leadership publishing mechanisms you have in place can all be put to use in your ABM campaign plan. But the content generated by these programmes will need some fine-tuning. And marketing may need to find funding for doing in-depth research for specific accounts. Our research has found that, ideally, that extra funding for ABM should come from the business unit and from sales, which often has more money and flexibility in its budget than marketing. There's also an important alignment factor here. Funding from sales helps ensure that sales will participate in and support the ABM programme. ABM leaders must decide whether to try to get funding from the current sales budget or lobby for a new line-item budget for ABM.

- **Train and educate marketers.** The leaders of the ABM programme must identify the skills needed for ABM, create training programmes and establish mentoring or buddy systems.

- **Deepen executive sponsorship.** To build a broad foundation for ABM, executive support must begin to radiate up (the chief marketing officer (CMO) and top sales executive must become firm believers). ABM programme leaders now also look at other areas of the company that could benefit from the programme and bring them into the fold. But don't just talk to the sales and marketing vice presidents. Find out who the influencers are within the target areas and talk to them about the pilot successes, the strategy and the goals of the programme and the growth criteria for the programme. Get them to the point where they fully understand the value of the ABM approach. Convince them that the programme is important to the success of the company – and that their sponsorship is important to the success of the programme. And come right out and ask for their sponsorship.

It also helps to get the support of executives outside of sales and marketing, such as finance (which will see ABM as a budget line-item at some point) and IT (which will need to help install tools and technology platforms and implement dashboards for tracking ABM). In these cases, however, it's less important to build outright support than it is to educate and build awareness that ABM is a programme that sales and marketing both support and believe is important to the company's overall success.

# Stage Three: Standardize

## Key drivers for standardizing the ABM programme

The ABM programme has grown to the point where it is being used with success across different parts of the company. The concept is proven, it is broadly accepted and the risks of adopting it are reduced. But the strains of adolescence are beginning to show. There could be more effective sharing of methods and best practices, and the company is starting to see jealous spats over resources. Here are some signs that it's time for the ABM programme to grow up:

- **ABM accounts outperform others.** One of the biggest pay-offs of ABM is a more effective and efficient sales process. Because companies invest up front in learning more about the accounts, sales proposals become more relevant to customers' specific needs. There is less back and forth and redoing of proposals that can drag out a selling cycle. When the sales cycle is shortened, the profitability of the deal goes up. ABM teams also waste less time chasing unprofitable or poorly-fitting opportunities because they have better insight into the specifics of new opportunities. Indeed, ABM teams may be brought in to help develop those opportunities, opening up the possibility for sole-sourcing the deal without any competitive pitch or tendering process (outside the public sector).

- **Account relationships improve.** ABM isn't just about winning more business this year. It's about building the relationships that are the foundation of winning more business every year, maximizing the lifetime value of the account. As ABM teams create more and deeper relationships with contacts at target accounts, they build the foundation for *sustainable* growth in mutual business value over time. When companies see the stability that ABM can provide, they look for ways to bring it to more accounts.

- **Account managers demand ABM.** The word is out among the salespeople: if we partner with marketing on accounts and take a more formal approach to researching customers' most important issues, we will win more business. That sparks a rush for ABM support. Companies must manage this demand carefully, however, because not all accounts will be good candidates for ABM. ABM leaders charged with managing the programme must have a fact-based reason for saying yes or no to requests for ABM support, such as that described in Chapter 4.

- **ABM sparks career interest.** Being an ABM marketer is a generalist's dream. It requires a broad range of skills, from strategic to tactical, and provides constant stimulation as marketers try to keep up with the changes going on inside large, complex customers. In ITSMA research, ABM is found to attract – and just as important, *nurture* – top marketing talent. Seeing the opportunities in both the job and the experience it provides, ambitious marketers will begin clamouring to get in, providing yet more impetus to expand the programme.

## What should you look for in an ABM marketer?

ABM marketers are consummate generalists who have enough knowledge of all the marketing specialties to have credibility and good judgement, while having the leadership and relationship skills to pitch and manage ABM programmes both internally across the company and externally with clients and partners.

From their positions within collaborative account planning teams with salespeople, these marketers need to do just about everything, from meeting with senior customer executives to tweaking PowerPoint slides for subject matter experts. They are helping manage the entire customer relationship. We think these people are living blueprints for future marketing leaders. Some of the key characteristics of these marketers based on our research with the ITSMA ABM Council include:

- **People skills.** ABM marketers learn to go toe-to-toe with sales and with the senior executives (inside the organization and at customer companies) while maintaining good relationships with the supporting groups and outside agencies that keep ABM programmes running. They gain valuable experience speaking in front of internal groups and partners, as well as clients, and have good presentation skills.

- **External focus.** ABM marketers develop as much passion for serving the client as they do for practising marketing.

- **Business understanding.** ABM marketers understand not just the customers' businesses but their own as well. They are able to engage customers in spontaneous discussions and offer insights and suggestions from both sides of the table.

- **Tolerance for the mundane.** The practice of ABM has a healthy mix of the challenging and the mundane. For example, ABM marketers have the breadth of experience to do high-level account planning but also have the patience and skills to proof a presentation or manage event logistics.

- **Knowledge of business development.** By working as part of a team with sales, ABM marketers gain an understanding of and empathy for the challenges that their business development colleagues face.

## *Standardizing the ABM programme*

When ABM has demonstrated repeated success across a broad range of accounts, the programme reaches a threshold: if ABM is to continue to grow effectively, it's time to think about ways to standardize the programme so that it can be as effective and as efficient as possible. Companies start to build ABM into their operating models. That means standardizing ABM processes across the company and getting serious about creating a formal governance structure.

Here are the key ways that companies standardize their ABM programmes:

- Create a programme management office (PMO) and governance model. A PMO is the management and control mechanism for maintaining quality and consistency across all ABM accounts and improving overall ABM programme performance. Starting a PMO means that you must settle on an overall ABM programme leader. PMO activities include:

  - project management;

  - integration across internal functions;

  - training, education and mentoring;

- execution and implementation;
- system and process infrastructure;
- metrics, measurement and reporting.

- **Determine standard metrics and success criteria across all accounts.** The company now has enough experience with a critical mass of ABM accounts to determine goals and metrics for the programme as a whole. The PMO plays a key role in vetting and gaining approval for the final set of success criteria and metrics.

- **Develop staffing processes.** Companies will need to come up with a set of criteria that will be applied to bring new people in and for defining the career paths of ABM marketers.

- **Integrate ABM into the overall reward/recognition system.** ABM places an emphasis on aspects of sales and marketing that aren't reflected in standard reward and recognition systems. For example, salespeople in ABM will be investing more time in building relationships than they would be if they were handling transactional sales. They must receive recognition and rewards for building relationships rather than simply making the sale; otherwise, morale will slip and the programme will likely fail. The PMO plays an important role in lobbying for rewards and recognition systems that are appropriate for ABM.

- **Leverage ABM practices to pursue large sales opportunities.** A growing number of companies use the practices and principles of ABM to go after major opportunities – even if they are not target ABM accounts. Large opportunities are worth the investment of an ABM approach, even if it is only for a limited time. The methodology and structure you've developed for ABM to this point can be adapted to an 'elite team' approach to opportunities on an as-needed basis.

# Stage Four: Scale

## *Key drivers for scaling up the ABM programme*

After ABM has been proven successful and has generated formal processes and governance structures, there comes a point when it becomes part of the company's DNA – a core way that it goes to market with customers. The value of ABM is such that the company considers scaling it to the fullest extent possible.

Here are some signs that the company is ready for scaling:

- **ABM results lift the overall business.** In many large B2B providers, the 80:20 rule applies – as in 80 per cent of revenue comes from 20 per cent of customers. ABM typically focuses on that 20 per cent. As relationships improve with those key accounts and sales cycles shrink, companies start to see a shift where the top accounts begin to contribute an even larger share of revenue to the business – more 85:15. Since ABM makes use of marketing programmes already in place, the business gains are often made with little additional incremental cost, which improves the profitability of the company.

- **Recognition of need to expand globally from original geography/sector.** Sometimes ABM grows up within a specific area of the business, such as a particular business unit or geography. But now that there are standard practices and governance in place, other areas of the company see less risk in trying ABM themselves. The PMO begins getting requests to roll out ABM in other areas of the company.

## Scaling up the ABM programme

When companies decide to deploy ABM as broadly as possible, they inevitably face a conundrum. There will be pressure on ABM leaders throughout the development of the programme to broaden the programme to cover as many companies as possible. Inevitably, someone in the company will say, 'If ABM is so good, let's use it with *all* our customers, not just the top 50.'

But the differentiator in ABM is that it focuses extra resources on the most important accounts where the extra investment can be expected to pay off. If you take those resources and try to spread them across too many accounts, the differentiation is lost and the investment will see a smaller return. This is where the different types of ABM can play a role.

As the ABM programme matures, companies are left with an important and politically difficult decision. How big should ABM get and how many accounts can we load into each type of ABM in our programme? In ITSMA's research we have found that individual strategic ABM marketers are able to handle between one to five accounts at a time. ABM Lite marketers typically manage around 25 accounts, clustering activity for groups of around five at a time. Programmatic ABM allows for hundreds of accounts to be targeted, monitored and communicated with using a range of technology tools, and its rising popularity may be at least partly as a result of the

**Figure 5.5** Important factors in scaling ABM

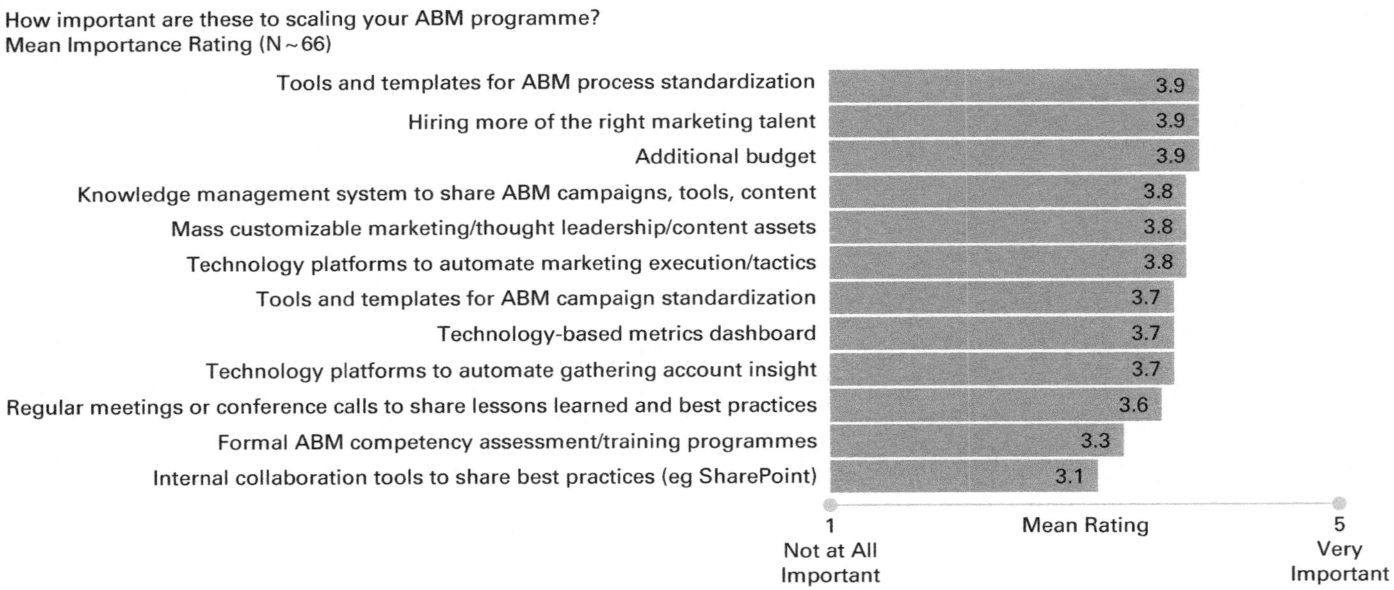

How important are these to scaling your ABM programme?
Mean Importance Rating (N ~66)

| Factor | Mean Rating |
|---|---|
| Tools and templates for ABM process standardization | 3.9 |
| Hiring more of the right marketing talent | 3.9 |
| Additional budget | 3.9 |
| Knowledge management system to share ABM campaigns, tools, content | 3.8 |
| Mass customizable marketing/thought leadership/content assets | 3.8 |
| Technology platforms to automate marketing execution/tactics | 3.8 |
| Tools and templates for ABM campaign standardization | 3.7 |
| Technology-based metrics dashboard | 3.7 |
| Technology platforms to automate gathering account insight | 3.7 |
| Regular meetings or conference calls to share lessons learned and best practices | 3.6 |
| Formal ABM competency assessment/training programmes | 3.3 |
| Internal collaboration tools to share best practices (eg SharePoint) | 3.1 |

Not at All Important (1) — Very Important (5)

Mean Rating

**NOTE** Mean rating based on a 5-point scale where 1=Not at all important and 5=Very important
**SOURCE** ITSMA, Account-Based Marketing Benchmarking Survey, March 2016

efficiencies it can offer as marketers look to scale ABM principles across more accounts in their programme.

In fact, ITSMA research reveals that tools and templates are thought to be the most important prerequisite for scaling an ABM programme (see Figure 5.5), followed by getting additional people and budget for the programme.

Here are some examples of how to drive efficiencies:

- **Achieve economies of scale through standard processes, shared services and automation.** As the ABM programme grows, companies can save by setting up centralized shared services and by automating some aspects of the process. For example, leading communications services company BT automates the account research process using agent3's Insight3 platform so that account managers automatically receive daily updates on the latest news and information on their accounts. This enables them to focus more time on relationship building and selling. Others use automation platforms like Demandbase to target and personalize digital advertising at scale.

## The potential danger points in successful ABM adoption

ITSMA has identified[1] two key points of failure when growing and scaling ABM:

1 Moving from pilot stage to build.

2 Moving from standardizing to scale.

### 1. Moving from pilot stage to build

**The problem:** You build a marketing programme that is in constant danger of being eliminated in the next round of budget cuts.

**The solution:**

- Position ABM as a corporate growth programme not as a marketing tactic. Too often programmes are tactical, marketing-centric initiatives.

- Align with sales to integrate marketing fully with the account planning process. Roles, responsibilities, and processes for creating and executing integrated sales and marketing ABM plans need to be understood by the account sales team.

- Measure and report interim results, both quantitative and qualitative. Most marketing campaigns have a short time horizon and concrete objectives. They are designed to drive demand for specific products and/or services, generate qualified leads and show results in 30–90 days. ABM programmes have a longer time horizon and the revenue opportunities aren't always known in advance. ABM is designed to change perception or positioning within accounts, build stronger relationships for ongoing collaboration and value creation and grow business with existing and new accounts through more targeted marketing.

### 2. Moving from standardizing to scale

**The problem:** Success creates enormous pressure to increase account coverage so you need to invest in people, process, and technology to achieve economies of scale.

**The solution:**

- Formalize your ABM programmes by establishing a centralized programme management office/centre of expertise, formal governance, and/or a marketing community. Centralized ABM programme management/community is a prerequisite for achieving scale.

- Develop your ABM marketers and create a formal career path.

- Implement technology for insight, campaign execution, orchestration, and metrics.

- **Create an ABM knowledge management system.** Having a central repository of ABM best practices and training materials helps teams sharpen their skills and get new accounts up and running faster.

- **Leverage ABM practices in other areas of marketing.** Companies often find that, when they have had ABM in place for some time, a trickle-down effect occurs. For example, the deeper relationships of ABM and specific company research done by account teams can help industry marketing teams make their content more relevant.

Remember that the commitment to build an ABM programme is thought of in years rather than days or months. But the benefits can be significant:

- greater account growth (versus non-ABM accounts);
- accelerated sales cycles;

- faster movement of opportunities through the pipeline;
- increase in number of client relationships;
- increased share of wallet;
- more sole-sourced opportunities;
- higher profitability in accounts;
- a single face to the customer;
- improved customer satisfaction;
- greater visibility and access to opportunities.

## Your ABM checklist

**1** The tried-and-tested ABM adoption model consists of four distinct stages: pilot, build, standardize and scale.

**2** Consider piloting all of the types of ABM that could be relevant for your company.

**3** As an ABM marketer you need to be a consummate generalist with enough knowledge of all marketing specialties to have credibility and good judgement, as well as having leadership and relationship skills.

**4** Note that there are two identified danger points in successful ABM adoption: moving from pilot stage to build and from standardizing to scale.

## Note

**1** ITSMA (2016) *Account-Based Marketing Benchmarking Survey*

# PART TWO
# Account-based marketing step-by-step

## Introduction to Part Two

We're now going to work through the seven-step process to develop and execute a strategic ABM plan for an individual account. These seven steps, shown in Figure P2.1 are:

1 Knowing what is driving the account.

2 Playing to the clients' needs.

3 Mapping and profiling stakeholders.

4 Developing targeted value propositions.

5 Planning integrated sales and marketing campaigns.

6 Executing integrated campaigns.

7 Evaluating results and updating plans.

While this process was developed for strategic ABM, the most resource-intensive of the three types, its principles apply equally to ABM Lite, and to a lesser extent, to programmatic ABM.

In strategic ABM, you work through the process for one account at a time. In an ABM Lite approach, you simply apply this process to a cluster of similar accounts rather than a single account. This means reviewing the business drivers, goals, strategies and major initiatives underway in all of the accounts in your cluster and identifying commonalities. Then reviewing your own portfolio (and that of your business partners if appropriate) to decide how and where you can help the companies in your cluster.

**Figure P2.1**   The seven-step ABM process

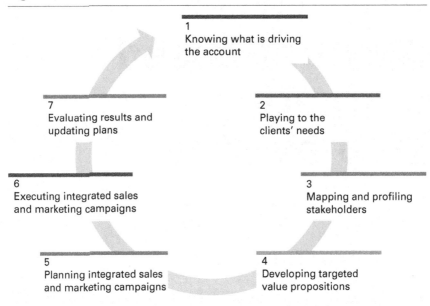

1
Knowing what is driving
the account

2
Playing to the
clients' needs

3
Mapping and profiling
stakeholders

4
Developing targeted
value propositions

5
Planning integrated sales
and marketing campaigns

6
Executing integrated sales
and marketing campaigns

7
Evaluating results and
updating plans

**SOURCE** © 2017 ITSMA

With that decided, you map out the stakeholders in each account whom you need to target, plus the influencers to whom this group of stakeholders listens. With this done, it's about developing a targeted value proposition for the group as a whole (or key segments within it), and then building a campaign with assets that can be tailored to each stakeholder in each company across your cluster. Your campaign can be tracked with a single metrics dashboard, reporting across all of the accounts.

If you are using programmatic ABM, you will probably collect less in-depth insight about what is driving the accounts in your programme – perhaps simple demographics on their size, location, industry type, number of employees, usage of a particular technology (eg Microsoft, SAP or Oracle systems) and growth rate – often used to qualify them into the programme. You will identify common issues facing them, such as digital disruption to their industry models, or the move to mobile multigenerational work-forces and match your portfolio to these issues. Then you will likely focus on specific job roles or buyer personas that you want to target and develop messaging for.

Your campaign planning is likely to focus heavily on digital media, with deepening personalization of messaging evolving as your engagement with individuals increases through the campaign. This will probably be supported by an inside sales or general salesforce, with whom your collaboration is mostly around the hand-off of marketing qualified leads to become sales accepted leads. Your metrics dashboard will be generic for all accounts and reported at a programme level.

For the purposes of this book, we will focus on the application of the seven-step process in strategic ABM, on the assumption that once you have learned to do it at its most in-depth, you can begin to apply less intensive versions of it for your own ABM Lite or programmatic approaches.

One final point to remember as you work through Part Two of this book is that this process is a generic one. Real ABM success comes when you develop your own process, linking it into the account management and sales processes that already exist in your company, and using the systems you have to provide the inputs and track the outputs from your process. In short, use our process as a starter for ten to develop your own way of doing ABM.

# Knowing what is driving the account

## Where are you today? Where do you want to be?

As we get started with the seven-step process of strategic ABM, this chapter guides you through acquiring the depth of insight you need to create and execute powerful ABM plans. Gathering and using account intelligence is the first step.

Once you have selected the accounts to include in your ABM pilot or existing programme, identified sufficient resources and assigned them to specific accounts, you are ready to carry out the primary and secondary research which lies at the heart of ABM activity.

Account intelligence positions you to:

- identify and proactively exploit new opportunities;
- enhance existing and build new senior-level account relationships;
- expand the scope and term of engagements;
- better align marketing and sales.

Your first job is to identify what you already know about your account and, critically, what you need to find out to fill any gaps. Start by assessing where you are as a provider today and what your objectives are for the account (Table 6.1). You probably already have some of this information from the account selection process described in Chapter 4. We know that this is an inside-out way of thinking, but it's important to set the baseline understanding of where you want to be and how far that is from where you are today. Once that's done, you can set it aside and get back to thinking from the customer's perspective.

**Table 6.1**    Starting point and current plans

| Where are we? | Where do we want to be? |
| --- | --- |
| • How big is the account for us? | • How big do we want this account to be? |
| • How profitable is the account? | |
| • What relationship do we have? | • How do we want to be perceived by the key stakeholders? |
| • How do the key stakeholders currently perceive us? | |
| | • What propositions do we want to sell (in an ideal world)? |
| • What do we do for them now? | |
| • Are we delivering well? | • What other goals or plans already exist for this account? |
| • How are we working with partners? | |

The best way to answer these questions is to meet with the account director and account team members close to the account day-to-day. This typically takes the form of a kick-off meeting, to confirm the ABM purpose and process for their account, and to produce a baseline for everyone's knowledge of the starting point and current plans for the account.

A typical kick-off meeting agenda may look something like this:

**1**  Introductions.

**2**  The ABM process.

**3**  Overview of the account:

   • Our history with the account.

   • Current status.

   • What do we do for them now?

   • Are we delivering well?

   • How big is this account?:

   – type of contracts;

   – value of contracts;

   – projected revenues over next three to five years;

   – number of people working the account.

   • Percentage of available budget owned by us.

   • Major competitors and their contracts.

   • Stakeholder relationship status.

**4**  Account goals.

**5**  Summary and next steps.

If an account plan already exists, much of the information you need may be in it – but beware, as this is not always the case. Our own experience of account plans is that they vary widely in quality, with some full of account intelligence but light on the strategy for the account and others light on intelligence but full of current project status reports and lists of what the client will be sold next… whether they want to buy it or not! Even when a company has a standard account planning template and process, the degree to which the process is followed and the template completed varies widely.

# ABM perception interviews

A key piece of information you'll need to understand about the account is how clients within it currently perceive you. This is important whether you are trying to change client perceptions or your position within an account, or your objective is to cross-sell, upsell or run a major bid into an account.

**Table 6.2**  Discussion guide for ABM perception interviews

1 How would you describe the services and solutions company X provides?

2 What business value does it bring to you?

3 How familiar are you with company X's solutions?

4 How effective is company X in educating you about its full portfolio of solutions?

5 How has your relationship with company X grown or evolved over the years?

6 How do you rate company X on the following: business knowledge, technical knowledge, ability to save you money, timeliness of delivery, and being proactive?

7 How satisfied have you been with your company X account team's ability to anticipate industry trends and future requirements and bring those perspectives to you?

8 How satisfied have you been with your company X account team's ability to present innovative solutions that address or enhance project needs or goals?

9 What solution providers do you consider to be most like company X?

10 In which areas do you believe company X is better than its competition?

11 In which areas does company X fall short of the competition?

12 If you were to look for a provider for these types of solutions today, which criteria would be the most important in your evaluation?

13 Do you consider company X to be one of your strategic advisors?

14 In what areas could company X do more?

Initial perception research will give you an understanding of how key decision makers and influencers feel about you today, and how big the gap is between what they think of you now and what you want them to think.

If you don't already have that information from your general brand research, customer satisfaction, net promoter or win–loss studies, it's worth considering some perception interviews to complete your baseline picture of your starting point. These interviews shed light on key stakeholder awareness of your company's successes in the account to-date, what you stand for and are best at, your competitive strengths, your range of solutions and the total value your company can bring to bear to help them achieve their business objectives.

Typically, a marketer or third party conducts six to eight interviews for each ABM account. The interviews can be repeated annually to gauge progress and provide an excellent set of metrics for reporting ABM impact and outcomes. Table 6.2 is a suggested discussion guide for use in these interviews.

# What is the account's context?

You have done all the foundation work to draw a baseline for your starting point. Now you can focus on the important stuff: what's happening in your account. To do so, you'll need to answer some fundamental questions about the context within which the account is operating and how it is responding.

This is not straightforward. These clients are usually large, complex entities with organizations in constant flux. What issues are they facing at this point in time? Are they going through a significant acquisition or divestment? Are there shifts in the whole business dynamic, including strategy, direction, operations and/or organization and staffing?

Essentially you will be doing a 'market audit' for the account, almost as though you were its marketing director or CMO. You'll need to collect information on:

1 How the wider world is impacting the account (a PESTEL analysis of the political, economic, social/cultural, technological, environmental, and legal issues that are affecting, or could affect, the account).

2 How market dynamics are impacting the account as its customers and competitors evolve (Porter's Five Forces of analysis of barriers to entry, power of buyers, availability of substitutes, power of suppliers, and the prevailing competitive intensity).

**Table 6.3** Key questions about the account context

| |
|---|
| **1** How is the account's industry landscape changing and what is emerging? |
|    a) Which elements are most important to the account? |
|    b) What is the impact of these changes on the account? |
| **2** How are they responding today? What are the major business, operational, and IT initiatives inside the account? |
| **3** Who are the key stakeholders that own the initiatives, and how do they fit into the organization? |
| **4** What are the decision-making criteria for each initiative, and how can we better understand them? |
| **5** Who are the perceived gatekeepers for the initiatives, and how can we work with or around them? |

**3** How the account is performing relative to its peers (especially as seen by investment analysts who advise individuals and institutions on its relative attractiveness as an investment vehicle in the short, medium and longer term).

**4** How the account is structured, its financial situation, its business divisions, geographical spread, mix of products and services, board and leadership team and its culture.

**5** The account's stated strategy and key initiatives and its progress against these.

**6** How the account buys services like yours, who it currently works with, your competitive landscape within the account and any plans for new contracts or contract renewals in your space.

The questions you are essentially trying to answer are shown in Table 6.3.

# A note on how today's buyers buy

One of the most important things for account-based marketers to understand, and one that is least well understood today, is how buyers consume information as they go through their buying process. For large purchases such as technology systems and complex professional services it is simply not true that buyers make up their mind whom to work with before they ever meet a salesperson, as some observers would have you believe.

When you hear someone say something like 'buyers are 70 per cent through the purchase process before they want to speak with a salesperson' be sure to ask which buyers they are referring to and what they are buying. It may be true for consumer goods, even high-value ones like new cars or kitchens, but ITSMA research shows that it is not true for high-consideration, high-value B2B purchases. People still play a major role in these purchase processes.

However, it is certainly the case that today's buyer has access to more content via more channels than ever before. Changing buyer behaviour and the sheer proliferation of marketing channels has led to some profound marketing challenges, including the need to create a seamless buyer experience and to optimize the marketing mix to reach those buyers effectively. Marketers need to know what content *their* buyers want and the channels *through which they prefer to consume it.*

At this stage, make sure that you understand how your buyers will make purchase decisions: what are the criteria they will use to select a supplier like you? This will inform both the content of your integrated sales and marketing campaign and the channels that you use to reach buyers.

**Figure 6.1**    How B2B buyers evaluate providers

When you were evaluating the providers on your shortlist and making your final decision for your most recent solution, how important were the following? (Rank order 1st, 2nd, and 3rd in order of importance) % of respondents (N=402)

| | |
|---|---|
| Knowledge and understanding of my industry | 25 |
| Knowledge and understanding of my unique business issues | 24 |
| Quantifiable value of the proposed solution | 24 |
| A proven track record backed by customer references from companies similar to mine | 22 |
| Fresh ideas and innovation to advance my business | 22 |
| Flexibility in their approach to working with clients | 19 |
| Available resources to meet deadlines and speed time to market | 17 |
| An existing relationship with the technology solutions provider | 16 |
| Proprietary IP, tools, and methodologies | 14 |
| Responsiveness of sales people and subject matter experts (SMEs) during the purchase process | 14 |
| Ability to share experience from working with companies across regions and/or industries | 12 |
| Endorsements from third parties such as industry analysts and/or sourcing advisors | 10 |

■ % Rank 1st     ■ % Rank 2nd     % Rank 3rd

**NOTE** Respondents were asked to rank in order of importance
**SOURCE** ITSMA, How B2B Buyers Consume Information Survey, 2016

Our own research suggests that the top three things to demonstrate through your campaign are your understanding of the buyers' industry, your understanding of their particular business issues, and the quantifiable value of your proposed solution (Figure 6.1). You should be well up to speed on the first two points through the analysis you've done, and we'll talk more about value propositions in Chapter 9. (There is more detail about the buying process in Chapter 10.)

# Information sources

If answering the questions in Tables 6.1 and 6.2 seems daunting, remember that you have many potential sources of information. And even if you don't have all the answers immediately, finding them may be among your early ABM objectives.

There is a flow (Figure 6.2) to this research process that's worth bearing in mind. Once you have had your kick-off meeting, you'll have a view of what secondary information is already available internally about the account. Review this in detail and identify the gaps before going off to fill those gaps with secondary information available externally. It's important that you understand all you can from this secondary information before you have in-depth, primary research-style conversations with your account team and partners about the account.

**Figure 6.2** The research process flow post kick-off

You'll be able to have a much better conversation once you have done your homework on the account. Only when you are fully briefed internally should you consider conducting primary interviews externally with the clients themselves.

## 1. Initial secondary research sources

To answer the context questions, first turn to secondary information sources (Figure 6.3). Some of these sources will be your internal systems or existing primary research that your company has conducted through other

**Figure 6.3**   Secondary information sources

| Internal | • Financial systems<br>• Delivery systems<br>• Knowledge management systems/intranets<br>• CRM systems |
|---|---|
| Publicly Available | • Company websites<br>• Press coverage<br>• Blogs/tweets/LinkedIn profiles<br>• Conference presentations and articles |
| Available to Buy | • Investment analyst reports<br>• Industry analyst reports<br>• Aggregators (Factiva, OneSource, BoardEx)<br>• Academic case studies<br>• Contract renewal databases<br>• Sales intelligence systems (iProfile, fresheye) |

initiatives, such as buyer persona research or customer satisfaction surveys. It's worth spending time with finance and delivery colleagues to understand the information they hold and their insights into the account.

Other sources are freely available externally. These include company websites, and in the case of public companies, investor relations pages are especially useful as they present the company's view of its market landscape, the challenges it faces, its strategies and priority initiatives. Still other public sources will offer information for a fee. These include investment and industry analysts, who regularly review public company performance and outline the actions company executives should be taking.

We see many ABM programmes turning to outside research firms to help build the background account profile information from a combination of sources. This can be a good strategy to supplement limited ABM resources and, if you're using a specialist tool or insight platform (see Chapter 3), make the information readily available to the sales and marketing teams.

## 2. Internal primary research

Salespeople are notorious for knowing far more than they will ever document in a sales system or presentation. As a result, they are often an untapped source of account information. Once you've done your basic background research, the next step is to interview the account team to find out what they know. Account teams are usually very happy to talk about what they know but rarely willing to make the time to write it down.

Using a semi-structured focus group discussion (Table 6.4) is the most effective way to extract this knowledge. Try to get people involved who work with the client day-to-day if possible, including delivery teams, commercial specialists, industry experts or consultants and HR people as well as sales people.

You might want to think about not having the account manager in the room during this discussion, since it may be harder for junior members of

**Table 6.4**  Sales/account team interview guide

| | |
|---|---|
| 1 | Introductions: What are your roles on the account and the areas you're most involved with? |
| 2 | What are the account's challenges and priorities as you see them today? |
| 3 | Please describe the culture of the account as you see it. |
| 4 | What is the status of the projects you are working on? |
| 5 | How would you describe the account's perception of what we are good at? |
| 6 | What projects do you see our competitors working on in the account and what's their status? |
| 7 | Why have competitors won (and beaten us) on specific deals in the past? |
| 8 | Where do our competitors have strong relationships/sponsors in the account? |
| 9 | How would you describe the account's perception of what our competitors are good at? |
| 10 | What is your understanding of the account's spending on relevant services today? |
| 11 | What is your understanding of their future spending plans and projects? |
| 12 | Where do you think we could be most successful in the account? |
| 13 | What do you think we need to do to be successful in the account? |
| 14 | Are there any other points of importance to the planning process? |

the account team to open up and say what they believe if they feel they have to toe the party line and not embarrass the account manager. This is particularly true in cultures where it is important to save face at all times and not be seen to be questioning authority.

Depending on the complexity and scale of the account, the size of your current business with them and the way that your organization manages large, international accounts, you may need to hold multiple discussions with teams working in different business units or regions on the account. Some of these may need to be via video conference, or you may decide to simply do telephone interviews.

Use your political judgement as to whom to speak to first and whom to invite to each discussion in order to keep the key stakeholders in your internal organization onside.

## 3. External primary research

It's easy to get the idea that ABM is a 'black ops' team which does everything covertly. In fact, some of the most successful ABM programmes have taken the opposite approach, openly discussing the ideas behind ABM with their accounts and using these discussions as a springboard for greater transparency.

This approach opens up an extremely valuable source of account insight: key contacts within the customer account. Once again, the most effective way to unlock this insight is through a semi-structured interview (Table 6.5). The idea is to have a clear idea of what you would like to know while remaining flexible enough to uncover information you might not have anticipated.

Remember: do your homework first via the secondary research and interviews with the account team so you can approach customers with ideas rather than simply asking for information.

The first two questions in Table 6.5 demonstrate how to use your knowledge during the interviews and avoid asking questions that the customer thinks you should already know the answers to. (You may decide to combine these questions with those in Table 6.2 if you need to also baseline perceptions.)

Primary research can sometimes be used not only to act as a baseline for current perceptions and future priorities, but also as a tool within an ABM campaign in its own right. KPMG successfully used a blend of primary and secondary research to uncover their client's focus on Sustainable Development Goals, and also then to build Sustainable Development Goal indices by industry to support the client in its work, repositioning itself in the account as a consequence (see the case study 'KPMG').

**Table 6.5** Suggested customer interview guide

| |
|---|
| **1** Can you confirm your business objectives for me? My research suggests they are as follows: ____. |
| **2** Based on my research, it seems that these are some of the main challenges and obstacles you face: ____. Which are most pressing for you? |
| **3** What are the resulting priorities you have for services or solutions? |
| **4** Thinking about these priorities for future services, which are the suppliers you might consider for them, and why? |

**CASE STUDY** KPMG LLP – Making a big impression at a key global account

KPMG International is a global network of professional services firms. In 2013, the US firm decided to make a concerted effort to enhance its brand visibility and deepen relationships at an important global humanitarian account by launching an ABM campaign strategy in support of the account's Sustainable Development Goals (SDGs).

**Ambitious objectives**

The ultimate goal was to transform the client's perception of KPMG as merely one of many undifferentiated 'professional services vendors' to one of KPMG as a true advisor with shared values and accountability in shaping the client's agenda – 2015 and beyond. KPMG in the US coordinated with multiple member firms to support this account globally.

The Global Account team accomplished a series of firsts by executing the SDG Industry Matrix campaign. Not only was this their first actual ABM campaign but they also broke new ground within KPMG's broader marketing organization in the following ways:

- This was the first account-based marketing campaign that combined a mix of digital and traditional media channels to drive brand, relationships, and sales at KPMG in the US.
- Seamless coordination within KPMG's marketing organization brought the best of the network's resources to the account. By leveraging internal market research tools, as well as local, national, global, and offshore resources, the team was able to achieve cost savings of approximately $225,000 in print production, event marketing execution, market research and campaign management costs.
- This was the first integrated client-centric marketing plan with a global reach and scale of this magnitude and prominence, drawing in C-Suite executives and global leaders across eight countries.

**Business results**

There were a number of key business results:

1 Lead acquisition that accelerated the account team's understanding of and connection to key buyers, influencers and coaches within the account.

- Approximately 85 new relationships were created.

- Eight new speaking engagements were identified and managed by KPMG marketing that 'credentialized' the Global Lead Partner as a leading subject matter expert in the post-2015 global debate.

- Using KPMG's US sales relationship scoring methodology, the campaign led to a 40 per cent increase in the relationship scores of post-2015 strategic contacts across this account's 10 largest entities.

2 Third-party brand perception study confirmed that the ABM campaign helped change perceptions of KPMG at the account:

- One director in the account noted that KPMG is 'an innovative interlocutor on a wide range of development-related topics' and credits the US firm and KPMG network with providing ideas on sustainable development and advocating for private sector-led, inclusive growth.

- Another leader from the account's Development Organization noted that KPMG is a 'leading professional organization in the area of global development' with the 'capacity and know-how to significantly contribute to pressing challenges around the post-2015 agenda'.

3 Positive media sentiment from the campaign enhanced KPMG's overall brand equity:

- Top KPMG executives were being covered across the media regarding their views on SDGs and how the private sector can guide the investment decisions of the sector while solving economic, social, and environmental challenges, thereby creating real, shared, tangible value.

- The views of KPMG's US firm on the SDGs garnered positive coverage on social and digital platforms, especially after the account's active involvement in creating high-touch event programmes, such as at the World Economic Forum.

- A total of 37 account-related events were identified and attended by the account team, 11 of which were hosted by KPMG in the US, yielding upwards of five million brand impressions in eight countries across six main industry verticals.

From a revenue growth perspective, the Global Account team expected the campaign to influence a 33 per cent US revenue increase by the end of FY15 and an increase in global revenue of 45 per cent over the same time period, given its proven effectiveness in building the team's continued exposure and credibility across the entire client organization.

Analysis of the figures from the account's 2014 Annual Report showed that KPMG had risen from seventh-place provider to be the third largest services provider to the account for applicable services and second largest provider within the Big Four professional services organizations globally.

### Lessons learned

Given the complexity of both the client account and the KPMG network globally, this was well executed, driving impressive results and competitive advantage. With relatively low penetration into the account, KPMG in the US used ABM to change perceptions of itself within the account from that of 'a good supplier' to one of 'a true advisor – a partner that really understood the account's organizational imperatives, and that could leverage its own wider business relationship to help support the client agenda.

There was also a good understanding of a large and dispersed client with many cultures and relationship/purchasing criteria. Finally, it demonstrated good coordination within the KPMG network of member firms.

## 4. Creating actionable insight

Now that you have a good understanding of what's happening in the account, you can turn the intelligence you've collected into actionable insight. There are (at least) two ways to do this. Most people typically use a SWOT analysis, highlighting their relative strengths and weaknesses in the account, the opportunities that exist in the account, and the threats to be avoided (see Figure 6.4).

Unfortunately, many SWOT analyses end up looking like laundry lists of information, with no clear indication of the relative importance of each item or of the actions that should be taken as a result. If you do use SWOT, try to keep yourself to the two or three most important factors in each box, and be clear on the implication of each one for your company and your ABM plan. Table 6.6 shows a Power SWOT framework with an example factor and implication in each category as an illustration of what you should be aiming for.

**Figure 6.4**    A typical SWOT analysis framework

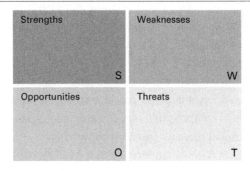

**Table 6.6**    An illustrative Power SWOT for an ABM plan

| SWOT Category | Factor | Implication |
|---|---|---|
| **Strengths** (where we are relatively stronger than our competitors) | We have a stronger reputation as an outsourcing partner than XXX and YYY competitors | Position for contract renewal opportunity in 18 months |
| **Weaknesses** (where we are relatively weaker than our competitors) | We are not seen as proactive or innovative | Develop a systematic programme of innovation and proactive contact for account stakeholders |
| **Opportunities** (where we can take advantage of something happening externally) | New government legislation will further increase pressure on the back office at account and drive an efficiency initiative | Take proactive, proven ideas for transformational change to account, reducing costs while achieving better customer experience through digital technologies |
| **Threats** (where we may be at risk from something happening externally) | XXX, YYY, and ZZZ competitors all have relationships with the person tipped as likely to be hired into the new CDO role in the account | Build executive relationship and visibility |

If you want to take your analysis even further, we recommend that you think about the imperatives facing the account and the initiatives they are or should be taking in response to these imperatives. The reason this is important is that it allows you to 'follow the money' in the account, since initiatives typically have an individual responsible for delivering them and an associated budget for that individual to use to get the job done.

A business or market imperative is a major dynamic, issue and/or trend that will have an impact on a company's ability to achieve its stated goals. An example from the telecoms sector might be their customers' increasing expectation to be able to watch videos while on the move through their smartphones or tablets. An example in the retail sector might be customers' increasing expectation to be recognized and complete a purchase across multiple channels, such as a website visited on a mobile phone where the purchase is made, followed by a store where that purchase is then collected.

A business initiative is an activity or set of activities taking place in direct response to one or more imperatives, and these initiatives can span financial, operational and technology functions in the organization. So, in the case of the telecoms company facing the customers expecting to watch videos while on the move, it's likely that initiatives to upgrade their network will be underway, together with billing system and CRM improvements. And in the case of the retailer dealing with its customer through several channels, an omnichannel initiative is likely to be underway, with changes to websites, customer databases and point-of-sale systems in store to deliver a seamless shopping experience along with staff training and supply chain improvements to allow swift delivery of goods.

By listing out the imperatives facing a company and the initiatives it is taking in response, together with the people and budgets aligned to them and their success criteria if known, you will be in a position to decide where you are best placed to help and understand the opportunities open to you in that account.

And to take this to the next stage, if you can identify the initiatives that the company should be taking but isn't as yet, you'll be in a position to proactively take valuable new ideas into the account. This latter approach, while more difficult, is where you are more likely to shape the account's thinking and position yourself as a trusted advisor in the process.

# Your ABM checklist

**1** Use a kick-off meeting with the account director to find out where your company is in the account today, where it wants to get to and by when.

**2** Think about using perception research to provide a baseline for how stakeholders in the account see your company before you get started with your ABM programme.

**3** Get yourself up to speed on the account by using the information that exists already in your internal systems, filling gaps with any external information you can find.

**4** If you still don't have an understanding of the account's context, objectives, strategy, key initiatives, stakeholders and the way it buys your services, consider doing primary research both with your internal account team and with the clients in the account.

**5** Draw out your relative strengths and weaknesses and the opportunities and threats that exist for you in the account using a Power SWOT.

**6** Remember: to create actionable insight identify the main imperatives facing the account and the initiatives they are running in response. By finding out the people, budgets and success metrics they've allocated to each initiative, you'll be able to 'follow the money' and decide where your best opportunities lie.

**7** To position yourself strongly as a trusted partner think about the initiatives they should be taking but aren't yet. This is where you can take in fresh thinking to add value to stakeholders in the account.

# Playing to the client's needs

## 07

## Changing your mindset

The second step in the ABM process for specific accounts is about defining and selecting 'plays'. A play is an offering or solution that addresses a specific imperative and initiative within your chosen account, as identified during Step One in Chapter 6. It can be narrowly applied (think of a single offer such as a consulting engagement) or comprise a complex solution (think of a technology-managed service that includes hardware, software, people delivering services and intellectual property based on best practice processes). It is the solution to the problem facing the account.

The defining factor in getting this step right is your mindset, or learning to think 'outside-in' rather than 'inside-out'. What do we mean by that? It can be altogether too easy, whether we are in sales or marketing, to focus on what we can offer without having first thought carefully about the client's challenges and context. We approach clients with our shopping list from which we hope they will pick and choose what they need.

We remember being bemused to hear the story of one accountancy firm whose head of business development described the challenge well, saying, 'If a client relationship partner has a deep knowledge of international tax services, that's what they try to sell all of their clients, even if the client wants to talk about corporate finance for an acquisition. They can't get out of their tax mindset and into the client's shoes.'

As we emphasize constantly throughout this book, account-based marketing is about understanding what an individual client needs and targeting or developing solutions to meet that need. This is what differentiates ABM from typical product or services selling. ABM is more suited to consultative selling methods, such as challenger selling or SPIN (situation, problem, implication, need pay-off) selling, where the focus is on the client and their issues.

Some people call it 'blank piece of paper selling' since the seller often goes in to give the client a good listening to, probing the issues the client faces and the implications of not dealing with them effectively before moving on to how their company could help. This is more about building long-term relationships that deliver mutual value than short-term, transactional selling.

So, once you have identified what the key challenges are, what the pressing initiatives are and who inside the targeted accounts feels ownership and is being held accountable for the successful implementation of those initiatives, your next step is to ask: What can we do to help them? What is our solution, our product or our service that meets that need? This is your play.

# Developing the play

Developing the play allows you to talk about what your organization has to offer in the context of what matters to the account. This is a long way from more traditional approaches to product marketing. Rather than swamping the client with a bewildering array of products or service features, which might or might not have any relevance, you have done the hard work of packaging up your products and services for them. This becomes the starting point of a much more effective conversation about the imperatives and initiatives you have identified for the client and your ideas about how you can help.

The play is a broad concept. It can be a product, a combination of a product and service, or a combination of product, service and the people necessary for their expertise. It can include intellectual property, frameworks and methodologies. It encompasses anything and everything you could possibly bring to bear to help the client address their imperative and implement their initiative successfully.

It can also include bringing in partners because complicated issues often demand solutions outside the scope of one provider. When you are moving into complex areas such as the transition to a digital platform, for instance, issues of security and compliance arise as well as technology.

So a solution may be made up of a number of hardware and software products, the services to implement them and the implementation expertise, which can also be a source of competitive differentiation. Remember: the play is about you. Everything else is about the client.

Best done in a workshop environment, the ideal way to identify potential plays that could be taken into an account is by mapping the imperatives facing the account and the initiatives underway (or possible) against your portfolio. Figure 7.1 shows how this mapping is done.

**Figure 7.1**   Mapping imperatives and initiatives to your portfolio

| Your offerings | Business imperative/ initiative 1 | Business imperative/ initiative 2 | Business imperative/ initiative 3 | Business imperative/ initiative 4 | Business imperative/ initiative 5 |
|---|---|---|---|---|---|
| Product 1 | Play #1 | | | Play #4 | |
| Product 2 | | Play #2 | | | |
| Service 1 | | | | | |
| Solution 1 | | | Play #3 | | Play #5 |
| Partner required? | No | Yes | Yes | No | No |

Marketers often facilitate this process, guiding the expertise of the account team and relevant subject matter experts from around the company. Occasionally, we have found it useful to have account managers from similar clients in the same industry in the workshop, since they may bring ideas of how the company has created plays for similar initiatives in a different account.

Use Figure 7.1 as a template to help cut through the detail and identify your headline plays. This should not be a 'laundry list' of part numbers, but focused at a high level on the appropriate solutions to the business imperatives and initiatives of the client. Define the challenge. Is it about security? Globalization? Mobility? Taking this approach raises the level of the discussions. It starts to shift thinking from what 'we' have to offer to what the client really needs.

For example, a leading professional services firm, investigating the challenges faced by its global media client, found that the client faced scrutiny for spending too much money on back-office activities rather than on developing and producing valuable content that could be sold around the world. As a consequence, the account had developed an initiative to reduce the percentage of its costs spent on sales, general and administrative activities from 12 per cent to nine per cent.

Meanwhile, its finance people were spending far too much time and too many resources on low-level administration rather than on supporting activities linked to creative content development and production. In addition to going against a stated financial initiative, it was alienating the young high-flyers on the finance staff, who resented having to deal with such routine jobs.

So the professional service firm suggested it put in some of its own junior finance people to do the low-level work. This would enable the media company to give its ambitious middle managers more time to spend on creative solutions geared to programme production, which added value rather than just kept the back office running. This targeting of such a specific need with the people who form a major part of the firm's offering wouldn't have happened without it understanding the imperatives and initiatives in the client.

Describe your plays as clearly as possible once you've identified them. Tables 7.1 and 7.2 show further examples of plays developed to meet specific imperatives and initiatives.

**Table 7.1**    Illustrative technology play supporting a globalization initiative

| Prioritized business imperative/ initiative | Play features |
| --- | --- |
| Globalization | • 24x7 localization platform<br>• Tailored security solutions<br>• Virtual support for each time zone; shift processing to different time zones<br>• Global commoditization<br>• Solution integration with local partners<br>• Localized software and services |

**Table 7.2**    Illustrative technology play supporting a risk mitigation initiative

| Prioritized business imperative/ initiative | Play features |
| --- | --- |
| Risk mitigation due to increased regulation and security mandates | • A secure platform<br>• Incorporate right rules to enforce current risk tolerance<br>• Security: can adjust to desire for risk mitigation<br>• Predictive modelling, be proactive in providing info to client, not after they have hit their risk tolerance<br>• Business process management – automated actions to address risk breaches<br>• Customized services |

# Prioritizing possible plays

You may find yourself in the position of having too many potential plays identified for your account. While this is a nice problem to have, the danger here is a lack of focus – of doing too much and doing nothing well. If this happens in an ABM workshop you're running it's time to prioritize.

**Table 7.3**  Illustrative approach to prioritizing possible plays

|  | Multichannel innovation | Cost reduction in payments | Business intelligence |
| --- | --- | --- | --- |
| Does it matter to the client? (0=No, 5=Fairly important, 10=Very important) | 10 | 10 | 5 |
| Do we have something different to say? (0=Nothing, 5=Broadly the same as competitors, 10=Different) | 5 | 5 | 10 |
| Do we have credentials? (0=None, 5=Same as competitors, 10=More than competitors) | 5 | 10 | 10 |
| Will it lead to a large-scale opportunity? (0=No, 5=Some opportunity, 10=Mega deals) | 10 | 10 | 5 |
| Will it position company more widely in bank? (0=No, 5=To some extent, 10=Definitely) | 5 | 10 | 10 |
| TOTAL SCORE | 35 | 45 | 40 |

The GE McKinsey directional policy matrix is one tool you could use here. But if that seems too unwieldy (and you don't have the time to go off and do the analysis needed to do it well), another, quicker, but still interactive approach is to prioritize on the basis of a few simple criteria. Table 7.3 shows the criteria used by one company in an ABM workshop for a bank, which threw up too many potential plays.

In this example, the company in question decided to pursue the 'cost reduction in payments' play, since it scored the highest in the prioritization exercise, with the 'business intelligence' play running parallel. The 'multi-channel innovation' play was not abandoned, but built into the plan to happen in the second half of the year once the two initial plays had been developed and tested with the account.

Companies using continuous insight platforms find themselves in the enviable position of being able to map their portfolio to account initiatives on a continual and systematic basis (see the BT case study). Systems can suggest what offers would resonate with clients in the account, what materials are available to send, the value proposition for the client and the proof points around where the product, service, or solution has been successfully delivered before.

There is a balance to be struck here around taking advantage of the opportunities as they present themselves in real time while being clear what you want to be famous for in an account, and the priority or long-term play that you are focusing on. Clear guidelines are helpful to salespeople working in an account about what types of opportunity will fit with the overall strategy the account director is executing.

---

**CASE STUDY**    BT – Creating more effective sales conversations with KAM Live

In 2007, leading communications services company BT decided it wanted to increase business opportunities in its largest accounts. A review of BT Global Services' marketing operations showed opportunities to increase share of wallet and drive a more profitable pipeline in the most important accounts. BT relied upon a portfolio-led approach to engage with customers. Salespeople focused on what they had to sell but were not always able to demonstrate in-depth knowledge of customers' needs.

'We realized that we would benefit from a more targeted approach to marketing and selling,' according to Neil Blakesley, then VP of Marketing of BT Global Services (BTGS). 'We said, let's focus on the individual and the company he or she is in. For companies that are selling to the very, very large organizations, the more you know about your customer, the better. And not just at an organization level but at the individual level. We decided to spend our marketing dollars on the customer rather than the billboard.'

In response, BT created the Key Account Marketing (KAM) programme in 2008 after a brief pilot testing programme. It began with an intense research effort for its top accounts. The researchers first performed an internal sweep, pulling information from BT's customer relationship management (CRM) system about each target account, including:

- current BT revenue with the account;
- level and areas of penetration within the account;
- customer service issues (do they like us or hate us, or are they indifferent?);
- relationships (whom do we know in the account and what are their roles, responsibilities and disposition toward BT?).

Next, the researchers gathered secondary information on accounts by crawling the web and other information feeds such as industry analyst reports, social media and financial information providers. The research team pored over the mountain of information for each account to create reports that identified compelling pieces of insight and mapped them to BT's strengths and portfolio.

The reports were delivered through a portal that divided the information into a number of key categories for each account, including:

- comprehensive business/IT update on each account;
- competitive intelligence detailing suppliers for the primary categories of IT;
- marketing resources to aid the engagement (eg case studies, events, relevant presentation materials, etc);
- potential conversations/opportunities.

The new programme was an immediate hit. BT sales teams outside the programme pushed to be included. Unfortunately, the tiny KAM team was already stretched to the limit. Given the large size of the target accounts, the amount of information generated by the searches was massive. And the search methodologies lived inside the minds of the researchers, who manually searched for insight on each KAM account across a wealth of criteria (ie manually typing in 'Joe Smith and company X' or 'company X and IT consolidation').

The task was extremely time consuming and the number of domains and criteria to be searched against was so difficult to manage that the KAM team could only update research on each account once per year. Adding more accounts would be impossible.

## Scaling the programme with no added budget

Yet that's exactly what the team was asked to do. The expansion would have to come with no added budget or staff. 'The only option we had was to innovate,' noted Richard Fitzmaurice, Global KAM Lead for BTGS, who led the development of KAM Live and managed the programme.

Necessity led Fitzmaurice to a strange source for innovation: price comparison websites. Seeing the websites' ability to quickly gather, process and update large amounts of price information from different companies' websites, the KAM team thought they saw a way to ease the load of their research team.

BT used the expertise in web crawling and web scraping behind the price websites to automate the information-gathering functions within KAM. The team worked with the world's leading search engines to pull information into the new KAM engine and integrated other information sources, such as social media and analyst websites. Developed over a period of about six months, the new engine automated the previously manual search for insight across hundreds of different criteria and domains.

## A pool of filtered information

Each day, the KAM engine created a pool of information on each account in five major areas for the KAM research analyst to review (Figure 7.2). The engine was designed to learn what information the KAM team had seen before so that it would never show the same information twice, ensuring that the information presented to the analysts was current and completely fresh.

The analysts then combed through the filtered information and compiled detailed reports on each account. Though the KAM engine was now doing more of the heavy lifting in terms of research, the analysts were more important than ever. They had to understand BT and its customers well enough to know whether the information being spat out by the engine would really be useful. 'We train our researchers as if they were a sales team,' said Fitzmaurice. 'We actually get the portfolio owners – the absolute number-one experts in BT in each area – to train the KAM team. The analysts are extremely bright MBAs and PhDs who are very technical and IT-literate.'

That kind of background and training was important because the analysts, the sales teams, and the sector marketing teams all had the ability to tune the KAM engine to produce the best insight for a particular company in a particular sector.

## An investment in the customer

The information generated by KAM Live changed the dynamic of the conversation with customers from one based on the portfolio to one based on empathy and

**Figure 7.2** Insight Analyst: Demo Account

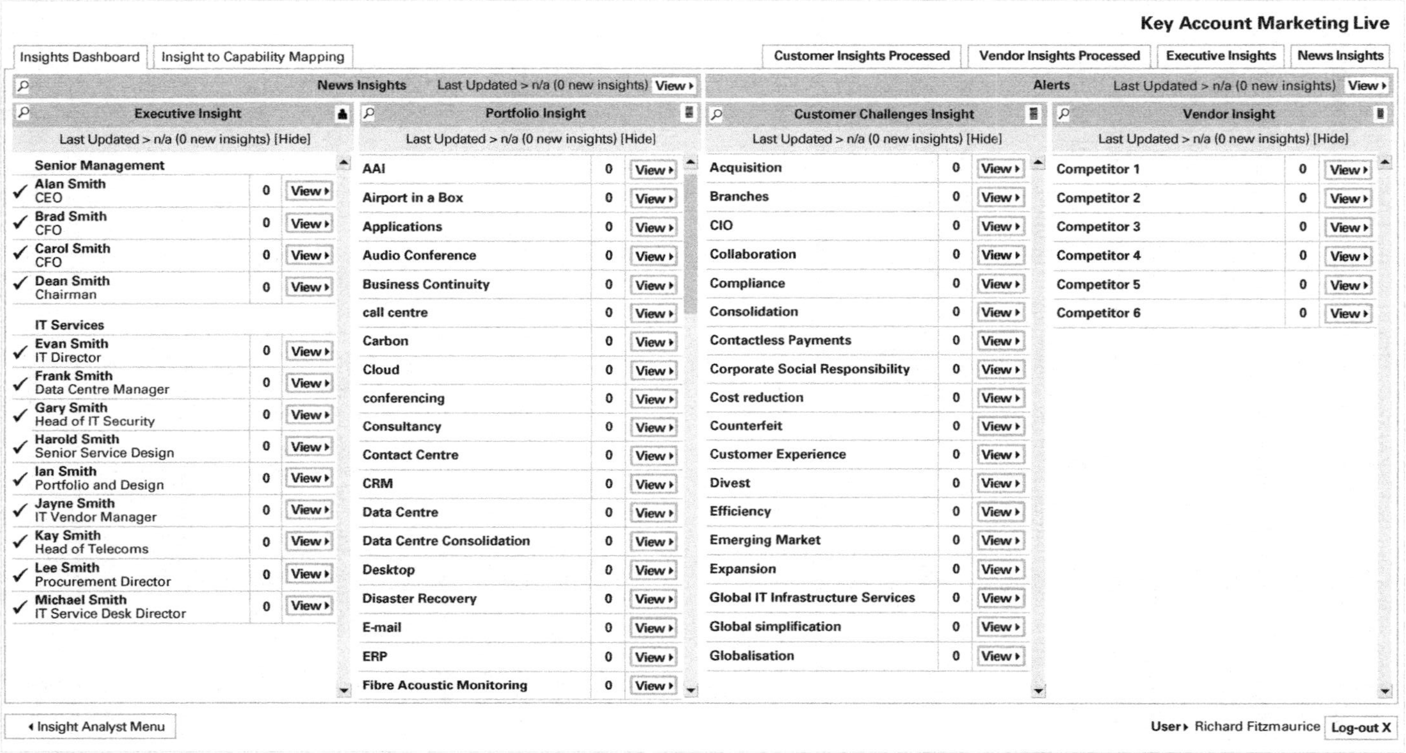

Insights Dashboard | Insight to Capability Mapping

**Key Account Marketing Live**

Customer Insights Processed | Vendor Insights Processed | Executive Insights | News Insights

News Insights | Last Updated > n/a (0 new insights) View ▸

Alerts | Last Updated > n/a (0 new insights) View ▸

| Executive Insight | | Portfolio Insight | | Customer Challenges Insight | | Vendor Insight | |
|---|---|---|---|---|---|---|---|
| Last Updated > n/a (0 new insights) [Hide] | | Last Updated > n/a (0 new insights) [Hide] | | Last Updated > n/a (0 new insights) [Hide] | | Last Updated > n/a (0 new insights) [Hide] | |
| **Senior Management** | | AAI | 0 View ▸ | Acquisition | 0 View ▸ | Competitor 1 | 0 View ▸ |
| Alan Smith — CEO | 0 View ▸ | Airport in a Box | 0 View ▸ | Branches | 0 View ▸ | Competitor 2 | 0 View ▸ |
| Brad Smith — CFO | 0 View ▸ | Applications | 0 View ▸ | CIO | 0 View ▸ | Competitor 3 | 0 View ▸ |
| Carol Smith — CFO | 0 View ▸ | Audio Conference | 0 View ▸ | Collaboration | 0 View ▸ | Competitor 4 | 0 View ▸ |
| Dean Smith — Chairman | 0 View ▸ | Business Continuity | 0 View ▸ | Compliance | 0 View ▸ | Competitor 5 | 0 View ▸ |
| **IT Services** | | call centre | 0 View ▸ | Consolidation | 0 View ▸ | Competitor 6 | 0 View ▸ |
| Evan Smith — IT Director | 0 View ▸ | Carbon | 0 View ▸ | Contactless Payments | 0 View ▸ | | |
| Frank Smith — Data Centre Manager | 0 View ▸ | Cloud | 0 View ▸ | Corporate Social Responsibility | 0 View ▸ | | |
| Gary Smith — Head of IT Security | 0 View ▸ | conferencing | 0 View ▸ | Cost reduction | 0 View ▸ | | |
| Harold Smith — Senior Service Design | 0 View ▸ | Consultancy | 0 View ▸ | Counterfeit | 0 View ▸ | | |
| Ian Smith — Portfolio and Design | 0 View ▸ | Contact Centre | 0 View ▸ | Customer Experience | 0 View ▸ | | |
| Jayne Smith — IT Vendor Manager | 0 View ▸ | CRM | 0 View ▸ | Divest | 0 View ▸ | | |
| Kay Smith — Head of Telecoms | 0 View ▸ | Data Centre | 0 View ▸ | Efficiency | 0 View ▸ | | |
| Lee Smith — Procurement Director | 0 View ▸ | Data Centre Consolidation | 0 View ▸ | Emerging Market | 0 View ▸ | | |
| Michael Smith — IT Service Desk Director | 0 View ▸ | Desktop | 0 View ▸ | Expansion | 0 View ▸ | | |
| | | Disaster Recovery | 0 View ▸ | Global IT Infrastructure Services | 0 View ▸ | | |
| | | E-mail | 0 View ▸ | Global simplification | 0 View ▸ | | |
| | | ERP | 0 View ▸ | Globalisation | 0 View ▸ | | |
| | | Fibre Acoustic Monitoring | 0 View ▸ | | | | |

◂ Insight Analyst Menu

User ▸ Richard Fitzmaurice  Log-out X

understanding. 'We've won deals where the customer noted that it was clear we were taking them seriously,' Fitzmaurice noted. 'They said we weren't just looking at the scope of the request for proposal [RFP] on the table, we were looking at the longer term of how we could help different areas of their business be successful. The information gives us more credibility with them.'

Best of all, the engine enabled BTGS to keep the insight in KAM continuously updated each day. The new speed and efficiency meant that the number of accounts covered by KAM could increase by 50 per cent without any increase in cost or headcount.

The new speed of the engine and the revamped portal, now (appropriately) dubbed KAM Live, meant that the BT teams could react to changes inside accounts on a near real-time basis. Blakesley explained:

> Let's say our salespeople are attending a conference where one of our customers is talking about expanding its capabilities over the next year. Now let's say someone tweets about the speech. Our web aggregation software will pick that up, our people in India will contextualize it, and then it will appear as a suggested conversation on the salesperson's BlackBerry. That's what we're working toward. The customer could step off the stage and our salesperson would be there waiting to talk about how we could help with the expansion plans.

This quest for real-time interaction led to a host of new features and tweaks of KAM Live's functionality:

- **News alerts.** When there was news that would have a big impact on an account, KAM Live would generate an automatic e-mail alert to the relevant salespeople.
- **Model conversations.** From the generated information, the tool built a profile of customers that helped salespeople understand how they should approach the account, such as what the account teams should be saying, to whom in the account they should be speaking, how they should position BT and what marketing tools they should use.
- **Win probability.** The tool signalled the chances of winning the business, including 'locked out,' 'possible,' 'won' and 'not determined'.
- **Individual profile updates.** The tool parsed information by specific individuals within the target account. Salespeople would receive updates on things like promotions and interviews with the press that the target individuals had given. If the information in KAM Live had relevance to specific products and services within BT's portfolio, the tool would alert salespeople, who would also receive specific guidance on how to proceed with the sale. Help might include

contacts within BT to go to for offerings, how to cross-sell and upsell the different offerings and success stories to help seal the deal.

- **Self-service search functionality.** BT salespeople didn't need to wait for the researchers to generate insights within KAM Live. They could search across all KAM accounts for information pertinent to them. For example, a CRM sales specialist focusing on the manufacturing sector in Europe, the Middle East, and Africa (EMEA) could use the search function to see a complete history of all KAM conversations (and accounts) meeting their criteria, which could be exported or viewed immediately. They could also subscribe to receive all future opportunities that meet their criteria.

### The secret weapon in account-based marketing

The speed advantage of KAM Live didn't just allow BT to scale the programme to more accounts. It also enabled a more thorough approach to its most important accounts. In 2011, for example, BT began a highly-targeted account-based marketing programme with a subset of its most important KAM accounts.

ITSMA research shows that on average, most companies assign between one and five accounts to each full-time marketer. With KAM Live supporting them, the marketers at BT could each support eight accounts. The process for managing each account included the following:

- **Examine current position in the account.** BT surveyed each member of the account team to see:
  - what the current strategy for selling in the account was;
  - what BT sold to the customer and whether BT was consistent in its approach across the different offerings.
- **Create a relationship map.** BT created a relationship map of the key executives within the target account. The purpose was to identify and prioritize key individuals within the target account and determine the strength of relationships. The results of the exercise were discussed so that account teams knew which relationships needed work and which were strong enough to be leveraged to deepen other relationships.
- **Determine hot issues in the account.** BT carried out a two-day workshop for each target account and then tuned KAM Live to track the hot issues identified by the team.
- **Create a workshop for the customer.** BT gathered together key individuals in the accounts and brought in external speakers from analyst firms to deliver presentations about trends and regulatory issues and to determine what was on the minds of customers. The agenda was what was happening

in the account. BT shared the results of its research from KAM Live and its relationship mapping exercise. The second day of the workshop was focused on creating an action plan. The team highlighted the 15–20 people within the account who were deemed critical to success and reviewed activities planned with them.

### A dashboard for measuring progress

KAM Live became so integrated into the daily workflow of the salespeople that it evolved into more than a tool for presenting information. It also became a dashboard for measuring progress. Here are some of the ways that BT was doing it:

- **Relationship scores.** At the end of each quarter, BT's KAM Live portal locked down the relationship scores for the programme as a whole and for the specific accounts. Marketers and salespeople then had to come up with plans for improving the scores during the next quarter (the scores were part of salespeople's review process). The scoring approach was so successful that BT rolled it out to 600 other accounts not covered by KAM Live.
- **Conversation tracking.** The structured conversations generated by the tool were tracked to see whether they were accepted by the account teams, what the current status of the conversation was, how other areas of marketing were supporting the conversation and whether the KAM programme identified new customer challenges/portfolio ideas/contacts. KAM Live linked with BT's Siebel CRM system to track the value and progress of opportunities. Conversation tracking was updated every eight to twelve weeks within BT's CRM system so that progress in the account could be monitored. For example, when account managers accepted a conversation generated by KAM Live, they were required to give updates on where they were in the process, whether they had read the materials and so forth.
- **Individual logins.** KAM Live user activity could be tracked to individuals and their regions.
- **Content consumption.** KAM Live could track whether individual pieces of insight generated by the tool had been read by salespeople (the text of the headline of KAM content changed from bold to regular when they did).
- **Content changes.** KAM Live tracked content contributions and changes by account teams by tracking when and how certain parts of the portal had been edited by the account team (such as the conversation tracking or account team insight priorities).

- **Account team feedback.** Account teams could contribute feedback on the success of the programme and ideas on how to improve it.
- **Value proposition tracking.** KAM Live tracked the popularity of value propositions that the tool had mapped to target accounts' challenges.
- **Automated reporting.** Metrics from KAM Live were automatically gathered and broken down into regions, sectors (such as verticals or markets), and solutions or portfolio areas and separated into individual reports.

### Not a replacement for salespeople

No matter how good KAM Live became, it was appreciated that it would never substitute for a good salesperson. All KAM Live could do was give suggestions and guidance. Success came from salespeople's ability to build a trusting relationship. 'You can't approach salespeople with something like KAM and say, "You've got terrible relationships with your customers and we're here to help"' declared Blakesley. 'Instead, you have to say, "Look, there are some opportunities to increase share of wallet, and we'll create an infrastructure for you that we will manage and keep maintained and updated. You concentrate on talking to the customer, and we'll focus on supporting your conversations." Who wouldn't be interested in that?'

However, Blakesley cautioned that salespeople had to have the consultative skills to be able to help customers come up with solutions to complex business problems. The insights coming from a tool like KAM Live would be of no help if salespeople are merely order-takers.

### Good relationships are critical

While building KAM Live had been a challenge, much more challenging was winning the hearts and minds of salespeople. Marketers couldn't have introduced a system designed to transform the sales process without first having good relationships and significant credibility within the sales organization. 'It's about credibility,' said Blakesley.

The credibility comes from having experience in the markets that salespeople sell to and demonstrating that you put your best effort into understanding their challenges. Then you need to go find the couple of people who are potential advocates for you because you've developed a strong relationship with them. Make a couple of people more successful than the others and the rest of them will come banging on your door.

# Your ABM checklist

**1** A play is an offering or group of solutions that addresses a specific imperative and initiative within your chosen account. It can be narrowly applied as a single product or service, or comprise a complex solution.

**2** ABM is about a change of mindset, from inside-out to outside-in. Developing the play allows you to talk about what your organization has to offer in the context of what matters to the account.

**3** Best done in a workshop environment, the ideal way to identify potential plays that could be taken into an account is by mapping the imperatives facing the account and the initiatives underway (or possible) against your portfolio.

**4** Marketers often facilitate this process, guiding the expertise of the account team and relevant subject matter experts from around the company.

**5** You may find yourself in the position of having too many potential plays identified for your account. While this is a nice problem to have, the danger here is a lack of focus: of doing too much and doing nothing well. If this happens in an ABM workshop you're running, it's time to prioritize.

**6** Where plays are mapped on a continuous basis through insight systems, clear guidelines are helpful to salespeople working in an account about what types of opportunity will fit with the overall strategy the account director is executing.

# Mapping and profiling stakeholders

08

*Don't count the people you reach; reach the people that count.*
DAVID OGILVY

## Understanding the decision-making unit

By this stage you should have a much clearer idea about which accounts are worth targeting in terms of the return on investment. You have done sufficient research into both the internal and external issues facing your priority accounts and the initiatives and solutions they are considering in response. This research has formed the basis of the plays you have devised to help them with their initiatives.

Each account will have designated one or more key people to oversee these strategic initiatives. You need to find out who these people are and much more about them, along with others likely to be involved in the buying process both directly and indirectly as influencers on the decision to be made. You might very well already know a number of the people involved, or this might be a new set of contacts that you need to cultivate in the account. In either case, it's time to do some in-depth research into who these individuals are and what makes them tick.

This is more than drawing reporting lines on the organizational chart (you should already have these from Step One, when you profiled the account). This is about understanding the actual decision-making unit (DMU) for your play(s). How will these people make a decision? Who has the final sign-off for a particular project? Who has influence on that decision, both at a high and a medium level? Who is responsible for the key business outcomes?

**Figure 8.1**   Illustrative decision-making unit

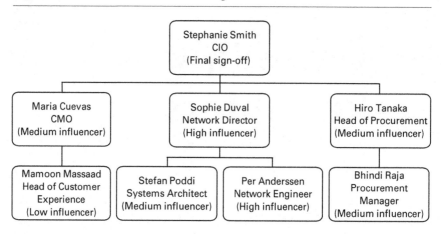

The best way to develop this picture is in a meeting or workshop with the account team. They will each know pieces of information that can be put together to form the whole – or as much of it as you collectively know today. From then on, it's a research and profiling process.

Figure 8.1 shows a simple DMU that you can use to map out the people likely to be involved in any decision around the play you would like to make to support a specific initiative.

This exercise is at the core of successful ABM because it encourages a much more targeted, thoughtful and ultimately relevant approach to all of your subsequent messaging and communications activities. It prompts you to think more deeply about who each person is, where they fit into the DMU and, crucially, how they want to receive any information you plan to send them in order to start to develop a conversation around your play.

## Building DMU stakeholder profiles

With most strategic ABM programmes the focus is on existing accounts: those companies you already have a relationship with but where you could potentially gain a much larger share of wallet. ITSMA research[1] shows, in fact, that almost three-quarters of those practising Strategic ABM do target existing versus new accounts (Figure 8.2), while in ABM Lite and Programmatic ABM the split is more even.

In existing accounts, this process of building profiles of your key stakeholders will inevitably be much easier. Your account team will know some of them already, or will know someone who they can ask.

**Figure 8.2** The focus of different types of ABM

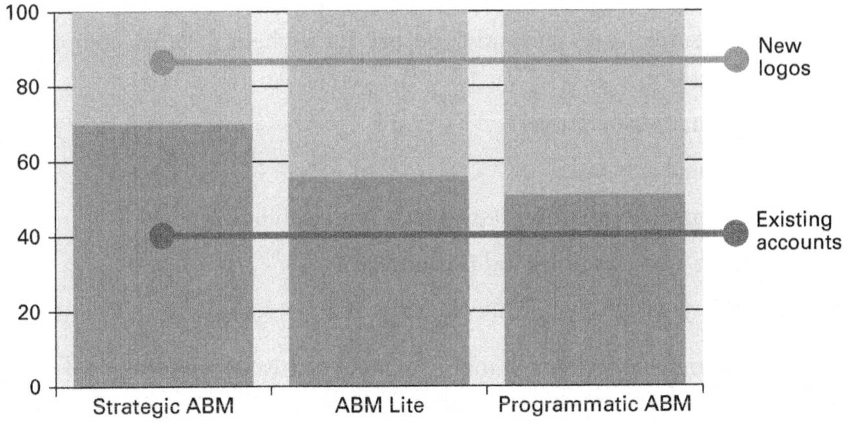

**SOURCE** ITSMA, Account-Based Marketing Benchmarking Survey, March 2016

Either way, start fleshing out your profiles by asking the account director, sales people, delivery team or subject matter experts about their contacts in the account. They may know the sort of information that won't necessarily be captured in a professional, public profile or within a sales automation tool, such as what charity they support, their wider interests or their hobbies.

At this point it is worth noting that the way you discuss and store this information is a privacy issue, subject to regulations and laws. Depending on the country you are working in and the country your stakeholders are in, there will be different privacy regulations that you have to abide by. In our experience, those countries with the strictest privacy laws (Germany, for example) will have the least public information available on the stakeholders you are trying to profile. If in doubt, seek counsel from your legal team before you start identifying, capturing and storing information on any individual stakeholders.

Assuming you can store some information as part of your account plan, ABM plan, or indeed in your CRM system, you still need to make sure with existing contacts that you have the most up-to-date information. With new contacts, once you have a database of names, you can start to populate the information you need.

Many ABM-ers look for the following information to complete their profiles where possible:

**1** A photograph (you want to know what your stakeholders look like before you bump into them!).

**2** Job title, scope of current role, and time in role.

**3** Previous roles held within the company.

**4** Previous roles held in other companies.

**5** Non-executive roles currently and previously held in other companies or in charities.

**6** Professional associations.

**7** Professional accolades.

**8** Professional contributions (speeches, articles, blogs).

**9** Academic qualifications and institutions.

**10** Personal demographic profile, hobbies and interests.

The goal is to develop a much more rounded picture of an individual than is typically held within an organization chart or an account plan. By doing your homework in this way, you have a much better chance of making sure your messages to each individual are not only framed correctly but delivered in the most effective way possible. This is about understanding the context in which your stakeholders will receive your message and making it as relevant and personalized as possible.

Increasingly, capturing information from social networks is making our job easier here. Social listening can be automated by selecting specific individuals and key words to monitor in the various conversations taking place online. But what if someone refuses to leave any sort of digital footprint? There are specialist agencies which can carry out qualitative research or access professional networks to help fill in the gaps but this can be expensive.

How you use the information you gather is just as important as how you collect it in the first place. It can take ABM experience to highlight the useful bits of data which are relevant to the client's initiatives and the play you want to make. The trick of being a good 'ABM-er' is knowing which insights actually count. Being succinct is critical, since few account managers are going to want to trawl through pages of information about specific individuals. Choosing those insights which will make a difference to your play can also make it apparent to colleagues just how marketing is adding value to the sales process.

Remember: this isn't a one-off exercise. The information you hold on key stakeholders should be continually refreshed as part of your ABM and account plan. Tracking each person's level of engagement with your company as you move into the execution phase of ABM should be a key performance metric. It will further enhance what you know about each stakeholder based on how they actually respond and behave.

# Mapping your stakeholders' wider networks

As well as those immediately involved in making a decision, you should understand the wider network of influencers who will potentially shape their perceptions and priorities (Figure 8.3). Some will have significant influence. Others won't be as influential but still should be included in your profiling and considered in your later messaging and communications planning if they impact decision making in some way. The evolution of social networks has increased the number of these influences substantially, while making the relationships that exist with your decision makers more transparent.

## 1. Significant influencers

Those who may have significant influence on your decision makers can include a range of individuals close to them in their professional and personal networks. Your job is first to identify them by looking through the public profiles and social-media activities of those decision makers and through conversations with people who know them and are happy to 'coach' you. Then you need to decide how important they are in terms of the degree of influence they will have over your decision makers for this particular play.

**Figure 8.3**  Stakeholders and their wider networks

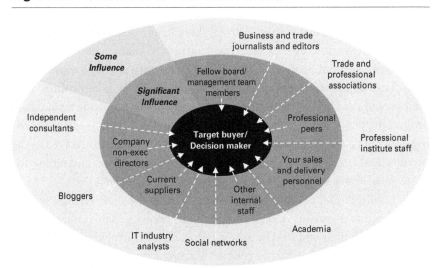

Finally, with this in mind, you can decide whether to create specific messages and tactics to reach these influencers as part of your ABM campaign.

## Fellow board or management team members

As part of a team, these people may be directly impacted by the decision your buyers make and will no doubt have some interest or concerns regarding that impact. They may look to shape the decision in their favour and so you will need to engage with them to understand their motivations and political intent, get their buy-in to your play and encourage them to shape the decision in your favour too.

## Company non-executive directors

These are often hugely influential people who bring fresh ideas from their experiences with similar initiatives in other companies. They will often have recommendations as to whom your buyers should consider working with based on their personal experience elsewhere and existing relationships. You need to understand if they are a champion or advocate for one of your competitors, or likely to recommend a 'do nothing' or alternative approach to the one you are suggesting. On the plus side, they may be people who have great experience of working with you, and so will influence in your favour.

## Your own salespeople, delivery personnel, and subject matter experts

No one is more trusted than delivery personnel, since they are seen to have the client's interests at heart, in contrast to many salespeople, who are usually suspected of having their own interests at heart most of the time. That being said, both of these may have existing relationships with members of the DMU and may be in a position to educate and engage them around the play you can offer to support them in their initiative. It's surprising how many account teams fail to make sure that everyone involved in the account and engaging with key stakeholders is 'on message' and telling the same story about how they want to help these stakeholders.

Your subject matter experts (SMEs) are seen as the most credible source of information about emerging business and technology trends, and potential solutions.[2] If any of your SMEs have relationships with key decision makers, these can be leveraged as part of your ABM campaign plan. If not, you should be thinking about creating these relationships through your plan.

## Other internal staff

Many of us who have worked in large, complex organizations know the informal power networks that can exist alongside the official 'hierarchy'. A great example of influencers that may not be immediately obvious is the network of personal assistants (PAs) in a company. These special individuals can ultimately decide whether your messages get through at all, can offer opinions on how your company conducts itself outside of the formal meetings you run and can tap into a network across the organization to share opinions and experiences from other business units.

Similarly, internal consultants, strategy advisors, or mentors for your DMU members can all have an influence on their thinking, providing a sounding board and a different perspective on the decision without being officially part of the DMU.

## Current suppliers

Most people within large companies will work with a number of suppliers to get their jobs done. Some of these may have stronger relationships than you do in the account, while not necessarily being one of your competitors or partners. A great example of this is the accounting firm working with your account. They will be interested in seeing the company make the best decisions for its shareholders, and may well be asked for their opinion on the initiative at hand and potential companies who could support it. You may or may not have existing relationships with these current suppliers (for example, you may have the same accounting firm, which is always great news), but the important thing is to first identify them and then consider how you can get them onside.

## Professional peers

Most executives use peers within and outside their company as a sounding board and source of advice and recommendations. This important, trusted word-of-mouth source is likely to be a key influence on their decision to take any initiative and on whom to work with to get the job done. They may be friends from college, ex-colleagues from previous companies or people the DMU has met through professional networks. They may be visible through social networks like LinkedIn, or they may need to be 'uncovered' through profiling. Once again, your job is to identify them and get them onside.

## 2. Those with some influence

It is significantly harder to identify those people who will have a lesser influence on your decision makers. It may not be easy to find out what associations they belong to, what journals or blogs they read or which independent consultants they work with. Follow the same process as you did for significant influencers. Explore what is already known by the account team, speak to any coaches in the account, look through your decision makers' public profiles and social-media activities for clues. Then, decide which, if any, of these lesser influencers should form part of your ABM campaign.

### Business and trade journalists and editors

Your decision makers are professional people, and so are likely to read at least some publications that relate either to their functional specialism or the industry their business is a part of. They may also look at general publications like *The Economist*, *The Financial Times* or other serious titles with broad business appeal. Even if you don't know exactly what titles they read, you can make an educated guess by exploring the list of titles targeted at people like them.

Then it's about finding out who the editors are, and which journalists write about the types of imperatives, initiatives and business solutions you are focused on. If they do exert some influence on your decision makers, you may need to add some broader media relations activities to your ABM campaign.

### Bloggers

Consider individual bloggers, outside of business and trade publications, who have influence over decision makers. An online search should reveal who is writing or speaking about the issue at hand. A quick look at their subscribers and the amount of engagement with their blogs will give you a feeling for how influential they actually are so that you can plan accordingly.

### Professional institute staff and trade or professional associations

Professionals within large, complex organizations tend to keep themselves up to date on the issues facing their profession and examples of how others have tackled them through membership of a professional institute. With institutes and associations for every industry, function, and role available in most geographies, you can make an educated guess about which ones your decision makers belong to and/or participate in.

Some decision makers will publicly announce their participation in their profiles, while others will reveal them through social media by belonging to a specific group on LinkedIn or following a particular Twitter handle. Once you know the institutes that matter, you can research them to uncover the individual staff members that you may wish to engage with as part of your campaign.

## Academia

Academic professionals can influence your decision makers in two main ways. First, they may be currently involved in a project to research an issue with your DMU. Many large organizations have academic arrangements like this, funding research programmes or being part of a research club (such as BAE Systems' and IBM's membership of the Cambridge Service Alliance in the UK run by Professor Andy Neely). Second, members of your DMU may be part of an academic alumni group. Again, those who participate actively in such groups often mention it in their public profiles. The degree of their participation with academia will influence your decision to make specific academics part of the target audience for your ABM campaign.

## Social networks

ITSMA research shows that LinkedIn is the preferred social network for business people to use as part of a complex buying decision (outside of China). LinkedIn has launched Sales Navigator to support 'social selling', allowing you to research and target those people you are most interested in engaging with. You can use this to understand your DMU's social networks to a greater extent. Where you have access to public profiles you can see which group networks someone belongs to on social media like LinkedIn and these can form part of your campaign plan.

## IT industry analysts

The power of analysts such as Gartner and Forrester should not be underestimated in the market for technology solutions. Simply by publishing their 'Magic Quadrant' or 'Wave' on a particular business solution area, they help decision makers narrow the pool of potential suppliers to consider. Both buyers and suppliers spend millions each year engaging with these analysts to be sure they get the right advice or are positioned in the right way, respectively. But the degree to which your specific DMU is consulting with analysts is something you need to understand. They may have actively hired them to advise on their particular initiative and procurement process (or they may have hired a third-party sourcing advisor firm like PA Consulting to support their procurement process).

Alternatively, they may simply read the relevant report from the analyst firm and perhaps have a short conversation with the author. Or they may not take the analyst firm's views into account at all. If the DMU is using an analyst firm to help in the decision making, the specific analysts involved form an important audience for you. And while you may have an analyst relations team to run your broader engagement with the firm, you will need to think about how to leverage them and potentially supplement their work around your specific play and account.

### Independent consultants

Sometimes independent consultants are brought on board specifically to help with an initiative. Working as interim resources, or freelance advisors, they can be hard to spot. In one instance, an IT supplier was engaging with a DMU for a technology solution without knowing that one member of that DMU was actually on secondment from their company's biggest competitor (and so unlikely to make a decision in their favour). Ask the account team and spend time researching the profiles of your DMU and any extended team members to uncover these independent consultants and understand how important they are to your play.

# A note on segmentation

In some accounts, you will have so many decision makers and influencers to deal with that you may want to segment them into groups with common needs or perceptions. This may be as simple as decision makers (who will need the most in-depth information about your play), significant influencers and those with some influence. (See the Juniper case study opposite.)

Or, if you are trying to recover your reputation in an account following a disruption in service, you may decide to group together those who were personally affected by the disruption and those who only heard about it. Or you may want to segment people who are advocates, people who are neutral or don't know you and people who actively brief against you. This is where initial perception research comes in handy. If you haven't done that, find out who is in which camp by talking to your account team and coach. You'll need a different strategy for each segment.

**CASE STUDY**   Juniper succeeds with ABM

Juniper Networks has been a market leader in network technological innovation since its founding in Silicon Valley in 1996. However, in 2013 the company faced an important challenge. It knew that its largest customer was evaluating potential partners for a critical project: its next generation virtualized, software-defined network.

This leading-edge project would likely set the direction and tone for the whole industry, defining the technology leaders in the process. Juniper's future success hinged on securing a partnership role. But the customer viewed Juniper as a small hardware vendor, not a strategic partner. Juniper's objective was thus to change the customer's perception of the company from a small hardware vendor to a strategic software partner that could support the customer's future business most effectively, even when compared to larger companies.

The first step was to form a customer team from multiple functions across the company, including marketing and sales. Juniper needed a dedicated marketing manager to oversee ABM activities. The team began by conducting extensive internal and external analysis to develop a comprehensive view of the customer's current and future state. The team then developed a three-year, integrated marketing plan, aligned with the sales plan and the customer's vision.

Marketing worked with sales to segment the account contacts into three groups: the decision makers, circle of influence, and operational teams. Each contact was assigned a mindshare score. All the ABM work was designed to improve these scores over time.

The key components of the execution strategy included a long-term communications plan, thought leadership through education, awareness building and sales-enablement tactics.

A multiphase communications plan included highly-targeted messaging for each individual. Communications were delivered through executive advisory boards, roundtables, briefings, newsletters, webinars and events. The team also communicated to the external circle of influence, including analysts, bloggers and technologists, followed closely by the decision makers. The team first determined whom they needed to reach based on their current mindshare status and then developed the appropriate content.

Juniper focused its thought leadership efforts on educating customers about new technologies and the implications of those technologies, rather than on products. Targeted audiences received the content through customized Innovation Day events, user groups, webinars, direct marketing and one-to-one meetings.

The marketing team also developed extensive customer insight reporting to enable sales to bring extremely relevant messaging to individual contacts.

Juniper became the second strategic partner selected in the customer's new network strategy and the first in its competitive set. Revenue from the account increased 30 per cent year-on-year. Marketing contribution grew to represent 30 per cent of a multibillion-dollar pipeline. Marketing also demonstrated a substantial increase in account mindshare. Juniper has since expanded its ABM programme into other accounts and vertical sectors.

# Stakeholder profiling for ABM Lite and Programmatic ABM

So far we have concentrated on strategic ABM in this chapter, dealing with profiling stakeholders in depth one account at a time.

Profiling is also important in ABM Lite and Programmatic ABM, but you have to decide how much time and money you are prepared to spend, particularly with new clients when the chances of winning new business aren't as high. As a minimum, you will need to understand which roles are usually involved in making decisions about the type of play you want to take in. Then some basic executive profiling of the people in those roles across your cluster of accounts is needed for ABM Lite.

You can look for commonalities in terms of the scope of their roles and any professional institutions or journals targeted to people like them. However, much of the more detailed personal information collected in a strategic ABM context will be wasted here, since you won't be customizing your messages and your channels to each individual in the same way, but rather building messages that resonate enough across the cluster and communicating through the channels they have in common.

Some ABM-ers use buyer personas at the volume end of ABM Lite and on into programmatic ABM. According to the Buyer Persona Institute,[3] a buyer persona tells you what prospective customers are thinking and doing as they weigh their options, based on interviews with real buyers (see box 'The power of personas'). The buyers' words reveal the attitudes, concerns and decision criteria you need to address to win their business. Using this approach can help you develop key messages and decide on appropriate communications channels for your campaign more quickly than trying to profile hundreds of individuals.

## The power of personas

Personas were first used in conjunction with application user interface design and later adopted by marketers. According to Kim Goodwin:[4]

> A persona is a user archetype ... By designing for the archetype – whose goals and behaviour patterns are well understood – you can satisfy the broader group of people represented by that archetype. In most cases, personas are synthesized from a series of ethnographic interviews with real people and then captured in one- to two-page descriptions that include behaviour patterns, goals, skills, attitudes, and environment, with a few fictional personal details to bring the persona to life. A good persona description is not a list of tasks or duties; it's a narrative that describes the flow of someone's day, as well as their skills, attitudes, environment, and goals.

Marketers can use personas as 'stand-ins' for real buyers. Focusing on the model buyer's wants, needs, goals, and motivations will keep the marketing team on an outside-in path when creating value propositions. Personas take market segmentation to the next level by bringing to life hypothetical individuals within the segment.

When using personas, companies often create primary and secondary personas. Primary personas represent the decision makers; secondary personas are the decision influencers.

When using buyer personas to scale up, think about leveraging marketing automation technology to continually refine the way you engage with decision makers and influencers based on their behaviour and response to you. What content are they interested in looking at? Do they prefer e-mail to social-media engagement? Your goal should be to 'qualify in' progressively the ones who are showing interest in you as you execute your campaign, to the point where you begin to treat them as individual people and no longer as personas.

# Your ABM checklist

**1** Each account will have designated one or more key people to oversee the strategic initiatives it is running in response to the business imperatives it faces. You need to find out who these people are and learn much more about them.

**2** This is about understanding the actual decision-making unit for your play(s). The best way to develop this picture is in a meeting or workshop with the account team.

**3** Identify the people who have significant influence over your DMU and those with some influence. These people should also form part of your ABM campaign plan, in addition to the DMU stakeholders themselves.

**4** The way you store information on stakeholders is a privacy issue, subject to regulations and laws that vary around the world. If in doubt, seek counsel from your legal team before you start identifying, capturing and storing information.

**5** In some accounts, you will have so many decision makers and influencers to deal with that you may want to segment them into groups with common needs or perceptions.

**6** For ABM Lite, look for commonalities among stakeholders to inform your campaigns. Much of the more detailed personal information collected in a strategic ABM context will be wasted here since you will be marketing to a cluster of accounts at the same time.

**7** For both ABM Lite and Programmatic ABM, consider developing buyer personas. This will help you develop key messages and decide on appropriate communications channels for your campaign more quickly than trying to profile hundreds of individuals.

# Notes

**1** ITSMA (2016) *Account Based Marketing Benchmarking Survey*

**2** ITSMA (2015) *How Buyers Consume Information Study: Moving towards an omnichannel experience*

**3** http://www.buyerpersona.com/

**4** http://www.cooper.com/journal/2001/08/perfecting_your_personas

# Developing targeted value propositions

## 09

## What is a value proposition?

While Step 2 of the ABM process focuses on describing the plays you could take into an account in terms of the tangible and intangible features of your solution to a client's problem, this fourth step in the process is about building targeted messages for the DMU identified in Step 3 to communicate the value your solution will deliver. This is represented graphically as shown in Figure 9.1.

The most successful value proposition starts with a customer's business issue, in *their* words and from *their* perspective. In ABM terms, this is the imperative that is impacting them and the initiative they are taking, or could take, in response. It describes *your* solution to their issue (your play), the particular benefits *your* solution provides over competitor solutions and the business outcomes they should expect by implementing your solution through a combination of benefits and price.

Value propositions should be simple, clear, easy-to-absorb statements, adaptable to specific buyers, credible and backed up by proof points. Wherever possible, they should be financially quantified when used in an ABM context. They should encapsulate the reason that your potential buyers should purchase your company's product, service or solution rather than anyone else's. And, in these economic times, communicating value that resonates with a customer is more than a goal. It is increasingly a matter of survival.

### A note on value

Remember, value is a subjective judgement.

Value is the client's assessment of cost versus benefits: benefits may be tangible, such as a percentage reduction in operating costs by using a

**Figure 9.1**  Solution, value proposition, and elevator pitch

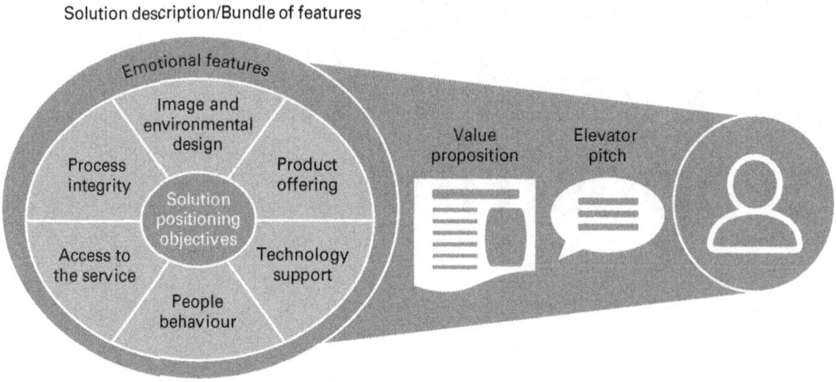

technology solution, or intangible, such as minimizing the risk of changing outsourcing supplier by staying with the incumbent. Wherever possible, if your value proposition offers tangible benefits to a client, you should try and quantify those benefits and show where other clients have received them from you in the past if you can.

Costs aren't always financial, of course. There are costs in terms of the time involved in supporting a particular solution, for example. And there may be other costs such as risks to operations or reputation to be considered. Your decision makers will have their own perception of the costs involved in a particular solution beyond the price.

Ultimately, clients will choose the proposition they perceive to have the greatest value for them relative to the available alternatives. For examples of both tangible and intangible benefits, see Table 9.1.

**Table 9.1**  Examples of tangible and intangible benefits

| Tangible benefits (can be quantified) | Intangible benefits (difficult to quantify) |
| --- | --- |
| • Increased efficiency | • Reduced risk and worry |
| • Increased revenues | • Ability to set new trends or be a market leader |
| • Increased sales | |
| • Market share growth | • Ability to be a hero in his/her own company |
| • Reduced time to market | |
| • Reduced costs | • Recognition, praise, esteem by industry, peers, or community |
| • Increased customer loyalty | |
| • Increased differentiation from competitors | • Ability to join a prestigious group of companies who use your services |

Remember the old adage that if a deal is won, it's down to the skill of the salesperson, but if it is lost, it's down to price? Let's be clear about this. Price is important, but winning or losing will be determined by value, not price. In many competitive situations, once two or more suppliers are relatively the same on price, a decision on whom to select will be made by the decision-making unit (DMU) based on their perception of who offers the most value.

Again, in many cases this will be subjective but is likely to reflect some of the more intangible elements of a proposition such as cultural fit, personal chemistry and track record, as well as tangible elements such as local decision making, access to innovation through the contract, or global reach and consistency of delivery.

That said, it is worth remembering that if the client's issue is urgent or important enough, price can become nearly irrelevant. A great example of this is where a company has had a cyber-security breach and is calling potential suppliers who can help recover the situation – fast. The buyer's focus will be on closing the breach quickly, recovering any data lost, reassuring those affected and ultimately on protecting their company's reputation and share price. Their personal priority will be to keep their jobs after such a breach happening on their watch! The company that can help them to achieve all this will be hired almost at any cost.

It sounds simple in theory, but writing good value propositions takes more than command of the language. To be effective, value propositions must uncover *unique* differentiation and quantify superior *value*. This is complicated by the long sales cycle in B2B, where there is often a need for several different types of value propositions to span the various stages of the buying process.

Furthermore, value propositions have to be more than words. They have to be based on tangible, proven and repeatable results. In our work with clients we have discovered that there needs to be more science applied to the art of writing value propositions. However, before we describe our six-step process for developing effective value propositions, let's first consider how *not* to do it.

# What's wrong with most value propositions?

It is sometimes easier to identify poorly-written value propositions than it is to write good ones. There are some common pitfalls:

- Inside-out focus: Have I told you enough about me?
- Too much jargon: Marketing-speak and techno-babble.

- No unique differentiation: Heard one, heard them all.
- No statement or quantification of value: Where's the content?

The problem with so many value propositions is that too often every sentence will start with 'we' or your company's name. Worse, the language is so full of jargon that everyone seems to be saying the same thing. It is not that what they are saying is wrong. It is the way they are saying it. Finally, value propositions are meant to provide a statement of value. Value exists when the benefits outweigh the costs. Therefore, the statements should make it easy for the buyer to determine the benefits. What will they get for the price paid? Again, nine times out of ten, the value is undeterminable.

If you listen in on a marketing planning meeting, you might hear the terms 'message' and 'value proposition' used interchangeably. Although messages and value propositions are both statements, the similarities stop there. Too often companies write messages or positioning statements and stop at that, never digging deeper to convey the unique value.

Messages are not value propositions. Messages are claims about capabilities. They are broad and generic. They are often inside-out statements about what a company can do. Value propositions, on the other hand, come from the outside in. Value propositions start with your buyer, not the offer, and provide a solution to a problem with identified results. Unlike messages built on claims, value propositions are supported by proof in the form of quantified results, testimonials, case studies and references.

## Three types of value propositions

Most sales and marketing professionals understand the need for value propositions. However, what many don't appreciate is how the nature of the value proposition must change with the stage of the buyer relationship in terms of its depth, quantification, and precision (Figure 9.2). As the relationship moves from an *epiphany*, or 'a-ha' moment, that the client has that they really need to take some action, through *awareness* of how they could take action and who could help them, through *interest* in finding out more about your company through to *confidence* that you are the one they should turn to for help, the level of detail they need about your proposition will increase.

Initially, broad value propositions with mostly qualitative benefit statements may suffice. But as they go through the buying process, buyers will

**Figure 9.2**   Three types of value proposition

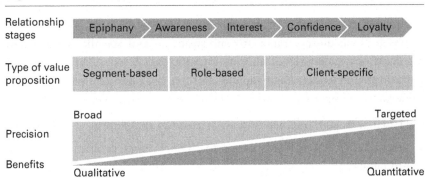

need much more targeted propositions with quantified benefits that help them to understand the value on offer beyond the price they will pay.

As you develop the value proposition for your specific play into a specific DMU in your account, you may draw on existing value propositions developed for the segment that account or those buyers are in, or indeed for the roles that they occupy, to create one that is targeted to your specific buyers. Your marketing colleagues representing your capability areas or your vertical industry sectors will hopefully have created both the segment and role-based value propositions for some if not all of the features of your 'play' already.

## Segment-based

With minimal client information, the value proposition is defined to address the needs of a specific market segment, such as an industry vertical. It is relatively generic, presenting hypothetical examples based on prior experience. The segment-based value proposition applies to a broad set of prospective clients. The benefits are likely more theoretical than factual and perhaps more qualitative than quantitative.

The segment-based value proposition is not designed to sell. The purpose of the statement is to get potential buyers to take action to learn more. That action can be going to your website, picking up the phone to call you, attending a webinar or reading a white paper. Marketing typically composes the segment-based value propositions and communicates them to wide audiences using broadcast communication vehicles such as the website, business press and company collateral. Nevertheless, they can be useful as a starting point for your client-specific proposition, if only to ensure that you are 'on message' with the wider communications to market.

## Role-based

With more contextual information about buyers available, value propositions become more targeted to sub-segments and specific roles within organizations, such as chief information officers (CIOs), sales management or business unit leaders. Such individuals often have different perceptions of value based on their roles and responsibilities. For example:

- IT manager: staff augmentation or access to capabilities;

- functional vice president: solution to an operational problem to increase productivity;

- business unit general manager: entrance to a new market and access to new streams of revenue.

Role-based value propositions resonate when they address the specific business needs of the buyer personas (see Chapter 8 on the power of personas) the company is trying to reach. They require a deeper level of understanding of the like-minded groups of people the company is communicating with, including their needs, desires, motivations, expectations, goals, fears, skills, and biases.

Role-based value propositions are usually 'narrowcast' via targeted advertising, media relations, analyst relations, speaking opportunities at third-party hosted conferences and seminars, company-hosted events and so forth. Role-based propositions like this can be useful in both ABM Lite and programmatic ABM, as well as forming a basis for the client-specific propositions used in strategic ABM.

## Client-specific

These value propositions are needed in strategic ABM to move prospects from interest to confidence or buy mode. The client-specific value proposition addresses the particular needs of the DMU in your account. They take into account the profile information you've collected, including the initiatives and the imperatives driving them, the initiatives they are responsible for, their business goals, how they are measured and their definition of success. In particular, they should take into account the language your buyer uses to describe their business issues and desired outcomes.

Armed with this knowledge, it is possible to quantify benefits in terms of actual cost savings, revenue growth or quality improvements. Once you know the buyers and can relate to them on a personal level, your message is more likely to resonate. You can position yourself as the partner who will help them achieve the business outcomes associated with the particular business initiatives they are working on.

Client-specific value propositions are communicated by an integrated sales and marketing campaign into the account.

# The six elements in a targeted value proposition

There are six elements to include in the value proposition you write for your buyers in an ABM context (Figure 9.3).

One of the most effective ways to work through these six elements and develop your proposition is once again with your account colleagues and subject matter experts in a workshop. With your account insight shared, priority plays agreed, and profiles of the DMU for each available, it's time to get creative and work through a series of questions that will give you the content you need for your proposition.

One word of warning: working through this process will give you too many words and not enough proof points, so your job after the workshop is to refine down to only the most important points, and find proof points to back your points up wherever possible.

Every company should have a template to help marketing facilitate this task. Over the years ITSMA has developed a simple yet effective template

**Figure 9.3**   Six elements of a targeted ABM value proposition

| | |
|---|---|
| 1 | Articulation of the needs/issues impacting them (the imperatives) |
| 2 | What actions are they taking to address these issues? (the initiatives) |
| 3 | Identification of the target. Who feels the pain? |
| 4 | A description of our solution to the problem(s) |
| 5 | Benefits the buyer will receive by selecting you |
| 6 | Needs to be equal to or superior (key differentiator(s)) to competitive offers |

**Table 9.2**  ABM value proposition template

| Value proposition element | Prompt questions |
| --- | --- |
| Business imperative | What are the issues impacting the account that they have to address? How would the decision makers describe them in their own language? |
| Business initiative | What initiative is the account taking to respond to the business imperative they face? What have they called the initiative? Have they set clear business outcomes or key performance indicators to measure their progress on it? OR what initiative could they take to respond to the business imperative? |
| Target audience | Who is working on this initiative, responsible for delivering the business outcome? Who else is involved in making sure the initiative is a success? How would they describe their involvement? How would they describe the issues or challenges they face? |
| Our play | What is the play we are making to support the initiative? Describe the solution we are offering to help the buyers achieve their planned business outcomes. |
| The benefits | What are the main benefits the buyers will receive from our offer? What language would they use to describe these benefits? Can we quantify the benefits on offer? Do we have proof points to back them up? |
| Differentiator(s) | How is our offer different or unique? Can we prove it? Why does it matter to the client? |

(Table 9.2). Crafting the value propositions is actually a multistep process. First, fill in the blanks on the template. This ensures that all the elements of a good value proposition are present. Next, write the story in prose, eliminating clichés and fillers and adapt it for the intended use, whether it is website content, sales presentation, glossy brochure or press release.

Let's work through this template step by step.

## Step 1: Define the business imperative

From your initial analysis of the account you will have identified the business imperative that is driving both the initiative the account is taking to achieve their desired business outcome and also the play that you have decided to take into the account. By including a statement about the imperative in your value proposition, you are demonstrating your understanding of your account's situation. In addition, by using the language that they are using about the imperative (in their statements to shareholders, for example), you are starting to build a rapport with key stakeholders because they will feel that you are listening to them and understand them.

As an illustration, Table 9.3 shows the imperative captured by one company making a play based on cloud computing to a professional services firm, allowing its people to access their information anywhere, anytime and on any device.

**Table 9.3**   Illustrative business imperative for 'Digital Workplace'

| Value proposition element | Description |
| --- | --- |
| Business imperative | Your people now expect to be able to access their information wherever they are, and from any device, whenever they choose. |

## Step 2: Identify the business initiative

If your play is targeting an existing initiative, make it clear that you understand the initiative, its scope, its objectives and the key performance indicators that will define its success. This should always be in the language the client is using to describe their initiative, so don't talk about cutting operational costs if they are talking about driving efficiencies in operations, for example. Once again, this will help you to appear more relevant to them and to build rapport.

If you are in the position of having identified a business imperative facing the client to which they have yet to respond and you would like to recommend a business initiative they should consider (along with your offer to support them in doing so), you will be bringing fresh thinking, or even thought leadership, into the account.

It's important to be clear about the initiative and why it is a good idea in response to the business issues they face. In effect, you need to educate your buyers on the route to action before you begin to sell your solution. Even so, use the language they themselves would use rather than your own terminology or jargon. You may also want to describe how others in their situation have responded in the same way, successfully, to a business imperative they share. Your target buyers may be aware they are behind the curve in terms of responding and will be interested to see how their peers are faring, particularly if traditionally they are 'followers' rather than 'innovators'.

However, if what you are recommending is completely innovative and new, and you are appealing to buyers who traditionally break moulds and lead the pack, the very fact that no one else is running a similar initiative will appeal. With chief executive officers (CEOs) around the world most worried about disruptions to their industries coming from new digital entrants like 'Uber', you will get their attention if you can recommend an innovative approach they could be taking to a common business imperative facing companies in their sector – particularly if it brings competitive advantage and a whole new revenue stream they hadn't considered.

Table 9.4 illustrates the business initiative part of the value proposition developed for our 'Digital Workplace' example.

**Table 9.4** Illustrative business initiative for 'Digital Workplace'

| Value proposition element | Description |
| --- | --- |
| Business initiative | 'Mobile professional' is our initiative to give our people the information they need to provide great client service, wherever they are. |

## Step 3: Talk to your target audience

Many value propositions are generic, talking to 'large enterprises' or 'government organizations'. This is poor even at a segment or role-based level. It is unforgivable at a client-specific level. You should be highlighting clearly that your proposition is for a specific buyer or group of buyers. So, use language like 'as a CMO in one of the world's largest banks', or 'as the management team tasked with transforming the way your people work', or even 'as a member of group of people responsible for outsourcing the management of your network operations around the world'.

**Table 9.5** Illustrative target audience for 'Digital Workplace'

| Value proposition element | Description |
| --- | --- |
| Target audience | As HR, IT, and finance leaders in your firm, you need to make the way your professionals work more flexible while improving profitability, but you have an aged IT infrastructure that is no longer supporting the firm as working styles change. |

Once you've identified them, connect with them by showing that you understand their main priority or concern. And again, use the language they would use themselves, not your own.

Table 9.5 illustrates how this might look for our 'Digital Workplace' example.

## Step 4: Describe your play

This step is about describing the offer you are making (ie your play, or solution) succinctly. It shouldn't be a list of features, but a summary of what you will actually provide to the buyer. Is it a simple product or service? Is it a more complex solution? Is it a solution that is bound up in a contractual offer such as a joint venture? This step is a balancing act between giving enough detail so that they are clear what you're selling but not so much that they're overwhelmed with the technical details.

You will have done much of the thinking about this during Step 2 of the ABM process, so use that thinking now to help you develop an overview for your buyer.

Table 9.6 illustrates how this might look for our 'Digital Workplace' example.

**Table 9.6** Illustrative play description for 'Digital Workplace'

| Value proposition element | Description |
| --- | --- |
| Our play | 'Digital Workplace' is a managed IT service that gives your people the tools and support they need to work flexibly on any device, anywhere.<br><br>There is no up-front cost, and you only pay for what you use. We give you real-time reporting and billing so you have predictability of costs each month. |

## Step 5: Explain the benefits on offer

Value propositions are most compelling when the target audience can clearly see the benefits they are getting for the price paid. As buyers move through the buying process, from epiphany and awareness through interest and confidence, their needs for quantifying the benefits of the product, service, or solution increase. Working with clients to gather the information to tailor the value quantification to their specific circumstances is a critical component of moving them through the buying process. This type of engagement can and should form part of your integrated sales and marketing campaign in the account.

The more you can quantify the value of the benefits on offer, the greater the interest generated. People like to see numbers – credible, hard numbers. However, even relative or qualitative numbers (eg improved efficiency and higher satisfaction), if backed up with proof, are acceptable. It is better not to use adjectives but to use stories that demonstrate your claims. Value propositions should be underpinned with real-life testimonials, success stories, and references.

We have identified four main areas of quantification (Figure 9.4):

- efficiency;
- quality;
- profitable revenue growth;
- value creation.

It is easiest to quantify the efficiency benefits such as impact on productivity, headcount and turnaround time. However, the more valuable benefits

**Figure 9.4**    The increasing impact of types of value

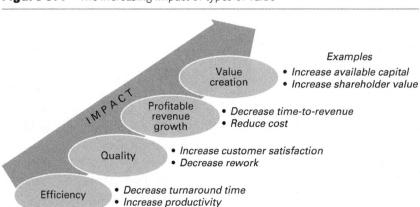

are the impact on revenue, especially profitable revenue, and actual value creation (eg new revenue streams, access to capital, attaining a leadership position). Solutions that address these areas are likely to be most relevant to senior manager, C-level executives and board-level executives and to command a greater price premium.

You may need to present your value in terms of a return on investment case, or net present value, as you progress through the buying cycle with your account. When this becomes important, the finance and commercial professionals aligned to the account will take the lead, along with technical experts, but marketing can still be helpful in ensuring the main messages are consistent, clear and in a language the client will understand.

Table 9.7 illustrates how this might look for our 'Digital Workplace' example.

**Table 9.7**   Illustrative benefits for 'Digital Workplace'

| Value proposition element | Description |
| --- | --- |
| Benefits | 'Digital Workplace' will improve your cash flow and switch IT costs from CapEx to OpEx, while giving you the flexibility to resource your business up or down immediately, with no constraints on growth or the way your people want to work. |

## Step 6: Demonstrate your differentiators

To be successful, value propositions must express why the company's products, services, or solutions are superior to those of the competition. What makes the company's offer unique? Differentiation is one of marketing's greatest challenges, topping the list each year in ITSMA's annual *Marketing Budget and Trends Survey*. Why is it so hard for companies to articulate their differentiation? In many cases an inside-out focus is to blame. Just as marketers need to take an outside-in focus to understand the account, they need to start with the market's point of view and examine what their competitors are saying.

In effect, you are looking for the 'sweet spot' here, where what your client needs overlaps with what you are better at than your competitors (see Figure 9.5).

Having examined your account in detail, you will have considered the competitors you face in the account. Review their materials to help you

**Figure 9.5**   In search of the sweet spot

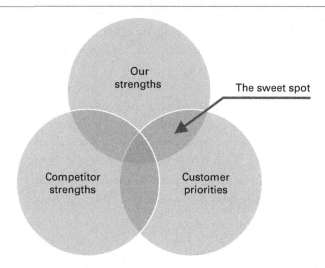

identify and prioritize your differentiators and build a case as to why the client should work with you and not them. What do they offer in the same area as your own play? What are their value propositions? What assets do they have in terms of client references, intellectual property or subject matter experts? What do they claim to be their key differentiators?

Present this information during the workshop: it's important that your workshop participants see how similar their messaging and value propositions are to those of competitors. For instance, it is common for every company to claim that it is global and innovative and to tout the expertise and experience of its people, but it is not always easy to identify unique differentiators.

Most are differentiators by degree. In other words, companies differentiate by being better. Nevertheless, being different by degree can still be good: being better than the competition provides an opportunity to lead, if the differences can be substantiated with proof. Table 9.8 will help you think through the nature and strength of the differentiators you develop and prioritize them for your value proposition.

In this example, the co-location of this company's data centres and regional offices with the client's main offices provides a comfort factor that is non-technical but potentially differentiating in terms of the day-to-day relationship between buyer and supplier.

Table 9.9 illustrates how this might work for our 'Digital Workplace' example.

**Table 9.8**    Prioritizing your differentiators: an illustrative example

| Play | Differentiator | Relative importance to target buyer (H-M-L) | Degree of uniqueness (1=me too, 10=unique) |
|---|---|---|---|
| **Cloud hosting service** | High security data centres | H | 5 |
| | Track record in client's industry | M | 5 |
| | Global footprint that matches client locations | H | 10 |

**Table 9.9**    Illustrative differentiators for 'Digital Workplace'

| Value proposition element | Description |
|---|---|
| **Differentiators** | We have already helped 75 companies and 1.5 million people work this way, using our global networking and security capabilities to give them faster and more secure access to the information their clients need than ever before. |

And with this final piece of the template in place, you can now work on building a simple prose statement to represent your value proposition, such as the final illustrative example for 'Digital Workplace' shown in Table 9.10.

**Table 9.10**    Illustrative 'Digital Workplace' targeted value proposition

| Summary statement |
|---|
| 'Digital Workplace' gives your people the ability to access the information they need anywhere, any time, and on any device, to deliver great client service. This pay-per-use managed service will improve your cash flow, switching IT costs from CapEx to OpEx, while giving you the flexibility to resource your business up or down immediately, with no constraints on growth or the way your people want to work. |
| Join the 75 companies and 1.5 million people successfully working this way today using our global networking and security capabilities. |

# Test, test, test

Once you have worked on the content from your value proposition workshop and developed more of a storyline for your buyer in simple prose, it's time to get feedback, both internally and externally. In an ideal world, the feedback would come from a coach within the account: someone prepared to be honest about how well your proposition will resonate with their colleagues.

More realistically, the value propositions should be tested with a select group of relevant stakeholders beyond those who attended the workshop and possibly external advisors, such as industry analysts or individual consultants or professionals from your network who understand the account you are focused on and can relate to the decision makers you are targeting. If your DMU is international, your value proposition should be tested in multiple geographies due to language and cultural issues.

Some questions to consider include:

1 Based on the wording, is it clear to you what I am describing? If not, what is unclear?

2 Were you familiar with this type of solution/offering (before reading the value proposition)?

3 Is this something you would be interested in learning more about after reading this proposition? Why or why not?

4 Do you think this solution is valuable to a business like the one we are focused on? How so?

5 Is it clear what is different or better about our proposition than similar propositions from other companies? How is that difference of value to companies like the one we're focused on?

Since it is the salespeople who communicate your value proposition one-on-one with buyers, you also need to validate it with them. Are the statements believable? Are they comfortable with the words and concepts conveyed? Can they communicate the gist of the value proposition using their own words?

Through a series of structured conversations your value proposition should be tested, revised and tested again. The validation process does not need to be onerous but it should be thorough. Value propositions are too important to be based on assumptions.

# Creating an elevator pitch

Any salesperson will tell you that when they're trying to get the attention and interest of a new decision maker in the hope of booking some time with them for a more in-depth discussion, they have less than a minute to make an impression. Even your value proposition will be too long for this type of encounter.

A classic example of this is when meeting a target buyer in an elevator. You have 20–30 seconds to make an impression – hence the term 'elevator pitch'. What you choose to say during that elevator ride will make the difference between a decision maker asking for a follow-up meeting as they leave the elevator, and one who is completely uninspired and who can't get out of the elevator fast enough!

We've seen examples of good account managers who put themselves in all sorts of positions to have a chance of meeting their target buyers. Ideally this is through an introduction, but where this isn't possible, then at a private or public event, or even in the office café or restaurant. There's no end to their creativity! The important thing is that they're ready with a proposition the target buyer can't refuse…

We can learn a lot from our consumer marketing colleagues here, who have had to put their value proposition across in 30-second commercials that get the consumer's attention and persuade them to buy. 'Three blades, fewer strokes, less irritation' anyone?

So, once you have developed your value proposition statement, it's worth going the extra mile and distilling it down into a short, powerful phrase that your account manager or salesperson can use in the elevator (or elsewhere in cultures where it is rude to talk in an elevator!). If we use 'Digital Workplace' as our example, the elevator pitch might be: 'Join the 75 companies that have already improved the flexibility of their workforce and the profitability of their businesses with our pay-per-use *Workplace as a service*'.

Of course, the best way to test the power of these statements is through role-play. If you can't make your pitch convincingly, you need to work on it until you can.

# Creating a hierarchy of propositions

Realistically, it's unlikely that you'll be taking just one play into an account at a time. So there's a risk that you might confuse stakeholders in the account

**Table 9.11**    An illustrative proposition hierarchy

| Your digital partner as you accelerate your growth around the world to 2020 | | | | | |
| --- | --- | --- | --- | --- | --- |
| **Improving your people's productivity by 20%** | | **Delivering a better customer experience to drive NPS scores up by 30%** | | **Modernizing your IT while reducing costs by 15%** | |
| Enabling your people to work anywhere, any time, and on any device | Keeping your people and your information secure around the world | Delivering a seamless, omnichannel shopping experience | Maximizing the efficiency of your supply chain | Increasing flexibility while reducing costs through a hybrid cloud model | Running your security operations centre |

with your range of propositions and associated messages (especially if some are in the DMU for more than one of your plays).

The best answer we've seen to avoid creating confusion is to develop a hierarchy of propositions, or a message house, for your account.

At the top of the hierarchy is your overarching company proposition for the account: what do you want to be famous for in that account in the coming years? This should be aligned to and leverage your brand proposition as far as possible.

Beneath that overarching proposition may come major theme areas where you plan to support the account, such as in enabling their people to be more productive, to improve the experience they give their customers and to modernize their IT estate. And beneath that layer, it's likely you will have one or more solutions or plays that you are taking in to the account, with their own specific proposition (Table 9.11).

Organizing your propositions for the account in this way allows everyone involved with the client to tell the same story, whether they are meeting the CEO and focusing on the overall company proposition and then working down to specifics, or meeting the IT manager to discuss one specific proposition and then putting it into the content of the whole story for the account.

# Your ABM checklist

1 Value propositions should be simple, clear, easy-to-absorb statements, adaptable to specific buyers, credible and backed up by proof points. Wherever possible, they should be financially quantified when used in an ABM context. They should encapsulate the reason that your potential buyers should purchase your company's product, service or solution rather than anyone else's.

2 Value is subjective. It is an individual's calculation of benefits minus costs. Benefits can be tangible or intangible while costs are more than just the price of a solution.

3 A compelling, targeted value proposition should define the imperative facing the business, identify the business initiative, resonate with your target buyer, describe your play, explain the benefits of your solution and demonstrate your differentiators.

4 Create your value proposition in a workshop with the account team and subject matter experts and then turn it into prose.

5 Test and refine your value proposition with internal stakeholders and then externally, with analysts or others who understand you, your client and your competitors.

6 An elevator pitch is a short punchy phrase that takes no longer than 20–30 seconds for a salesperson to deliver yet is persuasive enough to get the interest of your buyer.

7 Organize multiple propositions for your account into a hierarchy, or messaging house, that allows you to tell one, connected story in the account no matter whom you are meeting.

# Planning integrated sales and marketing campaigns

## 10

This chapter gets to the heart of account-based marketing campaigns: getting your targeted message across to potential buyers. It covers:

- ingredients of a successful ABM campaign;
- setting your campaign objectives;
- defining the audience for your campaign;
- creating personalized content;
- designing an omnichannel campaign;
- putting it all together in your campaign plan;
- visualizing your campaign.

## Ingredients of a successful ABM campaign

You know what accounts you want to target, have spent time understanding what drives them and selected the appropriate plays you could make to help them. You have mapped out in some detail the individual stakeholders relevant to your play and designed a compelling value proposition that differentiates you from your competitors.

Now it's time to design the campaign(s) to communicate your proposition. Some marketers are pressurized into starting ABM at this point by account teams who feel they already have a good account plan and simply need some marketing support to execute it. This could be the case, but make sure there is enough rigour in the planning process before you take on the 'communications' remit. Someone has to go through those initial steps if your campaigns are to be effective in the account.

There are a number of features which good ABM campaigns share:

- clear objectives that align with both the business and sales objectives for the account;

- segmentation and precision targeting of stakeholders and influencers;

- personalized content that leverages your understanding of the imperatives facing the account and the initiatives they are taking, putting your propositions into context;

- omnichannel execution, using online and offline channels seamlessly to deliver your messages.

We'll look at each of these features in this chapter.

## Setting your campaign objectives

ABM campaigns have clear objectives that are aligned to both the business and the sales objectives for the account. Often, a single ABM campaign will be part of a longer-term marketing programme into the account, such as to shift perceptions of your company from a transactional supplier to a trusted advisor and partner to the client during its digital transformation as a business. Or they may be stand-alone campaigns, focused on a more near-term goal, such as aiming at increasing mindshare within the decision-making unit (DMU) for a specific play so that your company is front of mind when the account decides to move ahead with a particular initiative and to investigate potential partners/suppliers.

When setting your ABM programme or campaign objectives for your account, start with the business objectives in mind. These are likely to be about the revenue and profitability of the account (and possibly its rate of growth), the extent of your portfolio the account is buying, your share of wallet in the account or your positioning in the account. Hopefully, the business objective will be SMART (specific, measurable, achievable, realistic, and time bounded), but if it isn't, you might want to develop some assumptions to make sure it is. Setting your marketing objectives will be much easier as a result.

To achieve these broad business objectives, there will be one or more sales objectives. These could be aimed at a single deal or contract related to your play (either win it for the first time or defend it at contract renewal), or could be about the number of deals at a certain size (two £1 million deals

**Figure 10.1**   A hierarchy of objectives for your ABM account

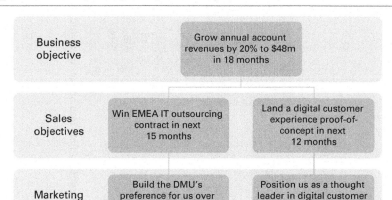

within the first 18 months, for example). They may focus on winning business in a different part of the account, such as a different business unit or geography. Or they may be about selling a different type of capability into the account, thereby breaking out of an area you've been boxed into and demonstrating what else you could be doing to help the client.

The objective you set for your ABM campaign should relate directly to supporting the sales team and the business to achieve their own objectives. Think of it in terms of a hierarchy, as shown in Figure 10.1. Again, the objective is to be as SMART as you can be, so that it's easy to develop metrics to track your performance and report progress to the business.

Marketing campaign objectives are usually geared to positioning your company in the mind of your audience, or informing and educating people in the account about your company and your offer or persuading the DMU to act in your favour.

It's worth getting your objectives reviewed and signed off by the account manager and his or her team, as well as agreeing them with your marketing line manager, so that everyone knows what you will be focusing on in the coming months (and what you therefore may need to stop doing!)

# Defining the audience for your campaigns

The best ABM campaigns are based on precision targeting which enables your proposition to stand out in a noisy and cluttered market because it is personalized and relevant. You will already have defined the decision makers

**Figure 10.2** Most credible sources of information for buyers

Compared with two or three years ago, how has your reliance on the following sources of information changed?
% of respondents (N = 402)

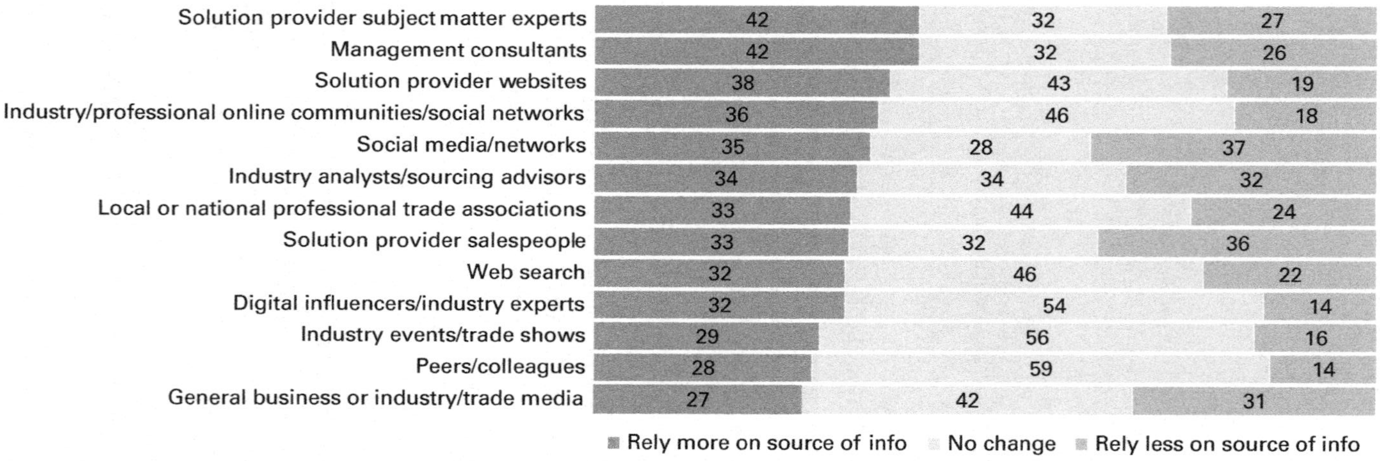

| Source | Rely more on source of info | No change | Rely less on source of info |
|---|---|---|---|
| Solution provider subject matter experts | 42 | 32 | 27 |
| Management consultants | 42 | 32 | 26 |
| Solution provider websites | 38 | 43 | 19 |
| Industry/professional online communities/social networks | 36 | 46 | 18 |
| Social media/networks | 35 | 28 | 37 |
| Industry analysts/sourcing advisors | 34 | 34 | 32 |
| Local or national professional trade associations | 33 | 44 | 24 |
| Solution provider salespeople | 33 | 32 | 36 |
| Web search | 32 | 46 | 22 |
| Digital influencers/industry experts | 32 | 54 | 14 |
| Industry events/trade shows | 29 | 56 | 16 |
| Peers/colleagues | 28 | 59 | 14 |
| General business or industry/trade media | 27 | 42 | 31 |

■ Rely more on source of info  ■ No change  ■ Rely less on source of info

**SOURCE** ITSMA, How B2B Buyers Consume Information Survey, 2016

and influencers for each of the plays you are taking in to the account in Step 3 of the ABM process, using the influencer map or 'onion diagram' seen in Figure 8.3 in Chapter 8. Revisit that map and the profiles you created so that you start your campaign planning with the audience in mind.

It's worth segmenting your audience in terms of the buyers and influencers for specific plays and other important groups that you need to communicate with, such as everyone currently delivering services into the account. Different audiences will warrant different levels of attention and need different messages, so be clear whom you will communicate with, when, and why.

Perhaps the easiest way of thinking about them is in terms of the investment in time and resources you will need to spend on them. While every member of your DMU will all need one-to-one attention, along with some of the significant influencers such as individual analysts advising them, others can be part of a one-to-few approach, such as your own delivery personnel, or even a one-to-many approach such as the members of influential groups on LinkedIn.

Some ABM-ers are tempted to leave out the external influencers in their campaigns, perhaps putting them in the 'nice to do' pile. But ITSMA research shows time and again that external influencers are important to buyers as they go through their purchasing process. Figure 10.2 shows buyers' increasing reliance on peers, digital influencers, online communities, and management consultants when purchasing complex business solutions worth over $500,000.

The good news is that your subject matter experts (who can identify trends for these buyers and recommend the best course of action, sharing thought leadership and pragmatic examples from other companies) were seen to be the most credible. But the third-party external influencers come after that: industry analysts and sourcing advisors, peers and colleagues of the buyers and management consultants. Ignore these powerful influencers at your peril.

# Creating personalized content

The very nature of ABM means that you are able to create content that is more personalized and relevant than that used for market- or segment-based campaigns. As a buyer yourself, you know how you are constantly bombarded with advertising messages or sales calls and you probably automatically screen out anything that isn't immediately relevant and of interest to you. Your buyers are doing the same.

**Figure 10.3**    The value of personalized content

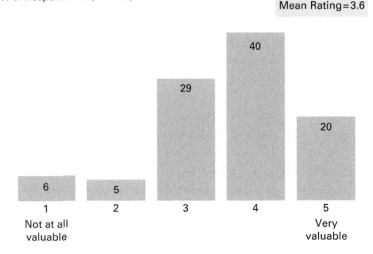

What is your perception of the value that solution providers deliver when they use technology to personalize content so it is relevant to your industry, company, role, and interests?
% of Respondents (N = 402)

Mean Rating = 3.6

40

29

20

6

5

1
Not at all
valuable

2

3

4

5
Very
valuable

**NOTE** Mean rating based on a 5-point scale where 1=Not at all valuable and 5=Very valuable
**SOURCE** ITSMA, How B2B Buyers Consume Information Survey, 2016

Our research shows that business solution buyers prefer to receive content that is personalized (Figure 10.3). In all types of ABM, marketers are using technology to personalize content as much as possible. This means not only ensuring that anything proactively sent out is personalized as a matter of course – both in terms of the identification of the recipient and also in terms of their business context – but also using technology such as reverse IP identification to recognize buyers or influencers when they visit your website so that they are served up more personalized content there too.

In this section we consider key elements in developing effective content:

- the right content at the right time;
- a note on thought leadership;
- the formats that buyers prefer;
- the power of storytelling;
- avoiding the pitfalls of marketing content.

## The right content at the right time

So, what types of content do buyers value? What should you be creating to support your ABM campaigns? What should you be personalizing? Well, it

**Figure 10.4**   The B2B buyer relationship model

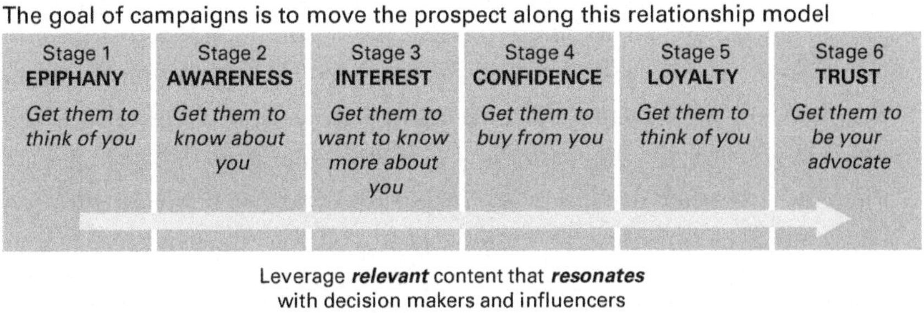

The goal of campaigns is to move the prospect along this relationship model

| Stage 1 **EPIPHANY** | Stage 2 **AWARENESS** | Stage 3 **INTEREST** | Stage 4 **CONFIDENCE** | Stage 5 **LOYALTY** | Stage 6 **TRUST** |
|---|---|---|---|---|---|
| *Get them to think of you* | *Get them to know about you* | *Get them to want to know more about you* | *Get them to buy from you* | *Get them to think of you* | *Get them to be your advocate* |

Leverage *relevant* content that *resonates*
with decision makers and influencers

depends on the objective of the campaign, and on the stage of the purchasing process your buyers are at.

The goal of your campaign should be to move the prospect along the relationship model shown in Figure 10.4 by leveraging relevant content that resonates with decision makers and influencers at the right time. This timeline may be extended, occurring over weeks or months, or it may be compressed, with your buyers absorbing all the available content in a day in order to accelerate their decision making. Whichever is the case, you need to be ready!

Let's look at the model in more detail and at what content works best, where.

**1 Epiphany.** Get them to think of you. This is about nudging customers to have that 'a-ha!' moment when they realize there is a business issue they need to confront. Thought leadership content can play a powerful role here, as happened when one national retailer became aware of how far behind it was in moving to a more international, multichannel platform and immediately started an initiative to catch up with and overtake its peers.

**2 Awareness.** Get them to know about you. Marketing content can ensure that your company is front of mind when the prospective customer starts looking around to deal with the issue. More in-depth thought leadership, including examples of how other companies have tackled the same issue and information about your company's expertise in this area, are all useful here.

**3 Interest.** Get them to know more about you with relevant information about how you can help with a challenge. This is about getting into your 'play', and calls for careful marketing and sales alignment as sales tend to get more involved with prospective buyers at this stage (once marketing has, in effect, warmed them up).

**4  Confidence.** Get them to buy from you. By now the customers have gained more confidence about putting you on a shortlist or, even better, selecting you as a supplier. The content you use here should convince them you know what you are talking about, which may mean that you ramp up the involvement of your subject matter experts and other customers who are willing to discuss what you have done for them. You also have to give them the tools they need, such as the business case, cost–benefit analysis, etc to build the same level of confidence in you with their internal teams. (Figure 10.5 shows the most effective types of information for buyers when they are selling a solution internally.) Again, alignment here is key, since your salespeople will play an important part at this stage.

**5  Loyalty.** Get them to automatically think of you. You want them to continue to buy from you, taking more of your portfolio as you move into a partner or trusted advisor relationship. The types of content that work here include partnership reports and case studies that show the value you have delivered to the account, along with thought leadership and ideas that continue to challenge and prompt the account on what they could do next.

**6  Trust.** Get them to be your advocate. A recommendation from a peer is one of the most powerful ways to attract new customers, as we've seen. What is less well known is that by building content that tells the story of how your client has succeeded with your support, you are also helping to build that person's perception that you are a good partner to work with and you are helping to build their career value.

**Figure 10.5**   Most effective content for buyers selling a solution internally

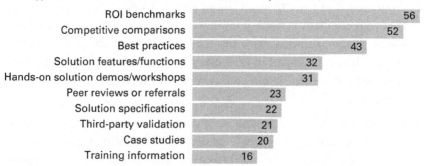

When you are 'selling' a solution internally to other members of the decision team, what types of information are most effective? % of respondents (N = 426)

| | |
|---|---|
| ROI benchmarks | 56 |
| Competitive comparisons | 52 |
| Best practices | 43 |
| Solution features/functions | 32 |
| Hands-on solution demos/workshops | 31 |
| Peer reviews or referrals | 23 |
| Solution specifications | 22 |
| Third-party validation | 21 |
| Case studies | 20 |
| Training information | 16 |

**NOTE** Multiple responses allowed
**SOURCE** ITSMA, How B2B Buyers Consume Information Survey, 2015

## A note on thought leadership

Of all the content types that work in B2B marketing, one of the most powerful is thought leadership. Defined by ITSMA as 'A set of ideas that educates customers and prospects about important business and technology issues and helps them solve those issues – without selling', you can see why it might be attractive to buyers.

Technology is changing so fast – social media, mobility, cloud computing and the era of big and fast data through the internet of everything – that buyers must educate themselves. To keep up in a marketplace inundated with me-too messaging, marketers are evolving their thought leadership strategy to be a key differentiator and integral part of the value proposition they provide to their customers.

Thought leadership is crucial to solution-provider awareness, interest, and consideration. The depth and quality of your thought leadership is one of the key criteria that will determine whether buyers want to learn more about you and who makes it onto the shortlist. Over the years, we've learned that:

- a thought leadership content development engine, supported by robust research and proof points, brings credibility to your company's point of view;
- engaging external networks as part of the thought leadership development process ensures that thinking is grounded and practical;
- best-practice companies have shifted from a publishing mindset to one of using thought leadership to support salespeople in their conversations with prospects and buyers.

You may wish to develop some customized thought leadership content for one strategic account if that account warrants the investment due to the size of the opportunity. Or you may develop it for a cluster of accounts, in ABM Lite, or more broadly, in programmatic ABM. Whichever is the case, we recommend you take the following steps to create this type of content:

1 **Develop a positioning statement.** It's not enough simply to identify a business issue that clients are facing and explain it. You need to take a strong point of view on why it is an issue, what's going to happen, and how to deal with the ramifications. Professional services firm EY created its '5: insights for executives series'[1] to help create short, impactful content for buyers that outlines the five questions thought leadership has to answer to be successful:

- What is the issue?
- Why now?

- How does it affect you?
- What's the fix?
- What's the bottom line?

This clear structure helps the firm develop its position on a range of issues, such as using predictive analytics to improve decision making.

2 **Gather proprietary evidence**. Ideas alone are not enough to convince clients and prospects to trust you. They need proof. Thought leadership seldom goes through the rigorous peer review process that academic papers receive, so evidence is needed in some other form.

3 **Build powerful examples**. Examples, ideally from named clients, should be significant stories that are easily understood and that customers can generalize across industries or markets. They should be unexpected and fresh. How many times have we heard the example of Target using big data to predict the pregnancy of a young lady before her parents found out?

4 **Elicit trustworthy testimonials**. Outside validation is also necessary to build credibility. Gather trustworthy testimonials from leading business executives, academics, scholars, government officials, industry analysts, or customers with experience to support your position.

## The formats that buyers prefer

It's worth noting that published presentations or slide sets featuring bullet points and visuals are the most preferred when thinking about the formats in which you should make your content available. This is followed by interactive visualizations of data with which buyers can engage. Next comes infographics and short-form web copy of two pages or fewer (Figure 10.6).

## The power of storytelling

Whatever forms of content you are creating, remember that the human brain is wired to listen for stories. If you use storytelling techniques in your content, you increase the chances that it will be seen or heard by your target audience. Stories reach three distinct parts of the human brain and directly connect to our instincts, our emotions and our higher-order, rational thinking. Over thousands of years of evolution, our brains have been wired to communicate in this way. Stories resonate with us. An increasing number of

**Figure 10.6**   The content formats buyers prefer

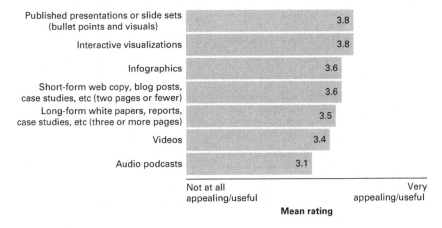

Based on your experience, how appealing and useful are the following content formats? Mean rating (N = 402)

| | Mean rating |
|---|---|
| Published presentations or slide sets (bullet points and visuals) | 3.8 |
| Interactive visualizations | 3.8 |
| Infographics | 3.6 |
| Short-form web copy, blog posts, case studies, etc (two pages or fewer) | 3.6 |
| Long-form white papers, reports, case studies, etc (three or more pages) | 3.5 |
| Videos | 3.4 |
| Audio podcasts | 3.1 |

Not at all appealing/useful — Very appealing/useful

**Mean rating**

**NOTE** Mean rating based on a 5-point scale where 1 = Not at all appealing/useful and 5 = Very appealing/useful
**SOURCE** ITSMA, How B2B Buyers Consume Information Survey, 2016

organizations, having observed the effectiveness of storytelling in B2C, now deploy the technique in B2B markets.

How do marketers go about creating stories? Simply put, stories have three components:

- **A plot or storyline.** This is the essence of the story, which, according to experts, can be articulated in as few as six words.

- **A story – or narrative – arc.** Starting with an opening scene, following various crises including a point of no-return, reaching a climax and finishing with the denouement, the arc is the journey you are taking the audience on.

- **A cast of characters with predetermined roles.** Having a hero and a villain is a good start. When they are joined by other archetypes, the story becomes more engaging.

As a technique for engaging an audience, stories have been used for years in commercials and other video-based content (we particularly love Adobe's range of humorous commercials for its marketing solutions). But stories are equally appropriate when planning how to make a presentation, how to write a customer case study or how to write a thought leadership paper.

**Figure 10.7**   Avoiding the pitfalls of marketing content

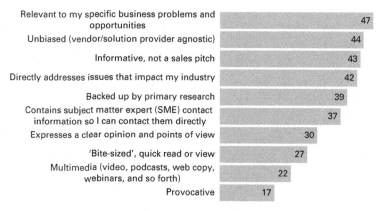

When looking specifically at solution provider content, which of the following content characteristics are most helpful to determine if reading/viewing the solution provider content will be a good use of your time? % of respondents (N = 402)

| | |
|---|---|
| Relevant to my specific business problems and opportunities | 47 |
| Unbiased (vendor/solution provider agnostic) | 44 |
| Informative, not a sales pitch | 43 |
| Directly addresses issues that impact my industry | 42 |
| Backed up by primary research | 39 |
| Contains subject matter expert (SME) contact information so I can contact them directly | 37 |
| Expresses a clear opinion and points of view | 30 |
| 'Bite-sized', quick read or view | 27 |
| Multimedia (video, podcasts, web copy, webinars, and so forth) | 22 |
| Provocative | 17 |

**NOTE** Multiple responses allowed
**SOURCE** ITSMA, How B2B Buyers Consume Information Survey, 2016

## Avoiding the pitfalls of marketing content

Buyers tell us that the biggest problems they find with the content suppliers send them are that it is too 'salesy', opinion-based rather than factual, and too long. They are looking for informative, unbiased content, relevant to their specific business problems and opportunities (see Figure 10.7).

# Designing an omnichannel campaign

ITSMA's buyer research has shown a slow and steady increase over the years in the amount of time buyers spend online when they are looking for information on trends to help them with a purchase. But, contrary to what you may read on the internet, they aren't spending the vast majority of their time online when considering buying a business solution worth more than $500k. Our research shows buyers spend almost half of their time offline when keeping up with industry and technology trends (Figure 10.8).

At the beginning of the purchase process the first three sources of information buyers turn to are their peers, management consultants, and your subject matter experts – in other words, people, as we discussed earlier in this chapter. This picture doesn't change all that much as buyers go through their purchase journey, with people at the forefront of the wide range of ways in which buyers get content and information from you (Figure 10.9).

**Figure 10.8**   Half the buying process takes place offline

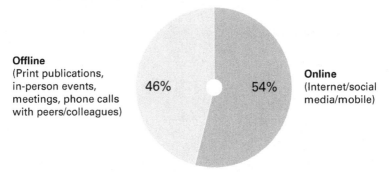

When you are keeping up with your industry and/or technology trends,
approximately how much time do you spend online vs offline?
Mean % of time (N=402)

**Offline**
(Print publications,
in-person events,
meetings, phone calls
with peers/colleagues)

46%

54%

**Online**
(Internet/social
media/mobile)

SOURCE  ITSMA, How B2B Buyers Consume Information Survey, 2016

**Figure 10.9**   Buyers turn to people for information early on

Thinking back to the beginning of the purchase process, what were the *first three sources of information*
you turned to when you began your solution research? (Rank order 1st, 2nd, 3rd)
% of Respondents (N=402)

| | |
|---|---|
| Peers/colleagues | 31 |
| Management consultants | 28 |
| Solution provider subject matter experts | 28 |
| Web search | 27 |
| Digital influencers/industry experts | 27 |
| Industry analysts/sourcing advisors | 26 |
| Solution provider websites | 26 |
| Industry events/trade shows | 20 |
| Solution provider sales people | 20 |
| General business or industry/trade media | 20 |
| Industry/professional online communities/social networks | 17 |
| Local or national professional trade associations | 15 |
| Social media/networks | 12 |

■ % Rank 1st   ▨ % Rank 2nd   ▢ % Rank 3rd

NOTE  Respondents were asked to rank order first three sources
SOURCE  ITSMA, How B2B Buyers Consume Information Survey, 2016

However, it's worth bearing in mind that 75 per cent of buyers expect an omnichannel approach. That is one whereby 'the people I work with at potential solution providers know what interactions (both on- and offline) have already occurred and what information has been exchanged'. Once again, technology can support you in this quest, from your marketing automation system through to your sales database, helping you take a more joined-up approach.

Social media is used by buyers during their purchase process, with LinkedIn and YouTube ranked the most useful (Figure 10.10). Almost one-third of buyers find social media useful for connecting with potential

**Figure 10.10**   The relative importance of social media

During your most recent purchase process for your most recent solution, how useful were social media channels and networks for helping you stay informed and make decisions? Mean rating (N = 402)

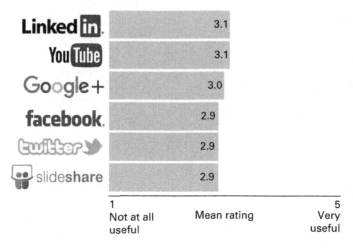

|  | 1<br>Not at all<br>useful | Mean rating | 5<br>Very<br>useful |
|---|---|---|---|

**NOTE**  Mean rating based on a 5-point scale where 1=Not at all useful and 5=Very useful
**SOURCE**  ITSMA, How B2B Buyers Consume Information Survey, 2016

solution suppliers (there are more direct ways for them to connect with existing suppliers). It also helps them connect with subject matter experts and keep up with industry trends, news and events.

When using social media in your ABM campaigns, bear in mind that ITSMA research tells us that the content buyers value most from you is original content authored by your people. After that comes curated content on a topic that interests them, which you have handpicked and introduced with some copy authored by you. The least valuable to buyers is filtered content that has been served to them based on their profiles.

As we all know, the real win comes when your content is shared on social media by the buyers and influencers you are targeting. Just over half of buyers do this at least sometimes and they are most likely to share when you present research-based facts or a new point of view on a topic they are passionate about. Just under a quarter will share, providing the content is entertaining or funny.

## Putting it all together in your campaign plan

Looking at the most effective campaign tactics for each of the three types of ABM reinforces the difference in both investment and depth in each one.

**Table 10.1**   The top five tactics used in different types of ABM

| Strategic ABM | ABM Lite | Programmatic ABM |
|---|---|---|
| **1** One-to-one meetings | **1** One-to-one meetings | **1** E-mail marketing |
| **2** Account-specific thought leadership | **2** E-mail marketing | **2** One-to-one meetings |
| **3** Innovation days | **3** Executive engagement plans | **3** Reverse IP/digital advertising |
| **4** Executive engagement plans | **4** Custom collateral | **4** Direct mail |
| **5** Private events | **5** Reverse IP/digital advertising | **5** Blogs/social engagement |

ITSMA's recent ABM benchmarking study shows that one-to-one meetings are the only tactic that appears in the top five of all three types, presumably because salespeople ultimately need to meet the client to make the sale (Table 10.1).

Strategic ABM and ABM Lite share only these meetings and broader executive engagement plans. ABM Lite and programmatic also share e-mail marketing and reverse IP/digital advertising. Programmatic ABM's tactics are more similar to those used in segment- or market-based campaigns, as you would expect. The tactics that work best in strategic ABM reflect the care and attention that is lavished on one account when you treat it as a market in its own right.

We will look at each of these in turn.

## The top five tactics for strategic ABM campaigns

These top five tactics are indeed a powerful mix for you to consider in your strategic ABM campaign plan.

### 1. One-to-one, face-to-face meetings

Peer-to-peer meetings are the best way to strengthen relationships, whether it is the account manager with the main buyer, your subject matter expert with the technical buyer or the mutual procurement or marketing directors – it should be with those considered best placed to make a difference. The mistake made in many account plans is to let the account manager 'own' all the relationships. Instead, you need a multilevel plan of meetings in most cases to develop a wide span of relationships across your buyers and influencers.

## 2. Account specific (bespoke) thought leadership development

Buyers want suppliers to demonstrate they can contribute genuine insights to improve their business performance. This is the conversation starter and it drives the epiphany moment discussed earlier. There should be close liaison between the subject matter experts who produce the insights and anyone charged with client contact, with the subject matter expert increasingly delivering thought leadership in person as the buyer moves through their purchasing process.

## 3. Innovation days

This is an increasingly popular way to position the capability of your company and deepen ABM relationships. Its aim is to create a shared vision of how to work together on a key issue to deliver a mutually beneficial business outcome and in the process deepening relationships and creating new opportunities. These sessions bring potential solutions (your plays) to life in a detailed action plan which both parties can then work on together.

The sessions should start with an exploration or recognition of the business imperatives and initiatives of the client, rather than jumping straight into your solution. This approach to co-creation of plans and value for both companies can be expensive. But most companies we speak to say that whenever they run one of these sessions, they strengthen relationships, improve their reputation and generate new opportunities for revenue (see the Cognizant case study below as an example). Figure 10.11 outlines a typical innovation workshop process and agenda.

**Figure 10.11**   Planning an innovation workshop

**Objectives:** To create a shared vision of how to work together on a key issue to deliver a mutually beneficial business outcome, deepening relationships and creating new opportunities

| Pre-workshop | Workshop | Post-workshop |
|---|---|---|
| Review account insight (do additional analysis/interviewing if appropriate) | Share insights around the issue(s) and outcomes | Collaborate on a project or projects identified in the workshop |
| Develop value proposition for the workshop | Highlight best practices from other companies/sectors | |
| Invite delegates | Explore potential ways in which technology can deliver the outcomes | |
| Circulate pre-reading | Prioritize ideas | |
| | Agree a broad route map for achieving the vision | |
| | Agree next steps | |

**CASE STUDY**   Cognizant – Strong growth through a focus
on innovation

Cognizant is a global leader in the provision of custom information technology, consulting and business process outsourcing services. The company's manufacturing and logistics practice has a diverse client base which includes one of the world's leading automobile original equipment manufacturers (OEMs) based in North America.

In 2014, Cognizant's success with one key client was driven mainly by an innovative ABM approach adopted by the engagement team. This strategic approach helped Cognizant bring greater business value to an important client by treating the account as a market of one.

### Building the framework

The Cognizant ABM team began this transformation by conducting a full-day event with the company's senior executives called Cognizant Partnership Day to map Cognizant solutions and capabilities with key business technology challenges. The goal was to change the client's perception of Cognizant from a transactional vendor to a key strategic partner.

The ABM approach with this account didn't directly pitch Cognizant's capabilities and service offerings. The content was focused solely in an external view of the client's existing state and strategic initiatives. It offered prescriptive suggestions on next steps.

The Cognizant team also adopted innovative practices such as personalized web pages for participants, targeted messaging about the event with delivery of related content, audience engagement using mobile-based gaming aimed at portable handheld devices, and information kiosks to enhance engagement. The entire campaign was tied together to deliver a consistent message on the client's strategy for the future.

### Hitting the right targets

To ensure precision execution:

- A core team of executives was identified from diverse Cognizant groups such as: business consulting; mobility practice; emerging business accelerators; social media, analytics, mobility and cloud centre of excellence; engineering and manufacturing systems; and manufacturing and logistics.
- Relying on key point persons of each group ensured executive buy-in within the organization, demonstrating Cognizant's leading-edge capabilities and its commitment to the event.

- Consistent messaging and event buzz was driven by creating a shared identity for every interaction with the client, 'save the date' mailers, and an innovative web page.

The Cognizant Partnership Day itself featured exclusive talks presented by the company's leadership on a variety of topics shaping the auto industry such as mobility, social media and emerging automotive technology. The mobility presentation, for instance, featured proprietary, custom-developed mobile apps, which were delivered through portable devices given to the audience. This ensured the highest levels of audience engagement and partnership.

Information kiosks were also set up on each of the core focus areas, where participants could gain specific information on the topic and also engage in meaningful one-to-one interactions with the leadership team and subject matter experts.

### Business results

Along with 100 per cent year-on-year revenue growth, with a headcount growth of about the same rate, this programme delivered the following results:

- Multiple prospects and follow-up calls in mobility, analytics, agile development and engineering, a 500 per cent increase in demand.
- Cognizant became involved in all of the client's major strategic business initiatives, a 400 per cent mindshare increase.
- A 500 per cent increase in new services opportunities and 300 per cent increase in new executive meetings.
- The company was now being shortlisted for every service opportunity (a 500 per cent increase) and in some instances as a preferred vendor.
- A change in perception from vendor to thought leader, taking conversations with leadership to the next level.
- Opportunities to engage with multiple product groups, multiple levels of the organization, and different functional lines.
- Client invites for pursuits in multiple lines of business of the client organization now became commonplace, including engineering, automotive technology, business consulting and mobility.
- Cognizant was being chosen as a preferred partner for the client's mobility projects.

In addition to now being among the top five accounts in the manufacturing and logistics practice, this account consistently topped Cognizant's annual customer satisfaction surveys conducted across all engagements. It scored about 7 per cent higher than the average customer satisfaction score of clients in the practice.

## 4. Executive engagement plan

Urban myth has it that whenever IBM was bidding for a large contract outside North America, 'the skies would darken with IBM executives flying in' at the later stages of the bid. This is not accidental. If you are preparing an integrated sales and marketing campaign to one of your most strategic accounts, it should include some of your executives. As suppliers compete for C-Suite positioning and relationships in their most important accounts, the people who can most effectively support these relationships are those who are, in effect, peers to the C-Suite executives in the account.

This is about balance and timing. Not all of your executives will have the time to be constantly out supporting your ABM campaigns. And not all executives will have the right chemistry with the client. The key here is to work with your account manager using the information you developed at the stakeholder mapping and profiling stage of the process (Step 3) to map your own executives against the key executives in the account, based on their seniority, role and likely personal chemistry.

Executive engagement can take the form of one-to-one meetings, or it may be private meetings about the governance of existing contracts or the bidding process for new contracts. It can also include hospitality events, or visits to executive briefing centres (including innovation workshops). Plan out the frequency and nature of your executive meetings as part of your campaign and make sure your executives are briefed before each meeting with the account, and debriefed afterwards.

## 5. Private/internal business events

This covers a broad spectrum of activities, from setting up a stall at the targeted client and running 'lunch and learn' events, to doing a thought leadership presentation to 20 people involved in a particular initiative, to holding all-day seminars targeted just at one account. Many large technology providers who have their enormous annual conferences and shows in places like Las Vegas' Venetian Hotel or San Francisco's Moscone Center each year organize private events alongside the public one to customize the content specifically as part of the campaign into one strategic account.

Of course, strategic ABM plans include more than just these five tactics and you can see the full range of the most effective tactics in Figure 10.12. They reflect the omnichannel nature of campaigns today, with a mix of both online and offline tactics present.

**Figure 10.12**   Most effective Strategic ABM tactics

What specific campaign tactics are most effective for Strategic ABM?
% of respondents (N = 48)

| Tactic | % |
| --- | --- |
| One-on-one, face-to-face meetings | 40 |
| Account-specific (bespoke) TL development and dissemination | 38 |
| Innovation days | 36 |
| Executive engagement plan | 34 |
| Private/internal business events | 26 |
| Microsites/website personalization | 15 |
| Hospitality events (eg sport, cultural, fine dining) | 15 |
| E-mail marketing | 15 |
| Direct mail | 13 |
| Custom collateral/videos/podcasts | 13 |

**NOTE** Up to three responses allowed
**SOURCE** ITSMA, Account-Based Marketing Benchmarking Survey, March 2016

Strategic ABM campaigns can cost anywhere from $25,000 to over $100,000 per account per year, depending on the amount of bespoke content created and the number and type of communications channels used. When planning your own campaign, bear in mind both the size of the opportunity, or potential lifetime value of the account and the budget you have available. As we said earlier, this is where business unit leaders and account managers often pay for some of the campaign out of their own budgets when the cost of what you need to do is beyond the budget you have available.

## The top five most effective tactics for ABM Lite

The most effective tactics for ABM Lite include two of those already discussed in the strategic ABM list:

### 1. One-to-one, face-to-face meetings; and
### 2. Executive engagement plans.

For ABM Lite, three additional tactics rank in the top five.

### 3. E-mail marketing

Here's where ABM Lite and strategic ABM diverge. However, while this is e-mail marketing such as you would use in broader marketing campaigns, it is with a bespoke twist to get the personalization ABM is built on. For example, you might be sending out an e-mail to a cluster of executives in the same industry with similar issues such as reducing operating costs in retail. It might lead them to a website, invite them to an event or share a relevant case study with the first and last paragraphs tailored to specific individuals. Don't forget that its effectiveness will depend on how relevant it is to the individual at this point, even if you are targeting 10 people in a cluster with your e-mail.

## 4. Custom collateral/videos/podcasts

This collateral can be targeted to specific accounts, especially when it is digital. It could be anything from printed material to a three-minute video of your CEO analysing key areas of value or a complete e-book. The opening and closing elements of the asset are usually customized for the individual account you are targeting within your cluster.

## 5. Reverse IP/targeted digital advertising/content

More and more marketers are getting involved in exploiting the power of this sophisticated technology. Doing a reverse IP look-up identifies the visitor by company and then provides demographic information, including industry, company revenue size and location by accessing third-party information held about that person or company.

By presenting more relevant information from the point of entry, your website can potentially minimize the time the visitor spends looking for ideas

**Figure 10.13**  Most effective tactics in ABM Lite

What specific campaign tactics are most effective for ABM Lite?
% of respondents (N=45)

| | |
|---|---|
| One-on-one, face-to-face meetings | 49 |
| E-mail marketing | 47 |
| Executive engagement plan | 23 |
| Custom collateral/videos/podcasts | 21 |
| Reverse IP/targeted digital ads/content | 19 |
| Microsites/website personalization | 16 |
| Hospitality events (eg sport, cultural, fine dining) | 16 |
| Innovation days | 16 |
| Custom e-newsletters | 14 |
| Blogs and social engagement | 14 |

**NOTE**  Up to three responses allowed
**SOURCE**  ITSMA, Account-Based Marketing Benchmarking Survey, March 2016

and solutions relevant to them, improve engagement with the visitor and increase the likelihood of conversion to a follow-up action or conversation. As the engagement develops, you can, of course, invite a client to register to be presented with specific content personal to them as an individual.

A full list of the most effective tactics used in ABM Lite campaigns is shown in Figure 10.13.

## The top five most effective tactics for programmatic ABM

The most effective tactics in programmatic ABM include three tactics already seen:

1. One-to-one, face-to-face meetings (as strategic ABM and ABM Lite);
2. E-mail marketing; and
3. Reverse IP/targeted digital advertising (as ABM Lite).

The two additional tactics marketers use most in programmatic ABM are direct mail, and blogs/social engagement.

### 4. Direct mail

Direct mail has a long history in marketing (and even stretches back, some say, to ancient Egypt). It has become more sophisticated as marketing technology and digital printing have evolved to support it. It is now possible to do completely personalized short print runs, while it can be seen as a novelty to receive a beautifully designed piece through the post. Little wonder that programmatic ABM-ers are taking advantage of this and relying on it in their campaigns.

### 5. Blogs/social engagement

With the rise of social selling (using social media to engage with prospects) and the increasing sophistication of social marketing, blogs and social engagement are an effective way to drive awareness and consideration among large groups of potential buyers in named accounts. This involves going beyond the 'broadcast' element of social media communications – which people do still use to announce new products or company initiatives – and moving into digital conversations. Malcolm Frank, EVP for strategy and marketing at Cognizant, and one of the authors of the recent *Code Halos* book[2] on the digital footprint we leave in our day-to-day lives, described the shift

**Figure 10.14**    Most effective tactics in Programmatic ABM

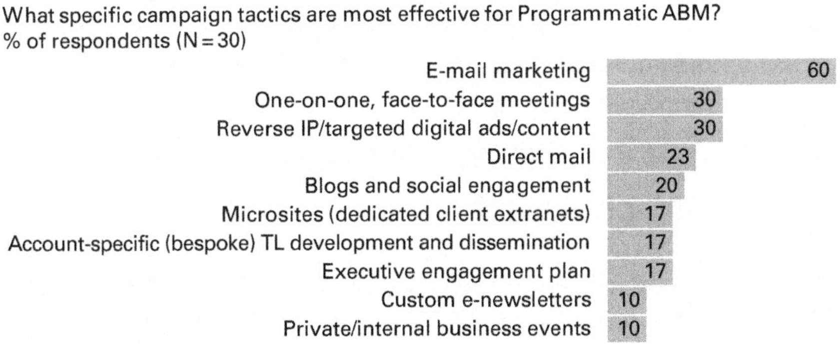

What specific campaign tactics are most effective for Programmatic ABM?
% of respondents (N = 30)

| Tactic | % |
|---|---|
| E-mail marketing | 60 |
| One-on-one, face-to-face meetings | 30 |
| Reverse IP/targeted digital ads/content | 30 |
| Direct mail | 23 |
| Blogs and social engagement | 20 |
| Microsites (dedicated client extranets) | 17 |
| Account-specific (bespoke) TL development and dissemination | 17 |
| Executive engagement plan | 17 |
| Custom e-newsletters | 10 |
| Private/internal business events | 10 |

**NOTE** Up to three responses allowed
**SOURCE** ITSMA, Account-Based Marketing Benchmarking Survey, March 2016

for marketers beautifully by saying that markets are now conversations, supported by social, mobile, analytics and cloud technologies.

The full range of most effective programmatic ABM tactics is shown in Figure 10.14.

# Visualizing your campaign

To bring your campaign to life for the account team and your wider business stakeholders, consider building a visual that represents the sequence of

**Figure 10.15**    An illustrative strategic ABM campaign

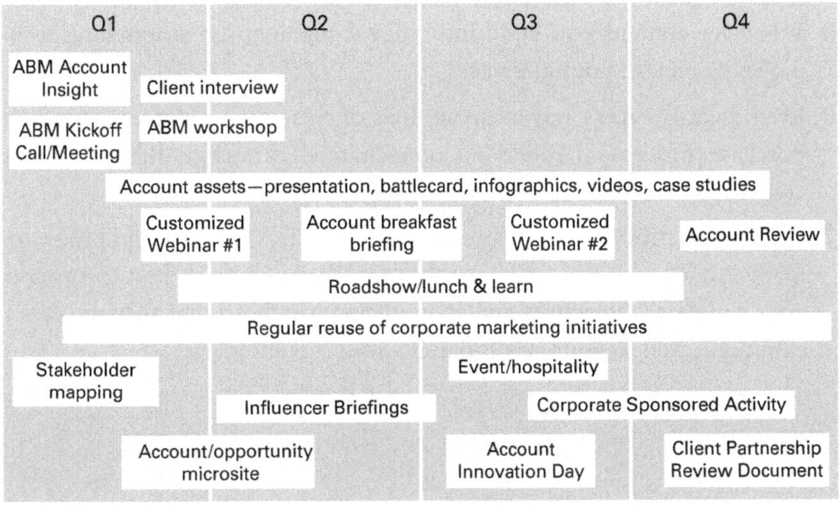

| Q1 | Q2 | Q3 | Q4 |
|---|---|---|---|
| ABM Account Insight | Client interview | | |
| ABM Kickoff Call/Meeting | ABM workshop | | |
| Account assets—presentation, battlecard, infographics, videos, case studies | | | |
| | Customized Webinar #1 | Account breakfast briefing | Customized Webinar #2 | Account Review |
| | Roadshow/lunch & learn | | |
| | Regular reuse of corporate marketing initiatives | | |
| Stakeholder mapping | | Event/hospitality | |
| | Influencer Briefings | Corporate Sponsored Activity | |
| | Account/opportunity microsite | Account Innovation Day | Client Partnership Review Document |

tactics you are planning to get your content across to decision makers and influencers. This 'campaign calendar' or 'flight path' can easily be included into the account manager's broader account plan, showing at a glance how marketing and sales are working together to execute the campaign designed to support the account objectives (Figure 10.15).

# Your ABM checklist

1 ABM campaign objectives should be developed to support both the business objectives for your account and specific sales objectives. They are usually aimed at positioning your company in the mind of your audience, informing and educating people in the account about your company and your offer, or persuading the DMU to act in your favour.

2 The best ABM campaigns are based on precision targeting which enables your proposition to stand out in a noisy and cluttered market because it is personalized and relevant. Revisit your stakeholder map and the profiles you created so that you start your campaign planning with the audience in mind.

3 The very nature of ABM means that you are able to create content that is more personalized and relevant than that used for market- or segment-based campaigns. Create content that resonates with decision makers and supports them as they move through their purchasing process.

4 Thought leadership content is a powerful way of connecting with buyers on the imperatives they face and the initiatives they are or should be taking.

5 Whatever content you build into your campaign, use storytelling techniques to engage your audience.

6 Even digitally-savvy buyers spend half of their time offline during their purchase process, so build an omnichannel campaign that gets your content across through both online and offline tactics.

7 Different tactics are effective in strategic ABM, ABM Lite and programmatic ABM campaigns. Choose the ones that will work best to support your campaign objectives and show them visually so that they are easily communicated to your account and wider stakeholders.

# Notes

1 http://www.ey.com/GL/en/Services/Advisory/5-insights-for-executives-series

2 Frank, M, Roehrig, P and Pring, B (2014) *Code Halos: How the digital lives of people, things and organizations are changing the rules of business*, John Wiley & Sons

# Executing integrated campaigns

# 11

## Aligning marketing and sales

Regardless of how impressive your ABM plan for an account is, remember that it is just a piece of paper until you execute it. There is no magic here. It all comes down to excellent project management, collaboration and implementation. Go back to the Fujitsu case study in Chapter 2. One of the key lessons learned from the company's experience with ABM was the critical importance of marketing integrating with the account planning process and working closely with the account team to ensure success.

In strategic ABM, ITSMA research shows that the second biggest challenge marketers face after securing adequate budgets to support programmes and resources is getting the buy-in of sales.[1] Further down the top 10 list of challenges, at no. 6 comes educating people (including sales) on what ABM is and how it is done. (It should be noted that the 10th greatest challenge facing strategic ABM-ers is keeping up with sales demand.) For ABM Lite these three remain challenges but are ordered slightly differently, with educating sales at no. 3, getting buy-in at no. 6, and coping with sales demand at no. 8 in the top 10 challenges.

That is why, before we look at plan execution, it's worth stressing the importance of sales and marketing alignment in ABM. As Figure 11.1 illustrates, this alignment encompasses a number of aspects, including both the skills of the account manager and the ABM-er, and the ABM process that they need to work through together. Not only will everyone be headed in the same direction with this alignment, but, if and when things change (and they will), the team will be agile enough to modify direction. The plan has to reflect reality or it will be ignored.

So how well aligned are marketing and sales today?

**Figure 11.1**    Sales and marketing alignment

| Account Management | Knowing what's driving the account | Marketing |
| --- | --- | --- |
| • Team formation<br>• Account knowledge<br>• Account plan<br>• Account relationship development<br>• Opportunity identifying<br>• Selling and closing<br>• Target and goal setting<br>• etc | Identifying and profiling stakeholders<br><br>Playing to the client's needs<br><br>Developing targeted value propositions<br><br>Planning integrated sales and marketing campaigns<br><br>Executing integrated sales and marketing campaigns<br><br>Evaluating results and updating plans | • Market intelligence<br>• Account intelligence<br>• Account relationship mapping<br>• Stakeholder analysis<br>• Marketing planning<br>• Value proposition development<br>• Thought leadership<br>• Campaigns<br>• etc |

ITSMA tested the alignment in its 2016 ABM benchmarking survey,[2] exploring the extent to which marketers agreed with these important statements:

1 ABM is widely understood to be a strategic business initiative rather than tactical sales support.

2 ABM is viewed as a corporate revenue acceleration programme rather than a marketing programme.

3 ABM is fully integrated with the account planning process.

4 Marketing is a member of the account sales team for ABM initiatives.

5 Roles, responsibilities, and processes for creating and executing integrated sales and marketing ABM plans are understood by the account sales team.

Let's look at each one in more detail.

## 1. ABM is understood to be a strategic business initiative

If ABM is positioned correctly, both in the business and in the sales and account management communities, it will be apparent to everyone that the marketer assigned to their account is not there to organize meetings, take notes, produce their presentations, add their client information into the sales system or generally take on the administrative burden for the team.

All ABM-ers have probably at some point been asked to create a 'newsletter' for their account, or run an 'event' without having been involved in the thinking around what the objective driving the tactic is and the other ways it could be achieved – nor, indeed, the broader activity mix into which this tactic fits. But the goal of an ABM-er is to be the marketing subject expert on the account team, recommending the most appropriate ways to achieve the business or sales objective (and probably helping to define those objectives). So, if you are responding to requests for tactical support, it's time to take a step back and take stock of your position on the team.

When asked if they agreed with the statement 'ABM is widely understood to be a strategic business initiative rather than tactical sales support', marketers agreed in the case of strategic ABM and ABM Lite (3.5 and 3.6 out of 5.0 respectively where 5.0 means 'strongly agree' with the statement). In programmatic ABM they neither agreed nor disagreed with this (see Figure 11.2). While this is encouraging, there is clearly more progress to be made here in all three types, but it is especially important in strategic ABM, where a one-to-one approach is being taken and ABM-ers can do so much more for the account they are working with. This positioning of ABM is not only a foundation for good marketing and sales alignment at an account level, but it is also a foundation for your whole programme and should be managed right at the programme outset, as we have discussed.

**Figure 11.2** ABM is a strategic business initiative

To what extent do you agree with the following statements?
Mean Importance Rating

| | | |
|---|---|---|
| Strategic ABM is widely understood to be a strategic business initiative, rather than tactical sales support. | N = 48 | 3.5 |
| ABM Lite is widely understood to be a strategic business initiative, rather than tactical sales support. | N = 49 | 3.6 |
| Programmatic ABM is widely understood to be a strategic business initiative, rather than tactical sales support. | N = 32 | 3.0 |

1 Strongly Disagree — Mean Rating — 5 Strongly Agree

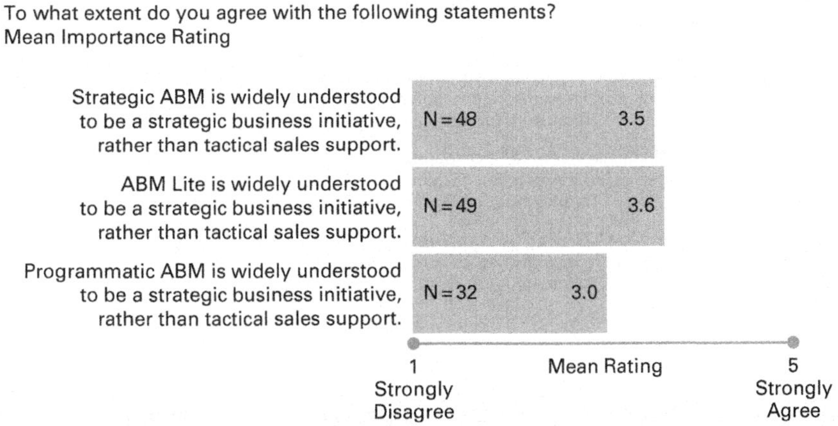

**NOTE** Mean rating based on a 5-point scale where 1=Strongly disagree and 5=Strongly agree
**SOURCE** ITSMA, Account-Based Marketing Benchmarking Survey, March 2016

## 2. ABM is viewed as a corporate revenue acceleration programme

Marketing and sales are part of the same business development value chain aimed at growing the revenues of the company. The same is true for ABM on a micro-level in your priority accounts. If ABM is seen as a marketing programme, with little need for sales collaboration, we will be back to the ludicrous situation many of us have seen before in our careers, where salespeople complain that they 'don't get any support from marketing' and 'don't know what they do all day', while marketers bemoan the fact that all the leads they generate for sales are left untouched and not followed up.

ABM is perhaps our best opportunity yet to close this traditional gap between sales and marketing, and jointly create new revenues for our companies. When asked about this in our survey, marketers were non-committal, neither agreeing nor disagreeing (see Figure 11.3). This is worrying, as it potentially means that salespeople feel they don't need to invest the time and effort needed to align with their marketing colleagues to execute on account campaigns.

Again, it is a question of getting the positioning right up front. But if this hasn't been done, you may need to revisit the education and positioning of ABM and how it works best for your account team.

**Figure 11.3**    ABM as a corporate revenue acceleration programme

To what extent do you agree with the following statements?
Mean Importance Rating

| | | |
|---|---|---|
| Strategic ABM is viewed as a corporate, revenue acceleration programme, rather than a marketing programme. | N = 48 | 3.2 |
| ABM Lite is viewed as a corporate, revenue acceleration programme, rather than a marketing programme. | N = 49 | 3.2 |
| Programmatic ABM is viewed as a corporate, revenue acceleration programme, rather than a marketing programme. | N = 32 | 3.1 |

1
Strongly
Disagree

Mean Rating

5
Strongly
Agree

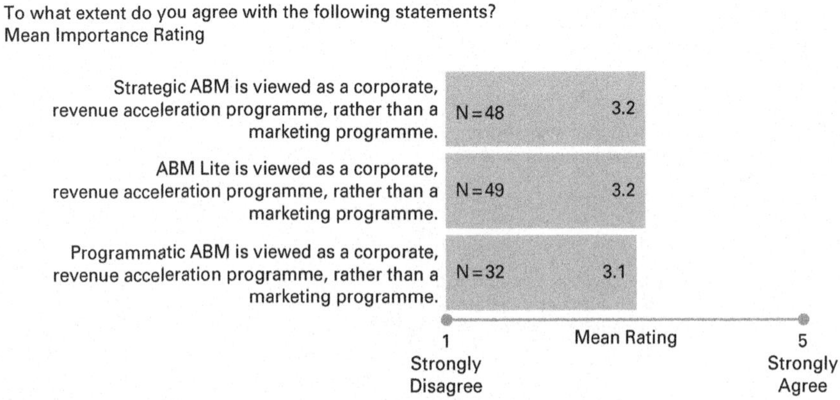

**NOTE** Mean rating based on a 5-point scale where 1=Strongly disagree and 5=Strongly agree
**SOURCE** ITSMA, Account-Based Marketing Benchmarking Survey, March 2016

## 3. ABM is fully integrated with the account planning process

Most importantly in strategic ABM, the integration of ABM into the account planning process ensures that you don't have two separate planning processes to develop the account plan and the ABM plan. It also means there is just one plan, or elements of the two plans that overlap and are shared – for example, by including the account plan's situation review in the ABM plan, or the ABM campaign calendar in the account plan.

Ideally, the ABM plan is also reviewed alongside the account plan as part of the normal account governance process in the business. In our experience, when a business unit leader or chief operating officer (COO) asks how the ABM campaign plan is doing each time they review the account manager's progress, that campaign plan quickly becomes something that's integral to both the account plan and the account manager's thinking.

The good news is that the marketers in our survey scored this statement 3.8 out of 5.0 (see Figure 11.4), meaning that they broadly agreed with it for strategic ABM. This is great news, but there's still room for improvement. The picture worsens for ABM Lite (3.5) and programmatic ABM (2.9), but given these are not one-to-one approaches, it is less critical in these contexts.

**Figure 11.4** ABM integration with account planning

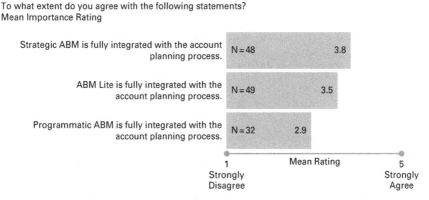

To what extent do you agree with the following statements?
Mean Importance Rating

Strategic ABM is fully integrated with the account planning process. N = 48 — 3.8

ABM Lite is fully integrated with the account planning process. N = 49 — 3.5

Programmatic ABM is fully integrated with the account planning process. N = 32 — 2.9

1 Strongly Disagree — Mean Rating — 5 Strongly Agree

**NOTE** Mean rating based on a 5-point scale where 1=Strongly disagree and 5=Strongly agree
**SOURCE** ITSMA, Account-Based Marketing Benchmarking Survey, March 2016

## 4. Marketing is a member of the account sales team

The most successful ABM-ers are seen as part of the account team: participating in its meetings, collaborating on the account plan development and execution, sharing the trials and tribulations of service or delivery issues, working flat out on major bids and celebrating success with the team. The pattern we've observed over the years is that the ABM-er tends to 'go native', identifying with the account team rather than the ABM or marketing community any longer, but this is a risk that's well worth taking. In fact, it may even be an indicator of success!

When asked to what extent they agreed with the statement that marketing is part of the account sales team for ABM initiatives, there was marginally more agreement in the case of strategic ABM than for ABM Lite, so 4.1 versus 4.0 out of a possible score of 5.0 (where 5.0 is 'strongly agree'). But, as you would expect, this drops dramatically in the case of Programmatic ABM, where the score was only 3.1, since it is less important in this context (Figure 11.5). The good news is that this indeed seems to be the case today with the strategic and Lite versions of ABM, where you really need marketers to be part of the account team.

**Figure 11.5**    Marketing is a member of the account team

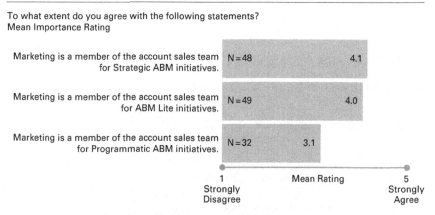

To what extent do you agree with the following statements?
Mean Importance Rating

Marketing is a member of the account sales team for Strategic ABM initiatives.    N = 48    4.1

Marketing is a member of the account sales team for ABM Lite initiatives.    N = 49    4.0

Marketing is a member of the account sales team for Programmatic ABM initiatives.    N = 32    3.1

1 Strongly Disagree    Mean Rating    5 Strongly Agree

**NOTE**  Mean rating based on a 5-point scale where 1=Strongly disagree and 5=Strongly agree
**SOURCE**  ITSMA, Account-Based Marketing Benchmarking Survey, March 2016

## 5. Roles, responsibilities and processes are understood by sales

With neither marketing nor sales known for their focus on detail and extensive project management skills, it can be easy for each side to make assumptions about the roles and responsibilities of the other. From our research, it seems that this remains a particular problem area around the alignment of marketing and sales in ABM. Marketers once again are on the fence about whether they agree with the statement: 'Roles, responsibilities, and processes for creating and executing integrated sales and marketing ABM plans are understood by the account sales team' in Strategic ABM and ABM Lite (Figure 11.6).

Clarity and transparency on these roles are important for a successful, integrated campaign. The best way to achieve this is to agree them up front in each account, even if they've been defined at a generic, programme level for all accounts.

At the first meeting between the ABM-er and the account team, it's worth discussing each person's expectations about the roles and responsibilities of the team members. Then, for each programme or activity you agree on, there's no harm in circulating notes from your discussion and being clear who has agreed to take on which actions, by when (this is only good project management, after all), building on those initial discussions about roles and responsibilities and making them real. A simple 'RACI' note, defining who is responsible, accountable, consulted on and informed of any task, is the easiest way to do this when mapped against the actions in a project plan.

Remember, since neither marketing nor sales is particularly process-oriented, simple visuals and project plans will help to make any collaborative processes easier to execute.

**Figure 11.6**  ABM roles and responsibilities are understood

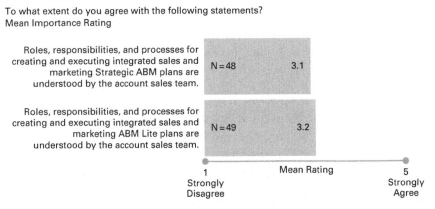

To what extent do you agree with the following statements?
Mean Importance Rating

Roles, responsibilities, and processes for creating and executing integrated sales and marketing Strategic ABM plans are understood by the account sales team.  N = 48   3.1

Roles, responsibilities, and processes for creating and executing integrated sales and marketing ABM Lite plans are understood by the account sales team.  N = 49   3.2

1
Strongly
Disagree

Mean Rating

5
Strongly
Agree

**NOTE** Mean rating based on a 5-point scale where 1=Strongly disagree and 5=Strongly agree
**SOURCE** ITSMA, Account-Based Marketing Benchmarking Survey, March 2016

# The role of the ABM-er on the account team

As you come out of the planning stage, you probably have both an account plan and an ABM plan. These need to be joined together for several reasons, both internal and external. Internally, linking these two documents encourages the account team to view the ABM-er and marketing activities as part of the broader approach to the account – one single approach, and not two. It also allows business unit management to review progress on the marketing plan while reviewing the progress of other work streams on the account. And finally, it allows marketing management to understand the broader context for the ABM plan. Externally, the client is more likely to see a joined-up approach from your company, making it easier to understand what you stand for and making you easier to deal with.

The account plan is the living document that captures all useful information needed to plan sales to a single customer. There are many different approaches to the design of an account plan, but they all have one thing in common: they review the current situation in the account, define the objectives for the account and set out how those objectives will be achieved.

Until relatively recently, marketers were more focused on looking at individuals, generating and nurturing 'leads' at the individual level rather than putting them into the context of an account. ABM is changing all of that, even at scale, where the availability of technology to help with this account-based approach is impacting the mindset of campaign planners.

Table 11.1 shows how the ABM plan can support and slot into the account plan, using a generic view of the typical contents within each.

But before you can do any of this as an ABM-er, you need to find out if an up-to-date account plan actually exists. Your initial role on the account team will be different according to the account plan's status, as shown in Figure 11.7:

- **Catalyst.** If there is no account plan, you have the opportunity to add immediate value to the account by using the ABM process to also develop the account plan. In fact, they can be done in tandem. The focus here is on introducing the methodology, demonstrating how it supports the account planning methodology (if there is one) and then using it to build an excellent account plan for the team, incorporating elements of the ABM plan that you also develop with the team and use to guide your own activities on the account.

**Table 11.1** The ABM plan and the account plan

| Strategic account plan (sales) | ABM plan (marketing) |
| --- | --- |
| Management summary | Account profile: Business imperatives |
| Revenue forecast | |
| Selected BUs/SUs | Identify target audiences |
| Account map | |
| Executive mapping | Relationship mapping: Buyers/ influencers |
| Value proposition | Targeted value proposition(s) |
| Goal and summary of objectives | Key business initiatives – plays |
| *Objective, strategy, and action plan* | *ABM campaign plan* |
| Resource summary and critical success factors | Programme operating model success criteria – metrics |

**Figure 11.7** Different ABM roles in the account

| CATALYST | INTEGRATOR | CO-CREATOR |
| --- | --- | --- |
| No account plan | Existing account plan | Account plan in process |
| • Seize the opportunity to provide value-add to the account team by using ABM | • Take the opportunity to integrate ABM and support/update the current plan | • Participate on the planning team |
| • Introduce the process as a way to map and drive engagement with key targets | • Provide hands-on support for specific account objectives | • Integrate ABM from the start as a key contributor |
| • Develop initiatives with key campaigns to directly assist the sales process | • Develop additional initiatives to round out the account plan and help drive the account to meet its revenue goals | • Be a partner on strategy and tactics |

- **Integrator.** When there is an existing account plan, you first need to gain access to it. This can be easier said than done. Alarm bells should ring if the account director is unwilling to share their plan. If they are embarrassed at the quality or age of their plan, that's easy to deal with once you've established that fact, since you're here to help them update and/ or improve it. If they simply don't see the point of sharing it with you, that indicates a broader unwillingness to collaborate. At this point, you need to re-educate the team on the benefits of ABM and/or escalate the problem to consider whether this account is the right one for you to be investing in. Assuming it is, your initial role is in integrating ABM with the current account plan, retrofitting it to complement what exists, and perhaps improving the existing plan where you can.

- **Co-creator.** If the account plan is currently being developed, you have the ability to make your mark on it as part of the planning team, integrating ABM from the start as a key contributor. You immediately set the tone for your ongoing relationship with the account team by co-developing both plans.

As you discuss your role on the account team with the account manager and your sales colleagues, you may want to make an informal contract with them so that they are clear on what they can expect from you and equally clear on what you expect from them. This can save a lot of heartache later on, when something starts to slip and one or more parties feel let down, since someone has failed to deliver on an unarticulated expectation held by another member of the team. This could be as simple as the account director being frustrated that you haven't delivered an e-book for their account in the way they've seen another ABM-er create one for another account (even if the account objectives mean that an e-book isn't the best tactic to use).

Some ABM-ers do this by creating 'service-level agreements' with their account team, covering response times, availability, typical assets that can be created, frequency of reporting, etc. Others have a contract document that lists the things they've agreed in an informal contracting meeting. You may wish to do neither, but just use your ABM plan as the contract between you. The important thing is to be aware of the need to surface any expectations and assumptions in the team about what you as an ABM-er will deliver, and be clear about the time and support you will need to execute the plan.

# Project management: making sure things get done

Skilled programme and project management are at the core of ABM success. A project is usually one initiative with a defined outcome while a programme is about managing a group of projects holistically, such as the various campaigns in your ABM plan.

Project management is now a sophisticated process built on well-accepted best practices. Programme management is a newer methodology, as the realization has grown that managing a group of related projects together can result in more than the sum of the parts in terms of both efficiency and effectiveness. Programme management focuses more on outcomes, which means the right governance is crucial to successful results, particularly since programmes can often include both internal and external players.

There are some basics for you to get in place before you execute your ABM plan with the account team and your sales colleagues. These should improve your chances of success:

- **Sponsor**. Good projects have a clear business sponsor who is ultimately responsible for delivering the project for the business. In the case of your ABM plan, this is likely to be the account manager or lead salesperson on the account. Agree with the sponsor how often they would like to be updated on progress on the account plan execution and in what format (eg by weekly e-mails, through a real-time KPI dashboard and perhaps by a quarterly face-to-face meeting with the steering group).

- **Steering group**. For much of your ABM execution the account team will be guiding your activities and reviewing their success with you to decide what to change, but they will not be delivering all of it. Usually, the account team is the steering group, possibly joined by business unit representatives, marketing management and other subject matter experts from around your company. This group is not responsible for delivering the plan, but for guiding those involved day-to-day in delivering it. You need to agree the format and regularity of steering group meetings and report to this group in the same way as you did with the sponsor.

- **Working group**. The working group consists of those individuals responsible for delivering the plan, including you as the ABM-er and the main salespeople and subject matter experts involved in taking your plays into the account. There may be multiple work streams in the plan that are owned by the working group, such as a major innovation workshop, or a campaign around a specific offer, and different people will be involved in different work streams. But each one will be led by someone on the working group, responsible for keeping the group updated on day-to-day progress and any issues arising. Once again, the working group needs to agree how often to meet. Someone should take responsibility for noting down the decisions made and actions agreed at each meeting, circulating these notes among the group and following up on the progress made on all actions.

- **Project plan**. Either contained within the overall account or ABM plan, or held separately as a spreadsheet document or more sophisticated project document, the project plan shows the sequence of activities you've agreed to do as a working group, who is responsible for each one and when major or minor milestones need to be hit. This is a live document that should be kept up to date as you execute your plan and learn from the success or failure of each action you take.

- **Communications.** Good projects rely on good communications. In addition to the face-to-face meetings you will schedule, you need to decide how you will communicate between these meetings and how you will share information on the account. There may be a shared folder or system that you all access and use for account documents, for example.

- **Performance metrics.** As a team, you should agree on the metrics you will use to track your performance and measure your success. You may have a wide range of metrics for the working group, tracking activity, outputs and outcomes, a subset for the steering group, tracking outputs and outcomes, and perhaps even fewer for the sponsor focused solely on business outcomes. The last one is likely to be responsible for delivering those outcomes to their business stakeholders, such as growth in revenues or profitability in the account. We'll discuss this further in Chapter 12.

The best project plans have a view of the key dependencies and risks that could impact the ability of the working group to deliver the project and thus the ultimate success of the project. It's worth thinking up front about the main dependencies (such as the budget and time you have available to deliver the ABM plan) and risks (your account gets acquired, your main stakeholders leave), to uncover any assumptions the team has made or likely events that others have not shared with you already.

## The marketer as facilitator

Marketers are noted for their skills in communications. They are usually very comfortable standing on a platform and getting their message across. But facilitating a group such as an account team is quite a different skill and one essential in ensuring that marketing and sales work together to fulfil your ABM objectives (see Figure 11.8).

A good definition of facilitation is: 'The art of bringing a group of people together to achieve effective learning and sharing, sometimes through self-discovery. In good facilitation the emphasis needs to be on both the acquiring and use of new knowledge, skills and abilities.'

With presentation, the focus is on the presenter and is centred on their knowledge. They are in control of the environment. With facilitation, on the

**Figure 11.8** Facilitation versus presenting

| A good **facilitator** | *versus* | A good **presenter** |
|---|---|---|
| • Focus is on the audience/ participants | | • Focus is on the presenter |
| • Creates and sustains interaction and a dynamic learning environment | | • Based on content and knowledge, expertise and delivery |
| • Fosters conversation and interaction | | • A presenter-controlled environment |
| • A shared-control environment | | • Interaction based solely on Q&A |

other hand, the emphasis is on interaction and dynamic brainstorming and learning as a group. It is a conversation and the focus is on the audience.

When you are facilitating a group like an account team there are a number of things to bear in mind:

- Make sure that everyone has the same understanding and buys in to the plan. You will need to 'sell' to the account team how integrating the campaign plan will help achieve the stated account objectives.

- Take note of what experience individuals bring and gather feedback from any interactions they have had with the account.

- Recognize that people sitting around the table could possibly have quite different motivations. While you might be thinking about client lifetime value on a three- to five-year view, the sales team will be thinking about chasing any opportunities.

# Agile working

Agility is becoming a much-prized attribute in marketing, particularly in getting a disparate group of people such as in an account team to execute plans effectively. If, for instance, something unexpected happens which has an impact on the account – interruption of service, for example – you will need to rethink the activities due for the account, perhaps delaying them or reshaping them so that they're appropriate given the service issue.

Learning good facilitation skills and the ability to keep projects and programmes on track are essential, as we've discussed. But increasingly, in today's fast-paced environment, these have to be accompanied by agility. We define agile marketing as improving the speed, predictability, transparency and adaptability to change in the marketing function. Success is gauged based on two key values: testing rather than opinions, and continuous experimentation rather than a few large bets.

We are seeing some organizations use methodologies from the software or manufacturing sectors, such as 'sprints', 'scrum', 'lean', 'Kanban' or 'Six Sigma'. Others adopt a more home-grown approach. But the benefits are felt relatively quickly. According to an ITSMA survey,[3] more cross-functional collaboration, more focus on the customer, and increased marketing productivity top the list of benefits (Figure 11.9) – all of which are ideal when you are executing your ABM plan.

**Figure 11.9**  Benefits of marketing agility

What are the primary benefits you have seen from your organization's efforts to increase marketing agility? % of respondents (N = 89)

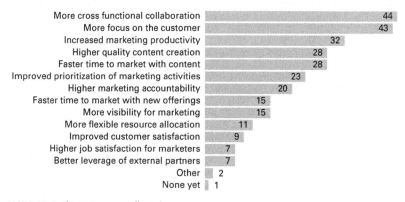

**NOTE** Up to three responses allowed
**SOURCE** ITSMA, Agility Survey, April 2016

# The politics of the account team

Every organization has a distinct political culture. Understanding what's going on can make a big difference to smooth plan execution. And yet few marketing or business courses actually teach you how to manage the politics of working in a large company or a senior team.

We recommend that you think about the two dimensions of power and sentiment for the internal stakeholders you are working with: how powerful is each member of the team, and what is their attitude to you and your ABM initiative? Ideally, you want the sponsor on board, supporting your initiative, since they will usually be the most powerful person involved (eg the business unit director or account manager for the account). But there

**Table 11.2** A simple power/sentiment matrix

|  | **Low power** | **High power** |
| --- | --- | --- |
| Positive sentiment | Keep informed of the progress of your ABM plan to maintain sentiment | Engage actively to create an advocate for your ABM plan |
| Neutral to negative sentiment | Monitor for potentially damaging comments and react quickly to limit damage | Communicate positive interim results on a regular basis to build positive sentiment |

may be other powerful players, such as an industry subject matter expert, or a heavy-hitting salesperson, who could derail the execution of your plan if you don't keep them onside.

Most people use a simple two-by-two matrix to map their stakeholders and decide what approach to take for those in each quadrant to keep the ABM plan on track (Table 11.2).

It's worth drawing this up immediately when you start to engage with the account team, and updating it regularly as your relationships evolve and your plan gets underway. One final tip: don't keep it in the office where others could stumble across it!

# Your ABM checklist

1 Regardless of how impressive your ABM plan for an account is, remember that it is just a piece of paper until you execute it.

2 In strategic ABM, one of the biggest challenges marketers face is getting the buy-in of sales.

3 Sales and marketing alignment encompasses a number of aspects: the skills of the account manager and the ABM-er, and the ABM process that they need to work through together.

4 ABM should be fully integrated with the account planning process, with the ABM-er a member of the account team and roles, responsibilities, and processes for creating and executing the integrated plan understood by all.

5 The role of the ABM-er on the account varies according to whether a good account plan already exists.

**6** Good project management will be needed to execute the ABM plan with sales, along with facilitation skills. It's not enough just to be a good communicator or presenter.

**7** Agile working techniques help to drive collaboration, increase the focus on the client and make the team more productive.

**8** As an ABM-er, you need to be aware of the political influence of the account team and wider stakeholders you are working with to get your plan executed, in addition to the extent to which they support your ABM initiative.

## Notes

**1, 2** ITSMA (2016) *Account-Based Marketing Benchmarking Survey*

**3**    ITSMA (2016) *Accelerating the Move to Agile Marketing*

# Evaluating results and updating plans

# 12

## Measuring the returns of ABM

As we have stressed throughout this book, ABM generates the highest ROI of any B2B marketing approach. This conclusion is based on ITSMA's extensive research on the subject over the last decade, including quantitative surveys, qualitative interviews, first-hand experience, annual marketing excellence award submissions and in-depth work with our members and clients.

But, if ABM really does deliver such consistently high returns, why isn't everyone doing it? And why aren't those who are using ABM doing more of it? The answers to these questions lie as much in how marketing organizations set expectations and communicate the impact of their ABM programmes, as they do in any of the practical challenges in implementing ABM. This is about measuring and communicating the results you're getting from your ABM investment, both at an individual account level and across your whole ABM programme, to ensure continued support and investment from the business.

There are three fundamental challenges that all marketing organizations face in delivering and demonstrating the powerful returns that ABM can generate. First, marketing must accurately measure and evaluate the ROI of ABM programmes, which is not always as straightforward a task as it might seem.

Second, marketing leaders must establish a point of comparison to other marketing programmes. It is often easier to determine the ROI of ABM than of anything else.

Finally, and perhaps most importantly, any organization undertaking ABM must set realistic timeline expectations with all stakeholders in order to achieve results. This is particularly important given that there is pressure in many organizations, typically from sales, for short-term results. The request to 'generate more qualified leads this quarter' is a familiar one.

Remember, ABM is not a short-term lead-generation approach. It is a strategic initiative that requires sustained investment to deliver maximum results. Organizations that position ABM as a company-wide strategic business initiative, rather than as a marketing initiative, are more likely to generate higher returns from ABM than from other marketing programmes and to be measuring the returns on their programmes in the first place.

# A word on ROI in marketing

It's worth considering a few of the logical challenges inherent in discussing return on investment in the context of marketing.

First and foremost, ROI is a finance calculation that measures the real or expected gains from a *capital investment*. But in finance terms just about everything marketing does is an *expense*. Does that mean we shouldn't consider the work we do in marketing as an investment? On the contrary, companies that 'get it' do consider marketing an investment. But it is important to remember the risks and limitations that emerge when we try to apply ROI calculations outside of their natural habitat.

Additionally, ROI is calculated for a defined period. Any ROI calculation will vary depending on the period over which it is measured. So if you are a widget company investing in a fancy new widget press, the return that you might expect on that investment will be different if you calculate it after six months, two years or five years. ROI does not stand on its own: it must be tied to a specific interval.

Finally, the point of calculating ROI is to evaluate multiple possible investments of the same size over a specific period to decide on the best one to pursue. In a world where there is no such thing as limitless resources, this is an important way to make trade-off decisions. It is sensible, then, that ROI measures are also used to evaluate the performance of an investment over a given period – presumably the one that was used to justify it in the first place.

The challenge we often have in assessing marketing programmes is that we fail to specify the period over which we are evaluating the performance of a specific investment. To make matters worse, we often try to compare the ROI of different scales of spending over different periods. This sets the scene for the all-too-common, typically fruitless debates on long-term ABM programmes versus short-term lead-generation campaigns.

That doesn't mean we should abandon use of ROI in marketing. Rather, ABM marketers must shape ROI discussions, in particular those related to ABM, to focus on measures and time frames that make sense for the objectives defined.

# Finding the right metrics and defining the time frames

If ROI is the main criterion for determining marketing priorities, it should be an easy decision to invest in ABM. But experience shows it isn't. Why? For one thing, ABM is a resource-intensive activity, but many marketing organizations have headcount limits. For another, the time required just to break even on your marketing investment is longer than with other marketing initiatives in general.

And, as we've already seen in Part One of this book, although nearly three-quarters of organizations that already had ABM programmes in 2015 were increasing their investment in them in 2016, the most significant challenge continues to be getting adequate budget to support programmes and resources.[1] There is a paradox here, in that the primary driver for scaling ABM is coming from the business as a consequence of the results that ABM programmes are delivering, and yet ABM programme leaders still face the challenge of getting enough budget to respond to demand.

Most marketing campaigns have a short time horizon and concrete objectives. They're designed to drive demand for specific services or solutions, to generate qualified leads and, typically, to show results in 30–90 days.

ABM programmes have a longer time horizon and the exact opportunities to generate revenue aren't always clear when you start. You may need to change perception or positioning within your account and increase awareness and understanding of the breadth of your offerings and strategy before results in terms of significant opportunities and growth in revenues start to come in.

Research shows that there is a correlation between the length of time ABM has been implemented and the proportion of companies achieving a higher ROI with it than with other initiatives. The bottom line is that companies that have had ABM programmes running for more than one year are twice as likely to reap the benefits of higher ROI. They are also more likely to achieve better results on key objectives, such as pursuing specific, identified sales opportunities.

The longer an ABM programme has been running, the more likely it is to generate higher ROI than other marketing programmes. But how can you justify the ongoing investments in an ABM programme to ensure that it is in place long enough to deliver results? This comes down to laying the appropriate groundwork with the stakeholders in sales and the business units and in defining a set of metrics that work at each account level and that expand as the ABM programme matures.

First, let's look at the metrics.

# Objectives and metrics

ABM metrics should cover three categories:

- relationships, which indicate deeper penetration within accounts;
- reputation, which may include perception and/or educating accounts on your offerings or capabilities;
- revenues, including pipeline as well as specific, identified sales opportunities.

Clearly, the metrics you choose to evaluate the success of your ABM initiatives should link directly back to the objectives you set for the programme as a whole and the individual objectives set for each account in the programme. Any ABM programme should regularly track performance on individual accounts and at a programme level.

Although the metrics used for account-level and programme-level evaluation may be the same, they tend to vary in importance across accounts. Hard metrics, like pipeline growth, total revenue tied to ABM initiatives, and revenue growth are among the most important programme metrics. Most of the programme metrics tend to be lagging indicators, that is, measurement of results achieved.

Account metrics usually also include a number of soft metrics, or leading indicators of ABM performance. These are things like number of new executive relationships within the account, number of executive meetings, number of new relationships in new lines of business, and quality of relationships. These metrics are predictors of future success, particularly where ABM has not been in place long enough to deliver concrete financial results.

## *Most common metrics in the three types of ABM*

In the ITSMA survey in 2016[2] respondents were asked which five metrics were most important to measure the success of their strategic ABM programme (see Figure 12.1). The most popular metric was pipeline growth, or growth in the size of the sales funnel, mentioned by over two-thirds of marketers. Next came revenue growth, mentioned by just over half. Around

**Figure 12.1**    Most important Strategic ABM metrics

Which five metrics are most important to measure the success of your overall Strategic ABM programme? % of respondents (N = 47)

| | |
|---|---|
| Pipeline growth (increase in sales funnel) | 1 — 68 |
| Revenue growth | 2 — 57 |
| Sales rep feedback/account team satisfaction | 3 — 34 |
| Engagement: event attendance, campaign response rates, number of meetings, e-mail opt-ins, etc | 3 — 34 |
| Customer loyalty/satisfaction: Net Promoter, referenceability of account, etc | 4 — 32 |
| Win rate/number of deals closed | 5 — 26 |
| Total revenue tied directly to ABM initiatives | 5 — 26 |
| Customer brand perception, awareness, and knowledge | 23 |
| Return on the ABM account investment (ROI) | 23 |
| Portfolio penetration, cross-sell/upsell | 19 |

**NOTE** Up to five responses allowed
**SOURCE** ITSMA, Account Based-Marketing Benchmarking Survey, March 2016

one-third of marketers mentioned account team satisfaction, engagement with the client and customer loyalty or satisfaction.

The same question was asked about metrics used for ABM Lite. The first two most popular responses were the same – pipeline and revenue growth – with roughly the same proportion of marketers using them. After this, however, the picture changes somewhat, with a third of marketers saying that the win rate or number of deals closed is the third most important metric in ABM Lite (Figure 12.2).

Next comes account team feedback, as in strategic ABM, but it is ranked equal with another new metric, the total revenue tied directly to ABM initiatives. These two 'new' metrics in ABM Lite reflect the fact that more scale is achieved through this type of ABM. This means that changes in win rates can be more meaningfully tracked across a wider sample of accounts, as can revenue tied directly to ABM initiatives (although this is much harder to track with confidence even in Lite, because of the close alignment between marketing and sales).

Finally, the top two responses from those using programmatic ABM are the same as the other two types of ABM, but with just over half of marketers quoting them this time (Figure 12.3). Then come two tied metrics, both with 41 per cent of marketers using them: client engagement, which appears in strategic ABM, and total revenue tied directly to ABM initiatives, which

**Figure 12.2**   Most important ABM Lite metrics

Which five metrics are most important to measure the success of your overall ABM Lite programme? % of respondents (N=45)

NOTE  Up to five responses allowed
SOURCE  ITSMA, Account-Based Marketing Benchmarking Survey, March 2016

**Figure 12.3**   Most important Programmatic ABM metrics

Which five metrics are most important to measure the success of your overall Programmatic ABM programme? % of respondents (N = 29)

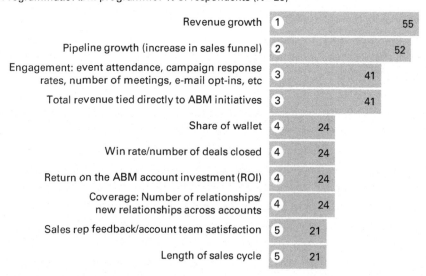

NOTE  Up to five responses allowed
SOURCE  ITSMA, Account-Based Marketing Benchmarking Survey, March 2016

also appears in ABM Lite. Tied for fourth place come four different metrics each used by just under a quarter of programmatic ABM marketers: share of wallet, win rate, ROI and number of relationships or new relationships across the accounts.

So, the type of metrics used varies somewhat by flavour of ABM. The number of metrics used also varies, from company to company, with an average of 10 metrics applied to individual accounts to evaluate ABM results.

The specific metrics often vary from account to account, reflecting the account objectives and maturity of the ABM programme within individual accounts. Those accounts that have been part of the ABM programme for some time will likely have metrics that span all three areas of relationships, reputation and revenues. Table 12.1 shows an illustrative ABM dashboard, showing some commonly-used metrics for evaluating ABM results grouped into these three categories.

**Table 12.1**   An illustrative ABM metrics dashboard

| KPI dashboard | Relationships | Revenue | Reputation |
|---|---|---|---|
| ABM pilot programme | • Coverage: number of relationships across accounts; new executive contacts<br>• Engagement: event attendance, campaign response rates, number of meetings<br>• Strength of existing relationships – negative/neutral/positive | • Pipeline growth<br>• Revenue growth<br>• Deal size/type<br>• Portfolio penetration<br>• Total revenue tied to ABM activities<br>• Share of wallet<br>• Win rate | • Sales/account team satisfaction<br>• NPS<br>• Brand perception<br>• Success story reference/ advocate |

# Demonstrating interim success

Since it typically takes about one year to generate significant business results in an account through ABM, we recommend defining a slightly different set of metrics for the short, medium and long term, especially if you are in a quarterly-driven business. Tailoring the metrics according to the maturity of the ABM programme – and its application to individual accounts – allows you to report on the progress of ABM as frequently as necessary (surveys show that nearly half of companies report on this quarterly) and still demonstrate results.

What's the best way to define a broad enough set of objectives to be able to track and report ABM success in the short to long term? Look beyond just the revenue-related goals (the lagging indicators of success) and be sure to measure the impact your ABM programme is having on relationships and reputation as well, as we've already recommended. The important thing is that the impact of these results increases with the duration of the ABM programme in individual accounts.

ITSMA has developed a simple model (Table 12.2) to define the appropriate set of metrics for accounts and programmes based on their maturity. It frames short-term, medium-term and long-term metrics across relationships, reputation, and revenues. Use this model, along with the range of common metrics from Figures 12.1–12.3, to establish the metrics by which you will evaluate individual accounts and your overall programme.

**Table 12.2**    Illustrative ABM metrics across time frames

|  | Short term (6 months) | Medium term (9–12 months) | Long term (18+ months) |
|---|---|---|---|
| Relationship | X new contacts<br>Stronger relationships with Y executives | X new contacts<br>Stronger relationships with Y executives<br>Z now a public advocate | X new contacts<br>Stronger relationships with Y executives<br>Z now a public advocate<br>Joint corporate social responsibility (CSR) programme in place |
| Reputation | N/A | X% familiarity/ preference<br>Y% NPS<br>Z% client satisfaction score | X% familiarity/ preference<br>Y% NPS<br>Z% client satisfaction score |
| Revenue | N/A | £Xm pipeline<br>Y win rate<br>Z revenue | £Xm pipeline<br>Y win rate<br>Z revenue |

# Using metrics in the account team

Regularly tracking the performance of your ABM campaigns against the objectives you've set with your account team is about more than just maintaining momentum and support. It's about keeping track of what is and isn't working so that you can adapt your approach as you go along. This is a key part of agile working methods, mentioned in the previous chapter, and something that is increasingly enabled through marketing technology.

Wherever possible, keep track of how clients in the account are responding to your sales and marketing initiatives: which messages are landing well, what content they are engaging with, which communications channels they use to contact you. Add this to your insight on the stakeholders and influencers that matter and continue to personalize your approach based on their preferences. Use the evidence you gather to justify any recommended changes in approach you want to make while the campaign is in flight, to reassure the account team that your decisions are insight-led.

# Using metrics with business leaders

The most important measure of success for any ABM programme is the amount of business that it contributes. A close second is how much it costs to generate that business contribution. But focusing on these criteria alone overlooks the critical aspects of *how* ABM delivers those results. Only by including the appropriate metrics for wider relationship development and reputation improvement (or perception change) will you be able to determine how well an ABM initiative is progressing. Indeed, these metrics, soft though they are, help to identify the concrete ways in which ABM generates opportunities and wins.

This brings us back to the starting point. To justify ongoing investments in ABM, you must not only be able to demonstrate interim success but also position the importance of those interim results with all of the programme's key stakeholders from the outset (see Microsoft case study overleaf). A key part of positioning ABM is to educate executives in the business units and sales teams on how ABM works. If they understand this, they are far more likely to buy into the validity of metrics that offer leading indicators of ABM success. Once everyone is on the same page, it is much easier to build consensus on the efficacy of ABM, even before programmes are mature enough to deliver measurable financial results.

The proof of ABM's success is in the numbers: it consistently delivers some of the highest ROI of any B2B marketing strategy. The compelling story is there. It just has to be communicated.

**CASE STUDY**   Microsoft – Making the case to scale up with ABM
                 metrics

It's often easier to start an initiative than to scale it up. In *Crossing the Chasm*[3] Geoffrey Moore argued that the most difficult step in marketing IT products was bridging the chasm between early adopters and the early majority. The same holds for internal programmes: even when pilots succeed, changing behaviour en masse requires proof of value. And when it comes to proof of value, the Holy Grail is a set of metrics that capture the programme's impact and link it to business results.

Microsoft was no newcomer to account-based marketing (ABM), called key account marketing or KAM internally. 'In 2009, the US Enterprise and Partner Group (EPG) began to invest in KAM to deepen relationships with existing customers, foster loyalty and build partnerships based on mutual trust,' recalled Nicole Summitt, senior marketing manager of US Relationship Marketing at Microsoft.

> Seven senior marketers worked with sales to invest in custom and scalable programs that would supplement the traditional event-oriented, product-focused, 'Microsoft-out' marketing agenda; understand and address each customer's unique business issues; and turn customers into advocates.

The goal was to create greater insight among customers and account teams so that both became more self-sustaining, with awareness of offerings, established communication channels in place, stronger contact databases, and an understanding of how to engage available Microsoft resources.

Then came the chasm. Feedback on the pilot was positive. The customers and sales leads involved in the pilot embraced the programme. The participating account team leaders were on board. But without quantified measures of the programme's effectiveness and return on investment (ROI), marketing could not justify the investment needed to roll out the programme beyond the pilot to new accounts. According to Summitt: 'To get the promise of continued funding, we had to demonstrate and quantify the KAM programme's contributions to Microsoft sales teams.'

The solution lay in a classic experimental design: treatment group, control group, measurement of results. (James Lind, a Scottish surgeon in the Royal Navy, created it in 1747 when he gave his treatment group oranges and lemons and watched their scurvy vanish.) At Microsoft, the pilot account supported by KAM comprised the treatment group. The control group was the broader group of all other US EPG accounts. The metrics came from both outside (scores on Microsoft's Enterprise Customer Satisfaction survey) and inside (scores on the internal Key Account Marketing survey).

### Metrics for the ABM programme

There are four steps to creating a metric. First, figure out what you want to happen. Second, decide what drives it. Third, separate out what people can control. Finally, devise a measure – something that can be counted – making sure that it's controllable and linked to results:

- **Figure out what you want to happen.** The sales team wanted to speed up existing buying cycles as well as identify new opportunities, take a bigger share of wallet and build stronger and deeper relationships.
- **What drives it?** In a word, engagement. Or, more specifically, customer conversations that are frequent, deep, and aligned with clients' needs.
- **What can people control?** Most aspects of the customer's business are outside the control of the sales team. But communication is well within anyone's control. It's reaching out, conveying useful information, and building relationships.
- **Devise a measure.** Microsoft's metrics were focused on customer-directed activity (number of touches, growth in new contacts) as well as the satisfaction of the account teams and customers. Both categories showed increases under the KAM programme. Note that these metrics related to process (what you do every day) rather than outcomes (new sales).

This is the central lesson of the *Moneyball* phenomenon. (*Moneyball: The Art of Winning an Unfair Game* by Michael Lewis was published in 2003 and adapted as a film in 2011. It told the story of how the manager of a struggling baseball team successfully used a particular analytical approach in assembling a competitive baseball team.)[4]

The key metric in *Moneyball* wasn't wins – it was runs. At an even more fundamental level, it was how often a player got on base. Sales are the equivalent of wins. Getting on base is akin to touches. Both can be measured, but touches are under the salesperson's direct control, can be done every day and ultimately lead to the more visible results of higher revenue, a shorter sales cycle, and more single-source contracts.

When the KAM accounts were compared to the traditionally managed accounts, KAM figures exceeded the national averages in every category. While often the difference wasn't large, there was consistency across all categories.

### Account team metrics

In addition to results from the annual Microsoft Enterprise Customer Satisfaction Survey, the KAM programme annually surveys Microsoft's US account teams to gauge progress against objectives. For example, the 2012 survey resulted in 136 responses representing 65 key accounts. Highlights included:

- **A record number of responses.** In FY2010 34 account team members responded. In FY2011 the number of responses had grown to 101, and in FY2012 the number had increased to 136.
- **Account teams liked both the KAM programme and the people who managed it.** Of the 136 responses, all but four said they were 'very satisfied' with the programme, and two of the 'satisfied' responses were outliers; other members of their teams said that they were 'very satisfied.' Respondents also liked the KAM managers: all but two said they were 'very satisfied,' and the other two were 'satisfied.'
- **New accomplishments.** The survey asked whether the account team had achieved things that would not have been possible without KAM support. Of the total, 98 per cent (133) said yes; three didn't answer the question.
- **Improvements.** Three-quarters said that they were happy or wanted more, with many of these respondents suggesting multiple improvements, while 42 said no changes were necessary – they were happy with KAM in its present form.
- **What customers thought.** When asked for 'insights into your customer's feedback/response', account teams were positive to the tune of 95 per cent (130) responses. The other six included three blanks, one NA, one yes, and one neutral comment.
- **Account executives valued KAM managers for strategic rather than tactical support.** When asked 'What are your top three critical success factors for key account marketing this fiscal year?' three of the top four responses reflected the more strategic areas of:
  - creating new/deepening existing/improving relationships (114);
  - delivering custom marketing activities (68);
  - providing a platform for MS thought leadership/improved perception (56).
- **Account teams were happy with the KAM programme and wanted more.** Of the 144 responses (some had multiple suggestions), almost half (66) wanted more from the KAM programme, including additional:
  - funding/resources for KAM managers (35);
  - time from KAM manager or fewer accounts per KAM manager (20);
  - KAM managers/expand the programme (11).

**The outcome**

As a result of measuring the KAM programme's impact and demonstrating its success, the programme gained approval of its recommendations for FY2013, including commitments to:

- invest in KAM support for two to five years, based on account size, complexity, maturity, and ability to sustain impact (the previous level was two to three years);
- Continue and/or enhance existing KAM offerings and launch new KAM services, including:
  - customized industry content;
  - reporting dashboards;
  - a contact management strategy;
  - coordination of speaking opportunities;
  - special treatment at onsite and on-campus briefings;
  - a speaker bureau and opportunity sponsors.

The new commitment enabled KAM-supported accounts to move to self-sufficiency, with the resources necessary to maintain and deliver at least a subset of KAM services after graduation from the KAM programme.

**Lessons learned**

- When pursuing a pilot, pick account teams with track records of working closely with marketing as a strategic partner rather than a tactical appendage.
- Screen customer accounts to ensure that they are:
  - ready for a deeper, longer-term relationship (satisfied but underdeveloped);
  - open to marketing managers learning more about them;
  - candidates for buying more.
- Scour the organization for existing metrics that can be used to compare the pilot with the broader universe of accounts.
- Customer quotes are invaluable. Although the focus should be on quantifiable metrics, verbatim comments from major customers add colour and impact. If the customers were well chosen at the start, there should be names that internal decision makers know and respect.
- Track the differences, refine your approach if necessary, and use the results to demonstrate proof of value and gain credibility when presenting recommendations for improvements and updates.

## Your ABM checklist

**1** This is about measuring and communicating the results you're getting from your ABM investment, both at an individual level and across your whole ABM programme, to ensure continued support and investment from the business.

**2** ABM marketers must shape ROI discussions, in particular those related to ABM, to focus on measures and time frames that make sense for the objectives defined.

**3** The longer an ABM programme has been running, the more likely it is to generate higher ROI than other marketing programmes.

**4** ABM metrics should track improvements in three categories: relationships, reputation and revenue.

**5** Since it typically takes about one year to generate significant business results in an account through ABM, we recommend defining a slightly different set of metrics for the short, medium, and long term.

**6** Regularly tracking the performance of your ABM campaigns will allow you to adapt as you go along to what is working, increasingly personalizing your marketing to your clients' preferences.

**7** A key part of positioning ABM is to educate executives in the business units and sales teams on how ABM works. If they understand this, they are far more likely to buy into the validity of metrics that offer leading indicators of ABM success.

## Notes

**1, 2** ITSMA (2016) *Account-Based Marketing Benchmarking Survey*

**3**    Moore, GA (1991) *Crossing the Chasm: Marketing and selling disruptive products to mainstream customers*, Harper Business Essentials

**4**    Lewis, M (2003) *Moneyball: The art of winning an unfair game*, WW Norton & Company

# PART THREE
# Developing your career as an account-based marketer

## Introduction to Part Three

The final part of this book is about how you get started and progress in your career as an ABM-er. People come from a number of different roles into ABM, drawing on technical marketing skills and personal attributes to be successful in the job. We will look at the competencies you need for ABM in Chapter 13, using the model that ITSMA built with members of its Global ABM Council. The proprietary ABM competency assessment based on this model is now used by companies to baseline the skills of their ABM team, to benchmark against ABM teams in other companies, and to prioritize areas for development.

This model spans the technical marketing competencies you would expect, including intelligence gathering, relationship marketing, value proposition development and marketing communications, together with business competencies such as work style, business acumen, leadership and cross-organizational collaboration.

Since ABM-ers by nature tend to be marketing generalists, it's common to work with specialists within the broader marketing function in your company, as well as with outside agencies and suppliers, to get the job done. Chapter 13 also takes a look at the agencies you might need to work with and how to brief and manage them effectively.

Finally, in Chapter 14, we look at how to manage your career as an ABM-er and where it might take you. Based on conversations with seven leading ABM practitioners, this chapter gives insights into the challenges you will face and how to overcome them. It looks at the typical career path, if there is one, open to someone with ABM experience. And it offers tips for you from the people who have 'been there, done that, and lived to tell the tale'. These are inspirational ABM-ers. We hope you enjoy meeting them.

# The competencies you need to do account-based marketing

13

## Your objectives

Being an account-based marketer is one of the most challenging, and at the same time most rewarding, marketing roles you can have. Challenging because, as this chapter will demonstrate, the skills and capabilities you need to do ABM successfully stretch far beyond perceived traditional, technical marketing competencies. Rewarding, because when you are at the top of your game, you have the satisfaction of adding real value to your organization and to your clients.

Let's look at that in a bit more detail. ABM-ers have two main objectives. The first is to increase your company's opportunity to build business with strategic accounts by strengthening relationships, building reputation and developing new and supporting business opportunities to help grow pipeline and revenue.

Secondly, and equally critically, is to deliver measurable value by providing a strategic marketing service that coordinates people across the company to deliver joined-up programmes at an account level. This involves the ability to collaborate, network and lead, since the account-based marketer provides insights for the development of the business strategy, creates the account-based marketing strategy working with the account team, and ensures the delivery of the marketing programmes and plans aligned to the account objectives.

Dr Charles Doyle, who has written the Foreword to this book and who appears in both Chapters 1 and 14, takes this idea of delivering value to the business even further. Just as strategic marketing adds significantly to the capitalization of a company by building shareholder value through intangibles such as brand and goodwill (strong client relationships), account-based marketers can add significantly to the long-term value of an account.

They do this by capturing a greater share of 'mind' in the account – such that stakeholders will choose your company before any other – and stronger relationships, providing the ideas that spark new conversations and the opportunities to meet and have those conversations.

## Your responsibilities

An ABM-er's life is never dull, as your responsibilities are wide-ranging. They include:

- forming a close working relationship with the account managers and their teams, as well as key members of sales and marketing;
- managing the ABM strategy locally, leveraging the thinking and approach from the group ABM programme as well as assets from other marketing groups;
- understanding account management and sales processes, the objectives of the account team and supporting their account strategy with marketing programmes that achieve their goals and grow their business;
- analysing the account and providing insight and interpretation of the current and potential future market environment facing stakeholders within it;
- developing and owning the ABM strategy, including identifying marketing tactics to provide proactive, structured, long-term support for the account objectives;
- working with the wider marketing function and external specialist agencies where required to deliver integrated sales and marketing campaigns;
- sharing local best practice and innovation with wider marketing and sales communities;
- tracking, measuring, and reporting on all ABM activity based on account KPIs and successes.

# The competencies you need

Finding the right people for this complex role, which sits at the boundary between marketing, sales and the client, has been a major preoccupation for the growing number of organizations that have embraced its tenets. This is why, a few years ago, ITSMA decided to work with its members, and especially those represented on its Global ABM Council, to define the competencies in more detail.

Not only would this help those looking to hire or promote people into the role, offering suggestions for role and person specifications and terms to use in competency-based interviewing, but it could also be used to assess the competency of those already in ABM roles and identify gaps where more professional development was needed to support them.

Since the ABM competency model and assessment was defined, around 100 ABM-ers have rated their own skills and capabilities against those a top-performing ABM-er should possess (Figure 13.1). As you can see, this is a powerful combination of both technical marketing competencies and the business skills needed to work as part of the account team to get the job done.

Looking at the responses of ABM-ers under each heading gives a clearer picture of the strengths of our sample of marketers currently working in ABM around the world and the areas where improvements could be made. But before we step into that, let's explore where ABM-ers tend to come from.

**Figure 13.1**   ITSMA's ABM competency model

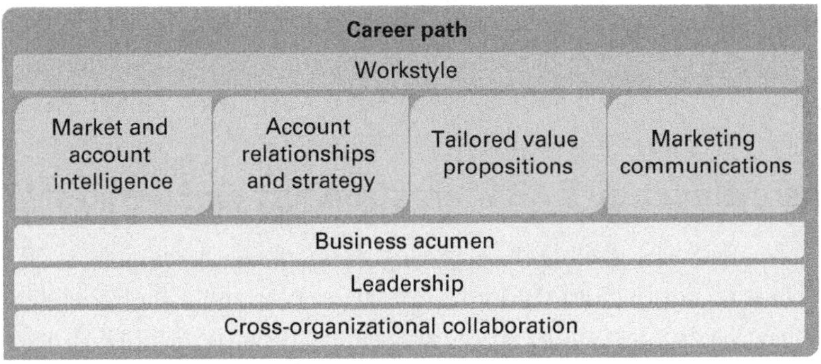

| Career path |
| --- |
| Workstyle |

| Market and account intelligence | Account relationships and strategy | Tailored value propositions | Marketing communications |
| --- | --- | --- | --- |

| Business acumen |
| --- |
| Leadership |
| Cross-organizational collaboration |

SOURCE © 2017 ITSMA

## Career path into ABM

First, as Figure 13.2 shows, the most common routes into ABM, apart from a previous account-based marketing role, are from field marketing, event

**Figure 13.2**   Career paths into ABM

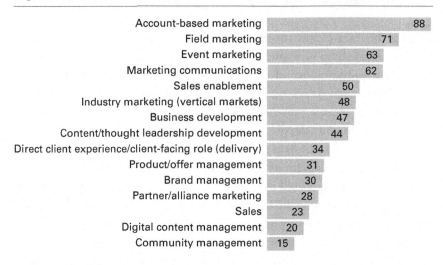

| | |
|---|---|
| Account-based marketing | 88 |
| Field marketing | 71 |
| Event marketing | 63 |
| Marketing communications | 62 |
| Sales enablement | 50 |
| Industry marketing (vertical markets) | 48 |
| Business development | 47 |
| Content/thought leadership development | 44 |
| Direct client experience/client-facing role (delivery) | 34 |
| Product/offer management | 31 |
| Brand management | 30 |
| Partner/alliance marketing | 28 |
| Sales | 23 |
| Digital content management | 20 |
| Community management | 15 |

**NOTE**  % of Respondents (N=108); Multiple responses allowed
**SOURCE**  ITSMA, ABM Marketer Competency Assessment, 2016

marketing or marketing communications. A background in field marketing is not surprising, since marketers in a field role are often closest to both clients and the sales team. In fact, many ABM pilot initiatives stem from field marketing organizations in a particular country or region who decide that a large, complex account should be treated as a market in its own right, given its potential to build the local business.

Half of ABM-ers have done sales enablement roles in the past, while a good proportion have held sales, business development or client delivery roles. This is good news, as it means that these ABM-ers will have a good understanding of the sales process and how to integrate marketing into it in ABM campaigns.

## *Where are today's ABM-ers strongest and weakest?*

When we look across all of the competencies in the model (Figure 13.3), the first thing to note is that ABM-ers are fairly upbeat about the competencies they have, with most mean scores at least a 4.0 out of 5.0. ABM marketers currently rate themselves highest in work style and cross-organizational collaboration. By contrast, the lowest mean scores across the ABM community are in the account relationship and strategy category. Next lowest is in business acumen and market and account intelligence. Both of these, while hitting a mean score of 4.0 out of 5.0, could be improved. In the middle

**Figure 13.3**    The competence of ABM marketers today

| | Mean Rating |
|---|---|
| Work style | 4.3 |
| Cross-organizational collaboration | 4.3 |
| Marketing communications | 4.2 |
| Leadership | 4.2 |
| Tailored value propositions | 4.1 |
| Market and account intelligence | 4.0 |
| Business acumen | 4.0 |
| Account relationships and strategy | 3.9 |

1
Don't Do This
But Should

Mean Rating

5
An Expert/Master
in this Area

**NOTE** Mean Rating (N=108); Mean ratings based on a 5-point scale in which 1=Don't do this but should and 5=An expert/master in this area

**SOURCE** ITSMA, ABM Marketer Competency Assessment, 2016

of the range of scores sit the marketing communications, leadership and tailored value proposition categories.

The real power of the model comes when you look below the category levels into the individual competencies. But, before we explore each of these categories in more detail, think about how you would rate yourself on these different competencies as you read through this section. It will help you to plan your own self-development. But don't panic if you're not good at everything. No one is! That's why you work in a team or community of ABM-ers and wider marketing specialists, so that you can draw on the skills of your colleagues to complement your own skills when you need to.

## Work style

Looking at the profile of an ABM-er based on the mean scores in this category is inspirational (Figure 13.4). It reveals a group of people with a passion for serving both the client and their own company, who prefer to look at the big picture and tackle strategic issues and with the persistence to stick with a programme and see it through to the end. They take the initiative to develop new knowledge and processes and don't rely on a manager for everything.

These are optimistic multitaskers who are analytical, building actionable insight from industry, competitor and account research. These are typically entrepreneurial people who fit in well with the action-focused environment

**Figure 13.4** ABM work style competencies

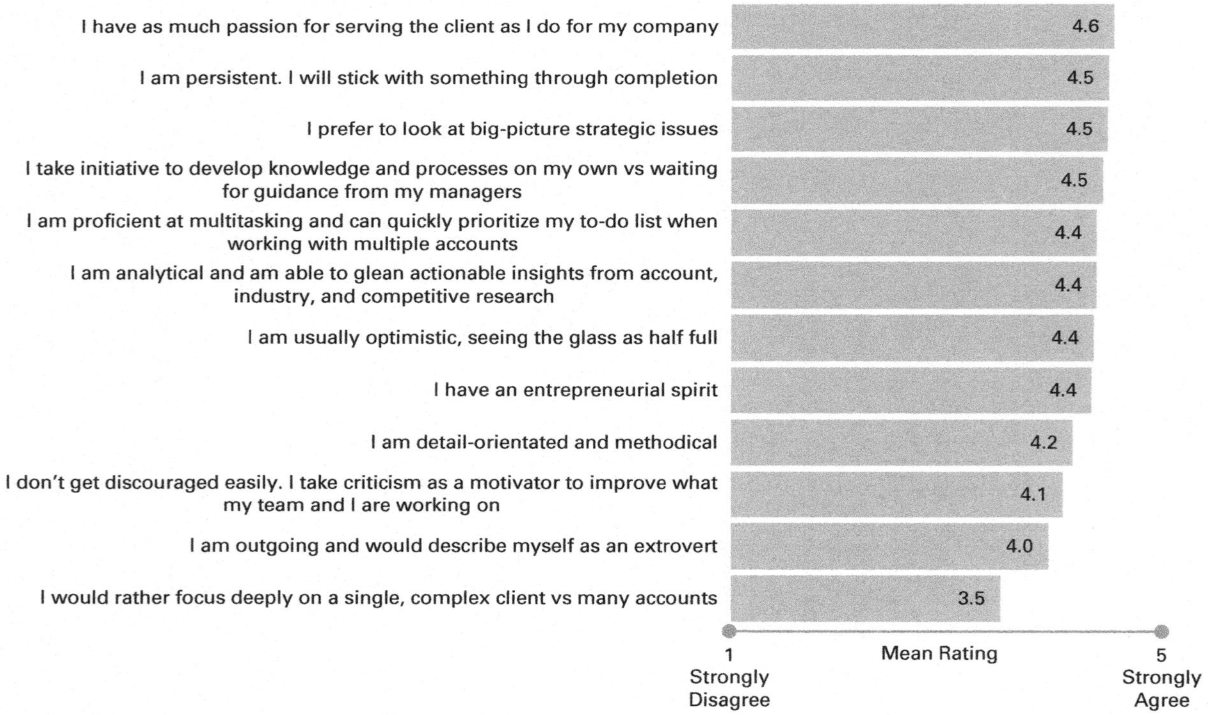

| Competency | Mean Rating |
|---|---|
| I have as much passion for serving the client as I do for my company | 4.6 |
| I am persistent. I will stick with something through completion | 4.5 |
| I prefer to look at big-picture strategic issues | 4.5 |
| I take initiative to develop knowledge and processes on my own vs waiting for guidance from my managers | 4.5 |
| I am proficient at multitasking and can quickly prioritize my to-do list when working with multiple accounts | 4.4 |
| I am analytical and am able to glean actionable insights from account, industry, and competitive research | 4.4 |
| I am usually optimistic, seeing the glass as half full | 4.4 |
| I have an entrepreneurial spirit | 4.4 |
| I am detail-orientated and methodical | 4.2 |
| I don't get discouraged easily. I take criticism as a motivator to improve what my team and I are working on | 4.1 |
| I am outgoing and would describe myself as an extrovert | 4.0 |
| I would rather focus deeply on a single, complex client vs many accounts | 3.5 |

Scale: 1 = Strongly Disagree, 5 = Strongly Agree (Mean Rating)

**NOTE** % of respondents (N=108); Mean ratings based on a 5-point scale in which 1=Strongly disagree and 5=Strongly agree
**SOURCE** ITSMA, ABM Marketer Competency Assessment, 2016

often found in an account team. This blend of attributes reflects both the character and the typical seniority of ABM-ers in roles today.

The lowest scoring competence in this category is 'I prefer to focus deeply on one complex account rather than work across many accounts'. With a mean score of 3.5 out of 5.0, this reflects the fact that many marketers need variety. But a large complex account often encompasses business divisions that are so varied that it feels as though you are working across a number of accounts anyway (as anyone who has built an ABM plan for a global bank or oil and gas company will testify).

## Market and account intelligence

As one of the core technical marketing competencies in ABM, the high scores in this category emphasize the priority ABM-ers place on doing in-depth research into both markets and the individual account. They then ensure that any useful insights are spread to other parts of the ABM team, particularly sales.

ABM-ers use data from analysis, third-party researchers and other outside sources to understand their account's business issues and the economic, industry and market trends impacting the account. They are continuously updating their insights based on these dynamic trends and the implications for their account of any changes in the external environment.

ABM-ers are sharing these insights with their sales colleagues to uncover new opportunities for growth in the account and to develop more targeted presentations and proposals that resonate with key stakeholders in the account.

The only worrying indicator in this category is that lower scores for understanding how clients buy and allocate budgets should be higher. Chapter 8 discusses the importance of understanding the customers' decision-making unit and creating buyer personas in more detail. This is becoming far more important as procurement becomes an increasingly sophisticated process across large accounts around the world. ITSMA's buyer research over the years has tracked a steady shift to seeing more people being involved in complex, high-consideration business purchases, decisions taking longer, and increasing use of third-party advisors, with more focus on the business case and financial justification for the purchase (see box 'Ask the right questions').

## Ask the right questions

We have come across the example of an account team in a competitive pitch situation about to respond with a proposal without knowing how many other companies they were competing with, never mind who their competitors were. It emerged that one of the competitors had been working with a member of the decision-making unit for the past 17 years. At the same time, the account team was unaware that it was standard practice in the procurement team to run two suppliers through the negotiation phase, with both thinking they were the preferred supplier.

The purpose of this was to get the best possible price out of the actual preferred supplier, but it meant wasted time and money for the second supplier. And, finally, the account team had put their best price in the proposal, not knowing that the procurement team in the account were incentivized on driving costs down and so had to be seen to have negotiated a discount on every purchase.

Once all of this information was on the table it changed the proposal, pricing and stakeholder communications the account team was planning. This information came from a coach in the account who was part of the ABM-er's network, but some pointed questions to the members of the decision-making unit (DMU) earlier on may have uncovered the buying process and priorities and may even have led the account team being more selective about which opportunities to really 'go for' in the account, and which to approach more tactically.

The lesson is that ABM-ers have to build insight into how an account buys, including how they bid for and allocate their budgets, early on, so that sales and marketing activities can align and support this process during the ABM campaign.

## Account relationship and strategy

While identifying key stakeholders and decision makers and participating in the development of the account strategy is something ABM-ers feel they do well, there are several areas for improvement across the ABM community in this category, which is why it sits at the bottom of the list in terms of ABM competencies today. Most pressing is the need to get better at tracking the touchpoints with a stakeholder to ensure that each one results in a positive experience and strengthens the relationship. This is something technology will increasingly make easier.

Another area to improve is the ABM-er's consideration of the client's wider ecosystem (suppliers, partners, key customer groups) as well as their own company's strategic partners when planning and executing ABM campaigns. With the bigger-picture thinking ABM-ers claim to possess, this shouldn't be too much of a stretch for them.

Finally, they would also benefit from learning how to project more confidence, which is essential when dealing with established account teams, and challenging them to see the art of the possible in creating mutual value for the account and their own company. At ITSMA we regularly work with a London-based company called Actors in Industry (www.actorsinindustry.com) to teach ABM-ers the soft skills they need in terms of assertiveness and communicating with impact in the account team. Both are vital for the success of your ABM programme.

## Tailored value propositions

Creating tailored value propositions (as described in Chapter 9) is a key step in the ABM process. But, while the scores in this category are mostly 4.0 or above, there are a couple of areas for development.

On average, ABM-ers are comfortable understanding client challenges and mapping them to their company's solutions and linking propositions to the client's business imperatives and pain points. There is a similar level of confidence in crafting differentiated, client-specific value propositions and making sure that the value propositions going into an account are aligned with each other and with the overall strategy.

ABM marketers are slightly less confident in communicating using the customer's language, with an understanding of both the client's needs and decision-making processes to facilitate true business-level conversations. This links back to their lack of knowledge about the procurement process, uncovered in the market intelligence category.

The main issue comes in approaching clients with unique insights about how they can achieve their strategic goals. Since this is one of the things clients say they value, it's important that ABM-ers get better at this. It's not something to be accomplished alone, but usually takes a network of people and a variety of perspectives to develop unique insights.

In the past, we've seen teams use the information they have from their own service delivery systems (sense and respond, root cause analysis) to generate new insights that could save the account money, increase productivity or bring it new revenue streams. Innovation workshops are also great sources of new perspectives and insights, with the account team and the client working together to review their current situation and future trends. Bringing together clients with similar issues can also be an effective way of delivering new insight to an account that helps them to achieve their desired business outcome.

Some of the insights generated by these methods may then form the basis for a bespoke thought leadership campaign into the account, which could subsequently be made more generic and taken out to a group of accounts with the same issue, through ABM Lite, or indeed a whole industry or market segment through sector or segment marketing.

## Marketing communications

The fact that this is one of the higher-ranked categories across the ABM community tallies with the fact that this is traditionally marketing's comfort zone and an area where ABM-ers feel comfortable.

ABM marketers are very strong in using existing marketing assets and programmes creatively to meet the specific needs of their accounts, as well as creating new account-specific assets. This is just as well, given the pressure on budgets most experience in their ABM programmes. Similarly, they can condense information into a format that is useful and effective for sales to use in conversations with the account. They can create customized content for each client and select the most appropriate communications channel through which to deliver that content.

Where this glowing picture falls down is in the ABM community's current ability to create multichannel programmes that build a progressively stronger relationship with the client. Given the need for omnichannel communications that we saw in Chapter 11, this is a serious shortcoming. The good news is that marketing automation and sales systems can help to sequence this kind of nurturing campaign. The bad news is that not all ABM-ers have access to the right platforms that give them account-level views as well as report on individual leads. It is nevertheless something to be aware of as an ABM marketer, so look for ways to improve your own competence in this area.

## Business acumen

Despite the fact that this category was second to bottom of the list for ABM-ers today, they reckon they are adept at understanding their

**Figure 13.5** ABM business acumen competencies

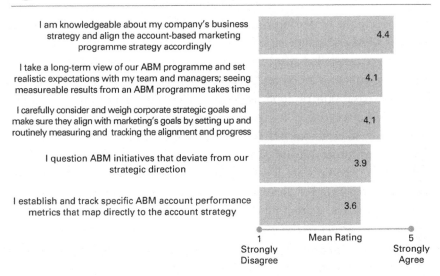

I am knowledgeable about my company's business strategy and align the account-based marketing programme strategy accordingly — 4.4

I take a long-term view of our ABM programme and set realistic expectations with my team and managers; seeing measureable results from an ABM programme takes time — 4.1

I carefully consider and weigh corporate strategic goals and make sure they align with marketing's goals by setting up and routinely measuring and tracking the alignment and progress — 4.1

I question ABM initiatives that deviate from our strategic direction — 3.9

I establish and track specific ABM account performance metrics that map directly to the account strategy — 3.6

1 Strongly Disagree — Mean Rating — 5 Strongly Agree

**NOTE** % of Respondents (N=108); Mean ratings based on a 5-point scale in which 1=Strongly disagree and 5=Strongly agree
**SOURCE** ITSMA, ABM Marketer Competency Assessment, 2016

companies' strategic objectives and can translate them into ABM initiatives (Figure 13.5).

They are also fairly adept at taking a long-term view of their ABM programme and setting realistic expectations with their team. Similarly, they are comfortable aligning marketing goals with corporate strategic goals and routinely measuring both ongoing alignment and progress.

One of the two lower scores in this category brings us back to the ability to challenge the account team. This time it is in questioning ABM initiatives that deviate from the strategic direction that the account team has set, such as when a marketer is being asked to create a single tactical response such as an e-book without being consulted on whether that is the best way to achieve the objective set for the ABM campaign. The ability to challenge, build rapport and communicate with impact are all important here.

The lowest mean score in this category is for establishing and tracking metrics that map directly to the account strategy (as discussed in Chapter 12). This highlights a priority area for improvement, particularly since we know that being able to demonstrate the performance of ABM initiatives and the value of the programme is key to the ongoing support of the account team and investment in ABM by the business.

## *Leadership*

The scores in the leadership competencies category fall in the mid-range in terms of ABM-ers' competence today.

ABM-ers are skilled at leading and facilitating meetings and navigating situations without a lot of guidance, and this talent for dealing with ambiguity is a basic skill of good leadership. They are comfortable in setting challenging marketing objectives and following them through to completion, getting others to buy into the game plan even without formal authority. They set clear processes and ensure the team is following them.

However, ABM-ers are less confident in their ability to coach account teams on preparing for client meetings and acting as an advisor for the account team. These are both critical skills that position the ABM-er as a consultative partner to the team rather than an administrative resource to help with sales support. If you feel the same lack of confidence or competence in these areas, it's worth increasing your knowledge of the client to be able to advise on engaging with them in face-to-face meetings. It is also worth improving your ability to challenge and communicate with impact, as we've already mentioned.

## *Cross-organizational collaboration*

The overall positive scores in this category (Figure 13.6) underline marketing's talent at acting as the corporate glue, able to look across the organization and network successfully. Being able to work effectively to overcome cultural, historical or organizational barriers to create more collaboration and productive working relationships bodes well for bringing a more customer-centric view back into the organization and being able to bring together the whole capability of the organization for the benefit of the client.

# Using and managing agency resources

One of your key skills as an ABM-er will be managing teams of people from different functions and backgrounds and who come from other parts of the organization and from external agencies. Using external agencies will play an important role in your ABM programme, since no one person can be a specialist in every area that an ABM campaign demands. Often the specialist skills needed for your campaigns either don't exist internally or are in short

**Figure 13.6** ABM cross-organizational collaboration, competencies

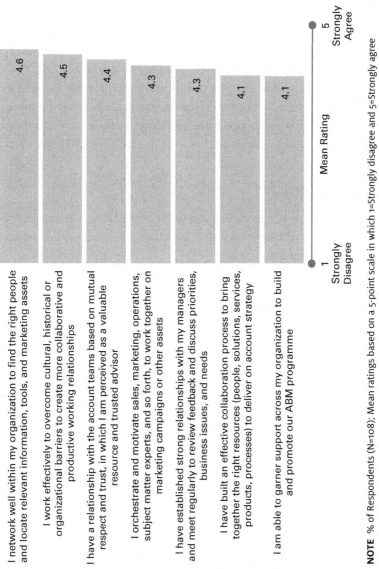

| | Mean Rating |
|---|---|
| I network well within my organization to find the right people and locate relevant information, tools, and marketing assets | 4.6 |
| I work effectively to overcome cultural, historical or organizational barriers to create more collaborative and productive working relationships | 4.5 |
| I have a relationship with the account teams based on mutual respect and trust, in which I am perceived as a valuable resource and trusted advisor | 4.4 |
| I orchestrate and motivate sales, marketing, operations, subject matter experts, and so forth, to work together on marketing campaigns or other assets | 4.3 |
| I have established strong relationships with my managers and meet regularly to review feedback and discuss priorities, business issues, and needs | 4.3 |
| I have built an effective collaboration process to bring together the right resources (people, solutions, services, products, processes) to deliver on account strategy | 4.1 |
| I am able to garner support across my organization to build and promote our ABM programme | 4.1 |

1 Strongly Disagree — 5 Strongly Agree

**NOTE** % of Respondents (N=108); Mean ratings based on a 5-point scale in which 1=Strongly disagree and 5=Strongly agree
**SOURCE** ITSMA, ABM Marketer Competency Assessment, 2016

supply when you need them. ABM is based on bespoke projects geared to the account and the account circumstances so the basket of skills you need over time can vary.

Another valid reason for using outside help is when you are setting about scaling up an ABM programme. As Chapter 5 showed, one of the two key points of failure ITSMA has identified[1] is when moving from standardizing to scale. You might well find yourself having to tap into agency resources to help with this, since you are unlikely to have a big team of specialists on hand to help to do what's necessary around the world.

For example, you might well call on research expertise to build account profiles for the next 20 accounts coming into your programme this quarter, or facilitation experts to run ABM planning workshops in another region during the year.

## Types of agencies

The list of possible agencies to draw on in ABM emphasizes just what a broad church it can be. It includes dedicated specialists such as Momentum ABM, plus experts in:

- training in the various competencies required of ABM;
- research and insight into accounts and stakeholders;
- workshop facilitation;
- messaging;
- content creation;
- creative assets;
- PR/analyst relationships;
- event management;
- digital marketing/social marketing;
- executive relationship management;
- advisory board building;
- technology, including the raft of suppliers first outlined in Chapter 3;
- direct marketing, including telemarketing.

## Selecting and briefing an agency

In an ideal world, choosing the appropriate agency should be done through a competitive process and a well-thought-out agency brief. While you may have a preferred agency or two that you've worked with over the years and who have learned your culture, a new, complex or significant project should be subject to competitive tender. The process of agency selection is outlined below.

## Step 1: Write the agency brief

This document is to be sent to agencies as a basis for their proposals. However, it is also useful as a mechanism to summarize the firm's view of the project. It should contain the sections listed in Table 13.1.

## Step 2: Create a shortlist of agencies

Create a list of potential agencies from recommendations, contacts and directories.

## Step 3: Contact agencies to see if they will compete

Make a telephone call or write an e-mail to the new business director. Not all agencies will be able to pitch because some will have a potential conflict of interest.

## Step 4: Send brief to agencies

The main elements of the brief are shown in Table 13.1, while more detailed examples of a research brief and a campaign brief are in Tables 13.2 and 13.3 respectively. However, note that the best agencies often have their own briefing formats, and some even refuse to engage with a client until the brief is completed to their own satisfaction. This is their way of avoiding risk by educating customers so that the creative execution, and the campaign over-all, have the best chances of success.

## Step 5: Create selection criteria

Define the pitch process by creating a set of criteria on which to rate agencies. This will help ensure objectivity on the day. Criteria might include: previous experience, understanding of the brief, etc.

## Step 6: Agencies present to team

Invite agencies to a day of presentations to a team of leaders.

## Step 7: Select final agency and engage

A contract should be negotiated using appropriate functions or skills.

**Table 13.1**   Generic agency briefing format

| Contents |
|---|
| Project objectives and key performance indicators |
| Other enterprise of business objectives |
| Description of target market |
| Message (if relevant) and desired take-out |
| Agency dynamics |
| Constraints |
| Timescale |
| Budget |
| Internal clients and resources |

Be clear on the quality of the deliverables you expect so that you can evaluate based on outputs rather than activities alone (although admittedly it can be a challenge to measure the results of strategic input). As with any external agency relationship, you need to look out for:

- over-promising: this is perhaps the most common trait;
- inefficiency: whether about returning phone calls or generally providing agreed levels of service;
- lack of knowledge about your business (or that of your client);
- using junior staff to do what senior staff should do;
- overcharging;
- preferring to chase new clients at the expense of building closer relationships with current ones (ie you!);
- unsound management of their own company, putting your programmes at risk.

This may all sound a bit melodramatic, but what you can't afford to do in a strategic ABM situation is put the relationships with the client, or your relationship with the account team, at risk. These accounts are, by definition, important to the future of your business after all.

**Table 13.2**   Research brief template

| Section | Questions to explore |
| --- | --- |
| Context | What is the current situation and what are the main drivers for this activity? |
| Business objectives | What do we want to achieve for the business with this activity?<br>What business outcomes will we look for? |
| Research objectives | What insight do we want to develop from this research?<br>What decisions will we take once we have the results? |
| Key questions to explore | What are the main themes and questions we would like to explore with interviewees? |
| 'Nice to have' information | What other information would we like to get from interviewees if possible? |
| Target audience | Who do we want to understand with this research?<br>What is their profile (demographic, psychographic, behavioural, contextual as appropriate)?<br>What split of interviewees do we want to achieve across different groups or accounts (hard or soft quotas)? |
| Available budget | How much are we able to invest in this research project? |
| Timescales and deadlines | What are the major milestones we need to meet with this project?<br>When do we want to have the final results available? |
| Constraints | What other constraints will the agency need to work within, eg not revealing the sponsor of the research, only contacting customers once account managers give their approval? |
| Contacts | Who is the marketing sponsor, business sponsor, and project manager for this activity? |

**Table 13.3**  Campaign brief template

| Section | Questions to explore |
| --- | --- |
| Context | What is the current situation and what are the main drivers for this activity? |
| Business objectives | What do we want to achieve for the business with this campaign? What business outcomes will we look for in the account(s)? |
| Campaign objectives | How do we want this campaign to influence the target audience in terms of increasing awareness, educating, or persuading them to act? How will the effectiveness of this campaign be measured? |
| Target audiences | Who are we trying to reach with this campaign and what are their profiles or personas? |
| Key messages and proposition | What are the key messages for this campaign (by audience type if applicable)? What is the messaging hierarchy? What is the value proposition? |
| Possible media | Which media are likely to be effective in reaching the target audience? What mix of online and offline channels will be used both internally and externally? |
| Available budget | How much are we able to invest in this campaign? |
| Timescales and deadlines | What are the major milestones we need to meet with this campaign? When will it launch? What are the phases or sequence of activities? |
| Constraints | What constraints will the agency need to work within eg brand guidelines, account procurement or hospitality policies? |
| Other third parties | Which other agencies will form part of the project group for this campaign? |
| Contacts | Who is the marketing sponsor, business sponsor and project manager for this campaign? |

# Your ABM checklist

**1** Being an account-based marketer is one of the most challenging, and at the same time most rewarding, marketing roles you can have. An ABM-er's life is never dull, as your responsibilities are so wide-ranging.

**2** Finding the right people for this complex role, which sits at the boundary between marketing, sales and the client, has been a major preoccupation for the growing number of organizations that have embraced ABM.

**3** You need a powerful combination of both technical marketing competencies and general business skills to get the job done.

**4** ITSMA's ABM competency assessment is an online test that covers all 50 competencies you need, from account insight, account strategy, tailored value propositions and communications, through to cross-organizational collaboration, leadership, business acumen and the way you work.

**5** When we look across all of the competencies in the model it's clear that ABM-ers are fairly upbeat about the competencies they have.

**6** One of your key skills as an ABM-er will be managing teams of people from different functions and backgrounds and external agencies – particularly as you scale your programme.

**7** To select the best agency to help you, run a competitive process using a solid agency brief.

# Note

**1** ITSMA (2016) *Account-Based Marketing Benchmarking Survey*

# Managing your ABM career 14

In this chapter we're going to hear the ideas and opinions of seven lead-ing ABM practitioners: our very own 'Magnificent Seven', if you like. In conversation with each of them, we asked about the backgrounds of the best ABM-ers they had worked with, what the salary and incentives look like for ABM marketers, how to stay fresh in an ABM role and what to do after ABM as you advance in your career.

The advice they give is equally applicable to a marketer doing ABM for one account as to a marketer running their company's whole ABM programme. It also applies whether you are thinking about becoming an ABM-er or thinking about hiring one.

While most of their advice is anonymous to protect the confidentiality of their own ABM programmes and staff, we've included a small vignette on each person in this chapter, setting out their own route into ABM, their current role and their top piece of advice for new account-based marketers.

And we end this book with the very person who started it for us in his Foreword – Dr Charles Doyle. His is the final vignette in this chapter and illustrates beautifully where you can take your career with ABM. He has had two global CMO roles since his pioneering work on ABM at Accenture, first at magic circle law firm, Clifford Chance, and currently at global real estate services firm, JLL.

## Where do the best ABM-ers come from?

Good ABM-ers are difficult to find and pursued eagerly because the skill set is so incredibly rare. It must be someone who 'speaks' sales, can function as a consultant to the sales team and the customer at a very high level, and at the same time be humble enough to get their hands dirty and execute campaigns.

There is clearly an advantage in hiring someone who has done ABM at another company. They can add some richness to the experience in their new company, which means they start adding value quickly. But, since the ABM population is still so small globally, most companies need to look elsewhere for their ABM team.

So where do good ABM-ers come from?

## A broad base of marketing experience

People are most effective in ABM if they come with a broad-based marketing background. The best ABM-ers are those who have done several of the marketing disciplines and then become a general marketer, such as looking after an industry sector. They need to be almost like mini-CMOs in their own right by the point that they become an ABM-er.

There are a number of areas that offer valuable experience. For example, starting at the marketing strategy and planning end of the marketing process, it's important that an ABM marketer has the strategic vision to see the interconnection between the individual stakeholder, the account and the market in which the account operates.

Because so very few clients are now unaffected by some global force or some trend outside their industry, ABM-ers have to immerse themselves in the client's world while also taking into account the quirks and differences that you'll get in every company, such as divisional rivalries or politics. Moreover, every client will be different even if they're in the same industry. That demands the ability and experience to recognize both those similarities and those differences, holding all these variables in their mind at the same time.

A good grasp of segmentation is essential as well since if the segmentation is not right everything else goes wrong. But always bear in mind that segmenting at client level is slightly different from segmenting at market level. ABM-ers need to use research to come up with the targeting and positioning for each chosen segment.

A field marketing role can also be valuable because it involves working extensively with sales teams, bringing an understanding of the complexity of a sales cycle and the different roles that are played both on the seller and the customer side.

In terms of more specialist experience in different aspects of marketing communications, good ABM-ers often have had public relations (PR), digital expertise and, increasingly, social media in their remit. In fact, PR is a really good grounding for ABM, partly because there is so much focus on content, which is a particular PR skill. PR experts are usually good writers, know how to ask the right type of questions and are also good at storytelling. Pitching a story to a journalist, which is what PR people do, is almost a mini form of ABM in its own right because they need to know the publication, the readership, what the journalists write about and how they like to consume information.

## An understanding of sales

Ideally the ABM-er has spent time in sales, whether managing a sales team, working in sales support or another aspect because that sharpens the understanding of how salespeople think and speak. After all, if you speak the language you can understand what sales are trying to accomplish and what their daily challenges are. If you don't understand that, you can't add value and if you can't add value, you have no credibility and you're going to fail.

The people who just naturally seem to 'get' ABM do tend to have paid their dues when it comes to sales in whatever aspect. Putting that knowledge together with their marketing expertise is very powerful.

## The value of partner marketing

Some outstanding ABM-ers have come from partner marketing roles because they have learned how to deal with the partner organization as a customer. The same philosophy applies as in sales: sitting down with partners every day, putting together co-marketing plans and understanding their challenges in the same way as treating an account in ABM.

## The importance of personal characteristics

ABM demands a certain breed of person who can gain trust very quickly. Winning trust is such a key issue in order to be successful as an ABM-er because you have to gain the account manager's confidence very quickly or you are not going to be successful.

Perhaps what really makes the biggest difference, however, is the degree of commitment to doing the job. You have to really want to do ABM, to get under the skin of the customer and always be thinking about how to make that relationship stronger.

## What doesn't work

Who shouldn't go into ABM? Typically, it would be those marketers who are sometimes described as 'corporates' ensconced in their ivory towers who prefer to focus on volume marketing and operate through PowerPoint presentations and data sheets. Also, people who come from more creative agency backgrounds tend not to fit in all that well because of the need for excellent project management skills.

## How does an ABM-er's salary compare with other marketing roles?

In most companies it seems that ABM marketers are on a comparable salary to other marketers at that level in the function, be they a manager, group manager, director, senior director or vice president. Within those levels salaries are broadly consistent across the band. It's unusual to create a separate grading structure or salary band for ABM marketers. However, bear in mind that ABM salaries tend to be slightly elevated since companies usually hire ABM-ers at managerial levels and above because of the strategic requirements.

This makes sense if you assume that the best ABM-ers have probably worked in a variety of different disciplines and marketing specialisms, have been promoted regularly and have taken on broader roles such as industry sector or country marketing. To have the ability to be able to deal with senior leaders in large and often global accounts demands the sort of experience that goes along with premium salaries.

Basically, someone with a strong combination of sales and marketing experience who has instant credibility with account teams they work with should have the sort of compensation package that reflects the fact that these are senior, strategic level roles that have to be paid accordingly.

## What is the best way to incentivize and reward an ABM marketer?

This is currently a very hot topic. A lot of ABM-ers argue that they contribute to revenue growth in a very similar capacity to the sales teams on the account without receiving the same rewards.

That's why companies try to avoid creating a barrier between sales and marketing through different account incentive schemes. It's a very delicate issue. If, for example, an ABM incentive scheme is too fully aligned with sales based on revenue targets, while the marketing is aiming at a big push on relationship building or reputation management, an uncomfortable disconnect can arise which can become a disincentive to achieving the goals of the account.

It's worth stressing as a point of difference that ABM-ers have chosen a marketing path rather than a sales path. They have more job security than someone in a sales role who is only as secure as their last few quarters. Because ABM-ers don't always face those risks it can be tricky to try and deal with rewards in the same way.

So how do some companies do it? Let's look at some of the ways this is dealt with.

## Bonus on a broader set of objectives than sales

Current wisdom is that it's best to have an ABM annual performance bonus that is linked to various objectives, including whether the account has hit its goals. So the ABM-er could be on an incentive plan for the account in the same way that the members of the account team are, but with tweaked criteria or KPIs. The right incentives for ABM-ers have to hinge on creating long-term value within the account. There might be a revenue-based compensation metric, but there will also be metrics for customer relationships, customer success and customer satisfaction, for example. For a salesperson, it's about completing the sale. For an ABM-er, it's about creating the environment for that sale to happen.

It's important to stress that credible measurement is critical in order to link incentives and rewards to outcomes, which is an area ITSMA research consistently finds companies struggling with. So measurements aimed at the three key outcomes of ABM – relationships, reputation, and revenues – are needed. It's not just about doing the deal at the end of the day.

In some large-bid marketing situations – a subset of ABM – there can be a specific incentive for the bid team, with the ABM-er included in that. While companies are starting to move towards this, it's still not the norm.

## Recognition is a key driver

Don't ever underestimate the power of recognition. Marketers tend to appreciate their work being recognized beyond purely financial incentives. They want to be seen as doing good work and helping to lead the organization forward. It costs very little to recognize someone, but can have a huge impact. For example, even hearing the sales team praise the ABM-er by saying they couldn't do their job without them can be a powerful incentive.

We have found that companies recognize their ABM-ers in various ways:

- ensuring that leaders publicly acknowledge what ABM-ers are contributing to wins;
- offering special training opportunities;
- inviting participation in internal strategic initiatives or work streams, where people can be exposed to senior leadership;
- providing spot bonuses, where an ABM-er has achieved something fairly extraordinary in support of account goals;
- awards and prizes.

The last of these can take a variety of forms. At Juniper Networks, for example, Raianne Reiss (see interview on page 248) was awarded with the company's Challenger Award for continuously challenging the status quo and looking for ways to innovate, and not being afraid to challenge to encourage people to think about things in a different way. Andrea Clatworthy at Fujitsu (see interview on page 252) was sent on an all-expenses paid trip as part of the sales incentive programme to reward outstanding success.

# How do ABM-ers stay fresh and avoid burnout?

Marketers tend to be people who get bored quickly. They like to be challenged all the time. They like taking on a new client and really digging deep, running the account based on all the detective work they've done.

But running these accounts can be pretty intense. Account-based marketers are often at the centre of everything in a lot of ways. They are multitasking, including working with senior leadership, focusing on strategic issues, dealing with the account team and being engaged in close client relationships. So there can be a risk of burnout, particularly with the larger accounts.

The consensus among the members of the ITSMA Global ABM Council is that there is a danger of burnout among ABM-ers after about two years. So how do you keep fresh during and beyond this two-year timescale? There are a number of ways.

## *Have multiple accounts*

The most straightforward way is to make sure as an ABM-er that you have a few accounts on the go since the accounts will most likely be at different stages of activity, with some in planning mode while others might be in full campaign mode, for example.

## Rotate account allocations

Accounts come into an ABM programme on a 24- to 36-month commitment, so changing account allocations every so often is a healthy thing to do. That may give ABM-ers a chance to gain expertise in a new industrial sector or through dealing with new individuals throughout the organization who provide a different perspective. The same thing happens with salespeople who may have had great success with the same account for several years but need a break to avoid getting stale.

## Promote within the ABM programme

At some point it will be time to increase the scope of an ABM-er's responsibility to prevent any danger of the job becoming too repetitive. Good people want to solve new problems and be faced with new challenges. These could include being charged with responsibilities on a broader basis outside the team, acquiring the knowledge to run a future ABM team or being given some vertical marketing roles. More senior ABM-ers can play an active role by supporting their more junior colleagues' professional development.

## Get involved with other work streams

ABM-ers are keen to add value while they also enjoy variety. Being involved with other groups keeps them interested, keeps them networked and gives them an opportunity to do something outside of their day jobs. This could be something like addressing the fact that the programme management office (PMO) needs to be reorganized or strengthened. Being able to pick those issues and work on them with others outside the day job add the variety that ABM-ers look for.

## Invest in continuous professional development

Think about your personal development as an ABM-er. What is it that you need to continually advance your skill? Make sure you are reading the right things, keeping in touch with trends, aware of new agencies on the scene and knowledgeable about the new technologies that are available to you.

## Leverage technology

If you have found some marketing automation that you recognize will make your job easier, build the right business case so that you can deploy it in your ABM organization. This is important in all areas of marketing. But it applies particularly to the hectic and stressful role of the ABM-er, who is essentially acting as a CMO but without a supporting team.

## Do a secondment

As an ABM-er, if you find yourself feeling jaded it can make a huge difference to do a stint working with the client you've been supporting. It helps you to see the account in a new light, having worked on it from the inside. It also starts to open up new career paths as well, such as client-facing roles. And, if this is simply not feasible, think about a secondment into another client-facing role such as sales, account management or delivery.

## Manage your health

Eat nutritious food. Exercise regularly. Meditate. Use all of your holiday allowance. This might seem obvious but the best ABM-ers stay on top of their game by staying in good shape.

# Where next after ABM?

You are one of the most senior ABM-ers on the team. While the discipline is probably at too early a stage to say what's next for you with confidence, we believe it sets up a multitude of paths for a marketer.

### Move up the ABM ladder

ABM-ers can start off with a very simple account and move on to a more complex one. Some of these organizations are truly global and have multiple brands. While as an ABM-er it would be physically impossible to address their entire business, you need to understand it or you can't decide where best to focus. That demands a more extensive approach to insight planning than with a local account that is reasonably regionalized and where you can quite easily understand what's going on with them and get to the right people at the right time with your messages. You may also take on the position of managing one or more junior staff.

You might well find that there is a call for your successful ABM programme to be replicated elsewhere in the business, since few ABM programmes start off truly global in nature. Companies are increasingly building global centres of expertise for ABM and are often keen to try to take some of what has been successful in one region and make it available in other parts of the world. Ultimately, you may find yourself leading a global programme office for ABM in your company on the marketing (and sales) leadership team.

## Move into a marketing leadership role

ABM-ers can become sector marketers, taking their knowledge into an industry vertical or business unit internationally. There could also be a path into central marketing, particularly in the product management area because you've demonstrated your ability to bring the rich voice of the customer into the company. This could channel into proposition development and roadmaps for the company's offerings.

In fact, ABM-ers are extremely marketable for other marketing functions because of their deep understanding of how the sales process and the company's strategic accounts really work. A lot of ABM-ers are recruited internally to go into leadership positions and into other areas within marketing because of this valuable experience and insight.

## Become a CMO

Moving towards a CMO role would be a logical career path because you have this multitude of experiences you are delivering at a very micro level. For example, you could become CMO of a regional business or business unit within your overall company, or join a smaller company where you are in charge.

## Move into account management

There is clearly a path into sales and account management. The money can be enticing, and some ABM-ers may be true salespeople at heart. They may initially gravitate towards marketing and ABM but then realize they are really drawn to sales.

Another option is a sales operations role if sales itself doesn't appeal. These roles act as the support to sales teams and sales cycles. Having spent some time in ABM you have a very thorough understanding of both. Another option is to act in a support role for a key account programme or strategic account programme. Don't be fooled by the word 'support', since these can be very senior roles and an ideal next step.

## Raianne Reiss, Director of Marketing, Juniper Networks

Contact: @RaianneR, http://bit.ly/2ep1lBh

### Awards:

- Juniper Networks' CMO Challenger Award 2015 for continuously challenging the status quo and driving innovation.
- ITSMA Diamond Award for Account-Based Marketing.

### My route into ABM

Early in my career, I realized that I had a different marketing mindset than other people around me. Regardless of the company or role, I always had limited resources – only so much budget, people and time to go around. Out of necessity, I had to ask myself: 'How can I focus those limited resources in the right places for maximum impact?' My peers were talking about volume marketing, such as number of leads, number of attendees, number of downloads and so on – with the hope that a percentage of the volume would land and translate to results. I wanted more assurance that my bets would pay off, and focused my resources on highly targeted marketing to the customers and prospects who had the highest propensity to buy. We were using terms like guerrilla marketing to describe this approach, which morphed into the 80:20 rule, and today, we call it ABM.

In a business-to-business model, we know that 80 per cent of our business is going to come from 20 per cent of our customers, so success is dependent upon what we are doing to support that effectively. This is especially true in technology companies, where we often have a few customers who drive roadmaps, strategies, and a large portion of the revenue. Some customers can produce more revenue than entire verticals, yet we often do not think of our largest customers in those terms.

As a marketing leader, I have always driven my organizations to identify the 20 per cent and ensure that we covered this appropriately, well before anyone used the term ABM. I remember years ago seeing an ITSMA course – I think the first one ever held – called 'Introduction to

Account-Based Marketing'. I had not heard this term before but the title resonated with me. As I sat in the class I thought: 'These people understand me!' I had been evangelizing that message of guerrilla marketing since the beginning of my career, and now I had a framework for it.

### Advice for new ABM-ers

My advice to people who are interested in a career in ABM would be to pursue positions that are as close to the customer as you can get. To succeed in ABM, it is critical that you can think like a salesperson, understand what they are trying to achieve, and speak the language of sales. In order to obtain these skills, you need to spend time as a quota-carrying salesperson, or in a role closely aligned with and supporting a sales team. Field marketing and partner marketing are often great roles for those who wish to pursue an ABM path.

## Dorothea Gosling, ABM & Pursuit Marketing Centre of Excellence Lead, CSC

*Dorothea Gosling, CSC*

Contact: @DoroGosling, https://ch.linkedin.com/in/dorogosling

### My route into ABM

I didn't plan on becoming 'an ABM-er'. That said, maybe there was an early hint, since as part of my degree course I picked what was then called capital goods marketing as one of my majors, and the other was production management.

In the early 1990s, I moved into IT marketing in Germany, loving the fast pace and culture of the industry, and the value-add IT gives individuals and businesses. Four years later, I was running marketing in Northern Europe, Africa, India and the Middle East for Micrografx. After a short stint of trying a version of 'The Good Life', I returned to IT, joining CSC's European Financial Services (FS) Group.

Initially, I worked for the European FS Legal Counsel, then spent some time with a sales leader, helping build a key account programme. From there, I returned to marketing, initially PR and analyst relations, then taking on roles in product marketing as well as becoming webmaster for FS globally. I'm a generalist at heart, and ever so slightly geeky!

In early 2004, I wanted a greater challenge and faster career growth. Just a month later, that opportunity presented itself, as CSC was looking for a bilingual Marketing & Communications lead for a Swiss account we were hoping to win. IT services outsourcing and transformation communications were new to me, but I was fortunate enough to do the role for CSC's Zurich Global Account for several years, working with and learning from amazing people in both CSC and Zurich, and becoming expert in seriously large pursuits.

In 2013, with CSC's transformation, yet another opportunity presented itself: running CSC's Global ABM Centre of Excellence. Today, we're constantly enhancing and tuning our programme in line with corporate strategy and market developments, and as ABM continues to evolve.

### Advice for new ABM-ers

If the opportunity arises to become an ABM-er, grab it! It's probably one of the best gigs in marketing right now. But don't expect any silver bullets: it's hard work and there are no shortcuts. Customer insight should be at the heart of your ABM programme and you need to understand how sales operates and speak the same language to be effective. Finally, never stop learning!

## Andy Pedack, Relationship Marketing Director, Worldwide Integrated Solutions, Marketing, Microsoft Services

*Andy Pedack, Microsoft*

Contact: @andy_pedack, https://www.linkedin.com/in/andypedack

### My route into ABM

I took an interest in ABM as a necessary extension of our approach to how we engage our top accounts. I found this was especially relevant in our services business as this is already in a way a nurture function for our company, focused on helping customers get the best from our technologies. In a cloud-first, mobile-first world, we increasingly need a connected conversation with the customer focused on their desired results, or business outcomes. So, the application of account-aligned everything is important: account-aligned delivery, account-aligned sales, and account-aligned marketing.

ABM has been a natural next step for many of our account engagements, even without saying formally 'here is our account-based marketing plan'. We incorporate principles of ABM increasingly in the way we plan and engage as marketers with our account teams to grow the relationship with our customers.

I think one of the things that helped me rapidly appreciate and adopt ABM was my past experience as product manager for Onyx Software, a leading customer relationship management (CRM) company in its time. At Onyx, we were inherently about the 360-degree view of the customer, connecting customer touchpoints into a cohesive brand experience and automating that through the software we were building at the time. This has been the basis for what I have done throughout my career in terms of keeping such a close focus on the customer and the business processes and functions that are the customer touchpoints.

### Advice for new ABM-ers

Start by asking yourself: 'Do I have the executive buy-in and mandate from my senior leadership for collaboration between marketing and sales in my role?' If so, great, you've already got the charter to drive the integration inherent in ABM.

If you don't, and if you're trying to create momentum, I think it's important to keep a balance so as to not over-extend or over-function beyond your current job description, but rather make it an extension of what you're already doing, with some experimentation to prove the value to the business.

Make sure that you pick the right partners for this experimentation, to help you get wins early on and develop the right proof points. I learned from my own experience the importance of solid internal partnerships to go push the envelope on something like doing content marketing in a different way. You need to establish what success looks like and go and make sure to get some good, hard, tangible facts to give back to your stakeholders. You need both, so I think it's really important to keep that in mind.

I'd say the other thing you could do is internally market ABM, through a campaign of thought leadership, providing expert articles from industry observers like ITSMA to help demonstrate the business impact, provide practical how-to guidance, and help with expectations setting.

## Andrea Clatworthy, Head of Account-Based Marketing, EMEIA, Fujitsu

*Andrea Clatworthy, Fujitsu*

Contact: @clatworthya, https://uk.linkedin.com/in/andrea-clatworthy-009133

### My route into ABM

I began my marketing career at Logica (now CGI) before moving to Fujitsu in 2010. I had become interested in what we call ABM very early on because we were members when ITSMA was first introducing it. My boss at the time was quite active in ensuring that his team was kept up to speed on new trends in marketing thinking.

What I most remember from my ABM training at ITSMA – which was about 2003, I think – was what I call the onion diagram. In the diagram you have the customer in the middle with two rings of influences around them. The emphasis on thinking about your customers, understanding them, and then understanding how they consume information enthused me about ABM.

Before moving fully into ABM, I worked in all different sorts of countries and on all different sorts of things, mainly in sector-orientated rather than portfolio-orientated marketing, but my passion for understanding the needs of the customer was always there. That has kept me enjoying ABM, because once you understand the customer, everything else is easy. Over the years I have spent a lot of time persuading colleagues not to say 'buy this service' but to make it easy for the customer to buy what we want to sell them, because we are talking their language and responding to their business needs.

### Advice for new ABM-ers

My number one piece of advice is to select your accounts very carefully. It might be that you currently have a small share and can see potential growth. Perhaps the incumbents aren't completely entrenched and you believe that you have something that is going to help customers and therefore they might buy from you rather than the incumbent. That's an important insight.

But the parallel process that you need to go through is to consider the account team that you're going to work with. ABM is about sales and marketing working together. If the sales teams don't get ABM, for whatever reason – they don't want to bother, they don't want the hassle, they don't want anyone helping them, they think you are taking over, they don't value marketing, all those things – if there's any sort of disconnect between the ABM-er and the account team, the sales team, then it won't work.

Selecting the right account where you've got potential for your organization with that customer and knowing you've got the right team that you can collaborate with is what counts. Then you are looking at something that could be wonderful. But if either of those doesn't work, you are going to have a failure on your hands. And nobody wants that.

One last thing: it's not for the faint-hearted!

## Eric Martin, Vice President Marketing SAP North America

*Eric Martin, SAP*

Contact: @myfavemartin, https://www.linkedin.com/in/ericmartinsap

### My route into ABM

My background has been in B2B marketing, most of it in the enterprise software space, and quite a bit of it at SAP. Many of my roles have been working directly with the field. I was initially exposed to ABM over a decade ago when I was at Deloitte Consulting, when some of my colleagues were doing some robust ABM programmes targeting a very small number of accounts. I didn't get to work directly on that project, but I attended a number of sessions with great interest and saw what they were doing.

In early 2015, I had an opportunity to take on the ABM programme office leader role at SAP North America. I had a predecessor who moved into a different role within SAP, and when I heard about the opening I jumped at it because I realized that ABM could have a significant impact on our business.

### Advice for new ABM-ers

My first piece of advice applies both to those who are starting out and those who have been in the role quite a while. Read as much as you can on the topic from a wide range of sources. For the new person, this allows you to come up to speed quickly on the topic. For someone who has been in the role for quite a while, it can give you a fresh perspective, an outside perspective, that may give you some new ideas. The field is evolving so fast that everyone has to stay current.

Look outside to organizations like ITSMA as much as possible. There's an awful lot that's being published, plus regular webcasts and conferences on the topic of ABM these days. Of course, you need to consume that information with some critical thinking, and apply some filters, so that you take only the parts that apply to your organization, and discard the rest.

I also have advice for a new ABM-er's manager. Despite the fact that the beauty of ABM lies in the customization and the bespoke nature of what you do account by account, we as managers need to pull together templates, programmatic approaches, and shortcuts, so that they can quickly come up to speed on how we do ABM within our organization and what tools are available to them. This will help them see some early success and build their credibility within the role.

## Julie A Johnson, Executive Director of Markets and Accounts, KPMG LLP

*Julie A Johnson, KPMG LLP*

Contact: https://www.linkedin.com/in/julieajohnson2

### My route into ABM

I've been with KPMG for almost nine years and have been involved in our evolution into account-based marketing from the start, since it began just about the time I joined. Before that, I was vice president of marketing for a professional services firm focused on the healthcare industry. I started at KPMG by managing our North American western region in the field marketing team, which is now about 140 people.

At the time, the partner who was leading marketing came to all of us marketing leaders and said we should be moving towards more of an account-based approach, instead of just doing things like random events. So, we went through a pretty exhaustive change management exercise with an outside consulting firm to refocus all of our energies around account-based marketing and account management. I was very much a part of that because I had a change management background.

It led to a redefinition of roles and responsibilities, including writing new job descriptions and interviewing people for account-based marketing positions. Did they have the skill sets to make the transition from being a broad marketer to being able to focus at the account level? We divided our organization up into people who could make that transition, and moved others to do more shared-service kinds of responsibilities.

Over the last four or five years, we have evolved to a strong focus on individual accounts. For many of those years, I too was assigned to accounts, as I had taken over field marketing responsibility for everybody. This proved too much: I just didn't have the bandwidth to support accounts because of the responsibility of managing the whole team, so now I am very much involved in driving what the organization does and overseeing our methodology.

Can I say I set out to be an account-based marketer? Not really. I've just been involved in the evolution of where we've gone as a firm, helping to get us where we are today, which is very much account-based.

### Advice for new ABM-ers

I stress this all the time: it is a relentless focus on understanding client issues, as well as having a relentless focus on being a student of what we do as a business, and really bringing that idea to the account. I think that's critical, and whether you're doing it for the first time, or you've been doing it for 10 years, having that relentless focus is key.

That's where I think our people can really differentiate themselves as they sit down with their engagement teams. Their account teams are so busy, so heads down delivering work day in and day out, that they often don't have the broader view of everything going on at the account, or everything that's going on within the firm that can be brought to the account.

That's what I coach people to do right off the bat. If you bring that to the account, regardless of your level or title, you are going to be seen to be contributing real value.

## Dr Charles Doyle, Group Chief Marketing and Communications Officer, JLL

*Dr Charles Doyle, JLL*

Contact: @CJADOYLE, https://uk.linkedin.com/in/dr-charles-doyle-477788

### My route into ABM

I started as an academic completing a doctorate in legal corruption during the French Revolution. A strange beginning for a CMO! Absence of serious and permanent academic opportunity in the UK led me to the UK Civil Service, working for the UK Atomic Energy Authority (AEA). Because of privatization, the electricity supply industry was changing dramatically and we had to find commercial uses for some of the nuclear technologies we had, such as industrial lasers and space technology, for different types of market and buyer. So, I had to learn relatively quickly about entering new markets, and was sent on a number of excellent courses to learn many different techniques of marketing.

After that, I moved on to do product marketing at what was then ICL (now Fujitsu), and eventually shifted to network services, a hybrid role that combined both product and services marketing in European markets. More training and development followed – including the Japanese approach to strategic marketing. From there I went to BT, which was in professional services marketing, but the role was mainly targeting acquisitions for BT to bolster its fledgling services offerings. That was followed by a move to Andersen Consulting (later Accenture), where I learned about how to build a coherent professional services brand across multiple industries and countries.

It was while I was at Accenture I realized that we needed to improve the industry-focused marketing that we were doing with a much deeper understanding of the individual client account within those industries. I realized that the business-to-business approach to traditional industry marketing was limited. It was always going to be difficult to be seen as an 'industry expert' if the service company was not actually part of the industry that they were targeting. Also, it was clear that, even within an industry sector, despite similar competitive dynamics, every industry player is different. Therefore, a much deeper understanding of the client was needed rather than a simple analysis of 'industry trends', in order to uncover more opportunity.

My study of history had given me an understanding and appreciation of the role that cultural differences played in the rise of nation states, and it seemed natural to apply this segmentation of different internal groups within clients to gain greater understanding. I could see the importance of understanding this interconnection between the individual, the institution, and the market. After all, at the core of client-centric marketing, or what we now call ABM, is deep research into how individuals react within institutions, and how both are affected by market dynamics. No one aspect is entirely independent of the other.

I built on that knowledge in my next position as global head of business development and marketing at Clifford Chance, one of the magic circle law firms, where we introduced many seminars with clients – often over weekends! In my current global CMO role at JLL, a global real estate services company, we try to work with our clients globally and seamlessly, reflecting how they wish to work rather than our internal geographical structure, so we can deliver the best of JLL, everywhere.

### Advice for new ABM-ers

I have learned about ABM on the job, but with some very good company training and by applying appropriate academic techniques. It has stood me in good stead. You should be thinking of getting into ABM and mastering it at an early stage to maximize your career potential. The exploratory and pioneering work into its impact has mainly been done, so make sure you use this existing body of knowledge. When you start out, apply an almost military-like strategy: occupy the strategic high ground even if you face pressure to just do the tactical stuff for the sales force. If you don't occupy that high ground fast, then you're condemned to being a tactical runner for salespeople. Long-term value and relationships with the client – and their continuing loyalty – depend upon it.

# Your ABM checklist

**1** Good ABM-ers are difficult to find, needing broad-based marketing experience, an understanding of sales and the soft skills to build trust with the account team fast.

**2** ABM salaries, while banded on the same group levels as the rest of marketing, tend to be higher simply because more senior people are needed for ABM roles.

**3** The incentives offered to ABM-ers are usually broader in scope than those offered to salespeople, since ABM-ers are tasked with creating long-term value in the account by influencing relationships, reputation and revenues.

**4** Non-financial recognition, such as the acknowledgement of their contribution by sales colleagues, is an important way to motivate and reward ABM-ers.

**5** To stay fresh in an ABM role beyond two years, rotate the accounts you work on, look for other initiatives you can participate in, invest in your self-development and look to manage and train more junior ABM-ers on the team.

**6** A range of opportunities await when you're ready to move out of ABM, from sales roles through marketing leadership roles right up to becoming a CMO.

# INDEX

Note: *Italics* indicate a Figure or Table in the text.

CPSIA information can be obtained
at www.ICGtesting.com
Printed in the USA
BVOW06s1726050717

488581BV00005B/222/P